An Introduction to Video Comp
C/C++

Fore June

An Introduction to Video Compression in C/C++

CreateSpace, a DBA of On-Demand Publishing, LLC.

ISBN-10:	1451522274
ISBN-13:	978-1451522273

First Edition:	March, 2010
Second Edition:	April, 2011
Third Edition:	December, 2016

Contents

About the Author

Fore June is an independent Internet Service Provider (ISP) who provides various kinds of Internet services to the public and information technology consulting to a couple of small companies. Fore has written a few books and holds an M.S.E.E. degree in Electrical Engineering and Computer Science.

Preface

The rapid advance in computing hardware technology has sharply reduced the cost of computing, and consequently, the computing capacity of PCs has become ever more powerful. This helps the spread of video compression technology that usually requires a lot of computing power. Many multi-media workers can now learn and experiment with data compression techniques in their own PCs. In recent years this computing-intensive technology has even sought its way to low-cost embedded devices. This book grows out of the author's experience of implementing a video compression engine to be used in toys for a toy manufacturer. Video games played in a toy are at the very low-end of any multi-media products; they are implemented in embedded systems and very often a significant portion of the code is written in assembly language. The engine designer must implement the code in a way that it minimizes the storage space and computing time. To make such an implementation, one must understand thoroughly the mechanism behind the technique. It took me a long time to get familiar with the subject but after the endeavor, I enjoy the happiness of solving the problems and finishing the task. In this book, I report and explain the techniques I have learned and used in the project.

I am grateful to many friends who helped shape the content of this book and provided valuable information of the technology used in my video compression project.

I very much hope this book is enjoyable, readable and useful to you. Above all else, I hope you could share my happiness of exploration and in turn can help others to explore this beautiful and exciting technology world and make the world better. The source code of this book can be obtained from the web site *http://www.forejune.com/vcompress* by entering the password 'democracy'.

Fore June
Jan. 2010

Chapter 1

Introduction

1.1 The Value of Knowledge

Not long after the birth of the Web, multimedia has become an inseparable part of it. As the growth of the Web accelerates, the demand of multimedia applications and the knowledge of this field explodes. Data compression is the soul of the engine that drives the rapid development of these applications. Audio and image data can be effectively transmitted across the Web or saved in a digital storage medium (DSM) only after they have been compressed.

Video compression can be considered as an extension of audio and image compression, whose applications go well beyond the Web. As one might have noticed, in recent years video compression products have experienced rapid growth in a variety of consumer products such as iPods, iTune, mobile phones, digital cameras, TV games, and many kinds of hand-held devices. All these products have employed video compression technologies to save storage space or transmission bandwidth. Moreover, as the cost of computing drops rapidly, sophisticated video compression technologies begin to seek its way into toys, hand-held devices and many innovative low-end new consumer products that add video features to attract customers. These low-end products are usually sold in very large volume and their production cost becomes a sole factor in determining the adoption of a technology. Very often, these products are built using embedded systems and the computing power and memory space of them are relatively limited. To develop data compression programs in such an environment, one must have a thorough understanding of the technology.

After many years of research by a large number of scientists and engineers, the methodologies of producing high-quality compressed video have become mature and well known. However, not many books discussing the implementation of the methods are available. Therefore, a book explaining the principles and implementation of video compression could be helpful and beneficial to the workers in this field.

Even though the book presents the materials at an introductory level, some readers may still find the materials difficult, depending on their background and willingness of paying efforts in learning. But your knowledge is valuable only if you need to pay effort to gain it. Topics that are easy to you are also easy to your competitors. In the coming decades, the competition between nations will be a competition of acquiring and utilizing knowledge. The more effort you pay to acquire knowledge, the wealthier and happier you will be.

Renowned management specialist Peter Drucker (1909 - 2005) had long advocated the emergence of knowledge society and the importance of knowledge workers. The social transformations from an industrial society to a knowledge society would be the most significant event of the century and its lasting legacy. Science and technology have been advancing so rapidly that manufacturing becomes irrelevant in the modern society. A DVD containing certain data that you pay twenty dollars to purchase may just cost a few cents to manufacture. Though it is very rare for the productivity between two labour workers differ by a factor more than two, the productivity of a good knowledge work can be easily a factor of 100 or higher than that of an average knowledge worker. To become proficient in a certain field, one must learn with his or her heart, overcoming difficulties, barriers and frustrations. After enduring the hard work, one would enjoy the pleasure of understanding difficult materials and acquiring valuable knowledge. While the position of a labour worker can be easily substituted by another one with little training, it is very difficult to replace a specialist of a field in the knowledge economy, for the new worker must also go through the same learning barriers and hard work to acquire the knowledge.

1.2 MPEG-4 and H.264 Video Compression Standards

The work on video compression was mainly developed in the 1980s by a numerous number of researchers, mostly working in universities and academic institutions. Effective and close-to-optimal generic compression models began to emerge from the researching results. These models eventually became today's compression standards, which allow different parties to develop individual applications and communicate with each other seamlessly. The standardization has been mainly done by the International Organization for Standardization (ISO) in cooperation with the International Telecommunications Union and the International Electrotechnical Commission (IEC). ISO/IEC Joint Photographic Experts' Group (JPEG) and Moving Picture Experts' Group (MPEG) produced the well-known JPEG, MPEG-1, MPEG-2 and MPEG-4 standards that form the basis of most image and video compression standards today. MPEG-4 was introduced in late 1998 and designated as a standard for a group of audio and video coding formats and related technologies under the formal standard ISO/IEC 14496. Uses of MPEG-4 include compression of AV data for web (streaming media) and CD distribution, voice (telephone, videophone) and broadcast television applications. **H.264**, also known as *MPEG-4 Part 10/AVC for Advanced Video*, is the latest video compression standard, resulting from the work of a joint project between MPEG and the Video Coding Experts Group (VCEG), a working group of the International Telecommunication Union (ITU-T) that operates in a way similar to MPEG. ITU-T has helped set a series of telecommunication standards and is the sector that coordinates telecommunications standards on behalf of ISO and IEC. H.264 is the name used by ITU-T, while ISO/IEC refers it to as *MPEG-4 Part 10/AVC* since it is presented as a new part in its MPEG-4 suite, which includes MPEG-4 Part 2, a standard used by IP-based video encoders and network cameras. It tries to improve upon the weakness of previous video compression standards including:

1. Reducing the average bit rate by 50%, compared with any other video standard for a specified video quality,
2. Using straightforward syntax specification that simplifies implementations,
3. Defining exactly how numerical calculations are to be made by an encoder and a decoder to avoid errors from accumulating,
4. Improving robustness so that transmission errors over various networks are tolerated, and
5. Increasing low latency capabilities and achieving better quality for higher latency. (Latency refers to the time to compress, transmit, decompress and display a set of video data.)

H.264 can support a wide variety of applications with very different bit rate requirements. For example, in entertainment video applications including broadcast, satellite, cable and DVD, an H.264 encoder-decoder (codec) may yield a data rate between 1 to 10 Mbit/s with high latency, while for telecom services, H.264 can deliver bit rates of below 1 Mbit/s with low latency.

MPEG-4 Visual, also referred to as *MPEG-4 Part 2*, is an earlier standard developed by MPEG that has significantly different goals than H.264. Though both standards deal with video data compression, MPEG-4 Visual emphasizes on flexibility whilst H.264 stresses on efficiency and reliability. MPEG-4 Visual provides a very flexible toolkit of coding techniques and resources that allow users to code a wide range of data types including traditional rectangular frames, video objects with arbitrary shape, still images and hybrids of real-world and computer-generated synthetic visual data.

Both MPEG-4 and H.264 are 'open' international standard. The term 'open' here means any individual or organization can purchase the standards documents from ISO/IEC, or ITU-T. Sample code of implementation are also available on the Web of MPEG.

The documents specify exactly what is required for conforming to the standards. Ironically, any implementation of these 'standards' utilizes certain methods that fall into the scope of a number of related patents. Any software developer who implements the standards needs to pay a certain royalty fee to a number of organizations coordinated by MPEG LA, which is regarded as the 'Standard of Standards' (*http://www.mpegla.com*), a leading packager of patent pools for standards used in consumer electronics, as well as eCommerce, education and other technical areas. It is fairly sad to see that we have to pay royalty fees to use a 'standard'. But the world itself, being in and around us has never been perfect. We have to accept this imperfectness in order to move on. Moreover, we have the choice if we want to use the 'standards' in our applications.

The principles and methods discussed in this book are similar to those 'standards' as they are the results of a numerous number of researchers and have been published in various scientific and technical journals. However, to avoid any possible royalty dispute, our methods deviate in many minor aspects and the implementations could be very different from the 'standard' code. Readers are free to use part or all of the code presented in this book. However, whether the implementations have used any algorithm that falls into the scope of any patent is beyond our knowledge. If you use the code for any commercial product, you do that at your own risk.

1.3 This Book

This book, *An Introduction to Video Compression in C/C++*, is written based on the author's experience of implementing a video codec in an embedded system some years ago. The materials are discussed at an introductory level and the code is presented in C/C++. The implementations of more advanced topics are not included. Also, we have only considered image compression; audio compression is omitted. The programs presented are mainly for illustrating the principles of video compression and how to implement them; very often error checking and handling are not included. For the purpose of making the materials easy to understand, sometimes the parameters are hard-coded. Nevertheless, the programs can be used as a starting point for further development. More advanced topics on video data compression are presented in the last chapter without actual implementation.

We have to admit that the programs were written over a period of time and thus the notations may not be very consistent. Also, we have not optimized the code for memory usage or computing time. However, coding is always the relatively easy part compared to understanding the algorithms. All the code presented in this book can be found at the site:

http://www.forejune.co/vcompress/

and you can download the programs using the password 'democracy'. The programs have been compiled and tested in the Linux environment. . The C/C++ programs of this book reside in subdirectories with numbering reflecting the related chapters. For example, the programs discussed in Chapter 5 will be in directory **5/**. If the programs of another chapter need to use the programs developed in Chapter 5, we just need to link their object files in **5/**. We also put most of the sample data files in the directory **data/**.

We hope you enjoy reading this book.

Chapter 2

Elements of Information

2.1 What Is Information?

Basically, everyone knows that this is an information era and every day we talk about the importance of information technology and its development. Now, let us confuse you with a simple question. *What is information?* Before continuing your reading, try to answer the preceding question. Like most programmers, you may be surprised to find that after so many years of studying or working in the area of information, you really could not answer the question unless you have taken a course in information theory or have studied the subject before. To understand how data compression works, we need to first understand what information is.

Some may think that information is simply a concept and we cannot define it quantitatively. Actually, not only that we can define information, we can define it quantitatively and measure it.

Many people, including some authors of books on image compression, confuse information with data and may mistaken that information is the same as data. Actually, data is different from information. Data are used to represent information. We can have redundant data but not redundant information. We can have a large amount of data which contains very little information. For example, we can use a pseudo random number generator to generate an abundant amount of data, tens of millions of bytes. However, all these data contain very little information because if we want to transmit the information represented by these data to another person, all we need to do is to transmit the simple equation of the pseudo random number generator. The receiver can generate the huge amount of data identical to ours. As another example, when we watch news, we feel that we receive a significant amount of information if the news gives us surprises, informing us something unexpected. On the other hand, if your friend tells you that she will eat dinner tomorrow, you do not feel receiving much information as that's what you expect. For instance, consider the following two sentences,

1. India will elect her next governing party by universal suffrage.
2. China will elect her next governing party by universal suffrage.

These two sentences have exactly the same amount of data (characters). However, there is a big difference in information the two sentences would convey. Should the event happen, the first one does not give us any surprise and would not appear in any newspaper as that's what we would expect. However, the second one would give a big shock to the world and every newspaper would report the event; it gives us a significant amount of information. From these examples, we can see that information relates to unpredictability and surprises. It is a measure of the decrease of uncertainty or the gain of surprise of a receiver upon receiving a message. A perfectly predictable message conveys no information. To quantify the measure of information, scientists borrow the concept of entropy from physics. We know that in physics, entropy is a measure of disorder or unpredictability. In information systems, we also refer to information carried by a message as entropy. However, the use of the term entropy to describe information content is artificial. There is not much relationship between the entropy of a message and the physical entropy of a physical system.

Claude Shannon, known as the father of information theory published his landmark paper in 1948 that led to the dawn of the information era. In the paper, Shannon defined the information I(E) conveyed by an event E, measured in bits as

$$I(E) = log_2 \frac{1}{p(E)} \tag{2.1}$$

where $p(E)$ is the probability of the occurrence of the event. In other words, if E is some event which occurs with probability $p(E)$ and we are informed that event E has occurred, then we say that we have received $I(E)$ bits of information given in equation (2.1). We see that when $p = 1, I = 0$. For example, if we are told that "The sun rises from the East", we do not receive any information as we are one hundred percent sure this happens. If $p(E) = 1/2$, then $I(E) = 1bit$, meaning that one bit is the amount of information we obtain when one of two possible likely outcomes is specified, like the case of examining the outcome of flipping a coin. We can also interpret I(E) given in (2.1) as the information needed to make the occurrence of E certain. Note that equation (2.1) can also be expressed as,

$$I(E) = -log_2 p(E) \tag{2.2}$$

We can also define entropy in terms of a discrete random variable X, with possible states (or outcomes) $x_1, ..., x_n$ as

$$H(X) = \sum_{i=1}^{n} p(x_i) log_2 \left(\frac{1}{p(x_i)} \right) = - \sum_{i=1}^{n} p(x_i) log_2 p(x_i), \tag{2.3}$$

where $p(x_i) = Pr(X{=}x_i)$ is the probability of the ith outcome of X. Note that a random variable is not a variable in the usual sense but rather a function that maps events to numbers. To simplify our notation, henceforth, we shall write the logarithm to the base 2 of x simply as $logx$, omitting the subscript on the "log".

Equation (2.3) can also be expressed as

$$H(X) = \sum_{i=1}^{n} p(x_i) I(x_i), \tag{2.4}$$

Therefore, the entropy of the discrete random variable X is the average information of its states.

2.2 Memory Source

Rather than using a discrete random variable to further study information, it is more intuitive and convenient to consider a model of discrete information source as shown in Figure 2-1. In the model, the source generates a sequence of symbols from a fixed finite source alphabet $X = \{x_1, x_2, ..., x_n\}$. Successive symbols are generated according to some fixed probability law.

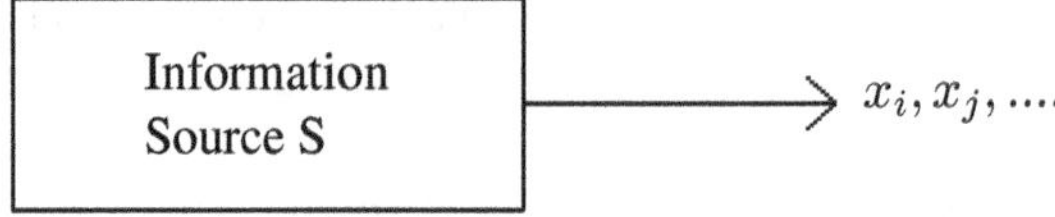

Figure 2-1. A discrete information source

For example, we can generate an English text message with a computer program; the alphabet X consists of letters {a, b, c, d, ...} and digits { 1, 2, 3, ...}. In this model we can also view each symbol $\{x_i\}$ as a state and the alphabet X as a random variable.

If the successive symbols generated from the source are statistically independent, the information source is referred to as **zero-memory source** (or order-0 Markov source), which is the simplest kind of sources one can have. Such an information source can be completely described by the source alphabet X and the probabilities with which the symbols occur:

$$p(x_1), p(x_2), p(x_3), \ldots\ldots, p(x_n)$$

If symbol x_i occurs, we obtain an amount of information $I(x_i)$ bits given by

$$I(x_i) = log\frac{1}{p(x_i)}$$

This means that if we receive a symbol z that is very unlikely to appear, $p(z)$ is very small; $\frac{1}{p(z)}$ and thus $I(z)$ is very large. In other words, we get a lot of surprise (information) when we receive something totally unexpected. On the other hand, if $p(z)$ is large, $I(z)$ is small. That is, we gain little information (surprise) when we get something we expect.

The probability for x_i to occur is simply $p(x_i)$. So the average amount of information per symbol one can receive from the source S is

$$\sum_X p(x_i)I(x_i) \quad bits$$

where we sum over the n symbols of the alphabet X; this average information is the entropy $H(S)$ of the zero memory source.

$$H(S) = H(X) = \sum_{i=1}^{n} p(x_i)log\frac{1}{p(x_i)} \quad bits \tag{2.5}$$

The source gives maximum entropy $H_M(S)$ when all symbols occur with the same probability $p(x_i) = \frac{1}{n}$.

$$H_M(S) = \sum_{i=1}^{n} \frac{1}{n} log\ n = log\ n \quad bits$$

Therefore, an alphabet with 256 symbols has a maximum entropy of 8 bits, which is the maximum amount of average information per symbol that the source can generate from it.

2.3 Markov Memory Source

In the zero-memory model, the occurrence of each symbol is statistically independent of each other. However, in reality symbols are statistically related to each other in most cases. For example, in an English text, the probability for letter 'u' to occur is quite small. However, if we receive a letter 'q', we know that the next letter that we shall receive is very likely to be a 'u'. If we have received the letters 'democrac', there is a large chance that the next letter is a 'y'. To better study the information content of this kind of symbol sequences, we need a model in which the occurrence of a source symbol x_i may depend upon m preceding symbols. Such a source is referred to as an mth-order Markov source and is defined by specifying the occurrence of source symbols with the set of conditional probabilities

$$p(x_i/x_{k_1}, \ldots, x_{k_m}) \quad for\ \ i = 1, 2, \ldots, n; \ \ k_j = 1, 2, \ldots, n \tag{2.6}$$

which is the probability of seeing x_i after we have seen m symbols.

It is often convenient to use finite state diagrams to illustrate an mth-order Markov source. At a given time, we can refer to the m preceding symbols as the **state** of the mth-order Markov source at that time; as there are n symbols in the alphabet, there are n^m possible states. Figure 2-2 shows a state diagram of a **second-order** (i.e. $m = 2$) Markov source with binary alphabet $X = \{0, 1\}$ and conditional probabilities

$$\begin{array}{ll} p(0/00) = 0.8 & p(1/00) = 0.2 \\ p(0/01) = 0.5 & p(1/01) = 0.5 \\ p(0/10) = 0.5 & p(1/10) = 0.5 \\ p(0/11) = 0.2 & p(1/11) = 0.8 \end{array}$$

In the diagram, states are represented by circles and state transitions are indicated by arrows labeled with the corresponding conditional probabilities. (This Figure and related examples discussed below are taken from the book *Information Theory and Coding* by **Norman Abramson.**)

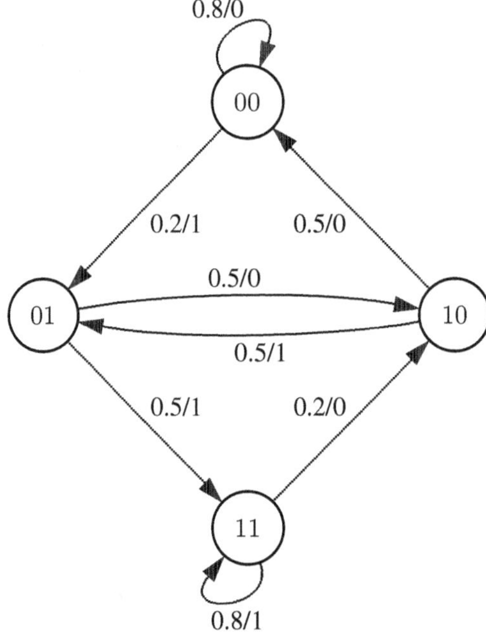

Figure 2-2. State diagram of a second-order Markov source with alphabet $\{0, 1\}$

In image processing, it is common to use a second or third order Markov model to predict a pixel value. That is, two or three previously occurred pixel values are used to estimate the value of a forthcoming pixel.

In many cases (but not all), the probability distribution over the set of states do not change with time. We refer to this kind of distribution as stationary distribution. In these cases, when we specify the conditional symbol probabilities $p(x_i/x_{k_1}, ..., x_{k_m})$ of an mth-order Markov source, we also implicitly specify the n^m state probabilities $p(x_{k_1}, x_{k_2}, ..., x_{k_m})$. The product of these two probabilities gives us the probability of the joint event "*the source is in the state* $(x_{k_1}, x_{k_2}, ..., x_{k_m})$ *and* x_i *occurs*". That is

$$p(x_{k_1}, ..., x_{k_m}, x_i) = p(x_i/x_{k_1}, ..., x_{k_m})p(x_{k_1}, ..., x_{k_m}) \tag{2.7}$$

The information we obtain if x_i occurs while the system is in the state $(x_{k_1}, x_{k_2}, ..., x_{k_m})$ is

$$I(x_i/x_{k_1}, ..., x_{k_m}) = log\frac{1}{p(x_i/x_{k_1}, ..., x_{k_m})} \tag{2.8}$$

and the average amount of information per symbol while the system is in the state $(x_{k_1}, x_{k_2}, ..., x_{k_m})$ is given by:

$$H(X/x_{k_1}, ..., x_{k_m}) = \sum_X p(x_i/x_{k_1}, ..., x_{k_m})I(x_i/x_{k_1}, ..., x_{k_m}) \tag{2.9}$$

where the summation is over the n symbols in the alphabet X. If we average this quantity over all the n^m possible states, we obtain the average amount of information, or the entropy of the mth-order Markov source S.

$$H(S) = \sum_{X^m} p(x_{k_1}, ..., x_{k_m})H(X/x_{k_1}, ..., x_{k_m}) \tag{2.10}$$

In other words, if we have a very long text consisting of n symbols which can be described by such a model, then $H(S)$ of (2.10) gives us the average information per symbol of the text. For example, in a long Internet message, we can take the alphabet as the generalized ASCII code, consisting of 256 symbols or characters (i.e. $n = 256$). To estimate the average information content of the message, we may take m to be 4 (i.e. using a 4-th order Markov model). There will be totally $256^4 = 2^{32}$, about 4 billion states. We have to collect the statistics over the 4 billion states to estimate the probabilities and use them to find the entropy given in (2.10), which gives us the average information per symbol. The total information of the message is then the length of the message times $H(S)$.

Substituting (2.9) and (2.8) into (2.10) and making simplifications, we can express the entropy (average information per symbol) in the following form:

$$H(S) = \sum_{X^{m+1}} p(x_{k_1}, ..., x_{k_m}, x_i) \times log\frac{1}{p(x_i/x_{k_1}, ..., x_{k_m})} \tag{2.11}$$

Example 2-1

Consider the Markov source of Figure 2-2, where the alphabet only consists of two symbols which are the binary digits, i.e. $X = \{1, 0\}$. Since the stationary distribution does not depend upon the initial states, we can calculate the probability for each state from the conditional symbol probabilities. One can show that the stationary distribution is:

$$p(00) = \tfrac{5}{14} \quad p(01) = \tfrac{2}{14}$$
$$p(10) = \tfrac{2}{14} \quad p(11) = \tfrac{5}{14}$$

We summarize the relevant probabilities in Table 2-1:

Table 2-1 Probabilities for Markov Source $X = \{0, 1\}$ of Figure 2-2

x_{k_1}, x_{k_2}, x_i	$p(x_i/x_{k_1}, x_{k_2})$	$p(x_{k_1}, x_{k_2})$	$p(x_{k_1}, x_{k_2}, x_i)$
000	0.8	$\frac{5}{14}$	$\frac{4}{14}$
001	0.2	$\frac{5}{14}$	$\frac{1}{14}$
010	0.5	$\frac{2}{14}$	$\frac{1}{14}$
011	0.5	$\frac{2}{14}$	$\frac{1}{14}$
100	0.5	$\frac{2}{14}$	$\frac{1}{14}$
101	0.5	$\frac{2}{14}$	$\frac{1}{14}$
110	0.2	$\frac{5}{14}$	$\frac{1}{14}$
111	0.8	$\frac{5}{14}$	$\frac{4}{14}$

Note that $p(x_{k_1}, x_{k_2}, x_i) = p(x_i/x_{k_1}, x_{k_2}) \times p(x_{k_1}, x_{k_2})$. We can now calculate the average entropy of the system using (2.11):

$$H(S) = \sum_{X^3} p(x_{k_1}, x_{k_2}, x_i) log \frac{1}{p(x_i/x_{k_1}, x_{k_2})} \tag{2.12}$$

Substituting the probabilities in Table 2-1 into (2.12), we obtain

$$\begin{aligned} H(S) &= \tfrac{4}{14} \times log\frac{1}{0.8} + \tfrac{1}{14} \times log\frac{1}{0.2} + \tfrac{1}{14} \times log\frac{1}{0.5} + \tfrac{1}{14} \times log\frac{1}{0.5} \\ &+ \tfrac{1}{14} \times log\frac{1}{0.5} + \tfrac{1}{14} \times log\frac{1}{0.5} + \tfrac{1}{14} \times log\frac{1}{0.2} + \tfrac{4}{14} \times log\frac{1}{0.8} \\ &= 0.81(\text{bit / binary digit}) \end{aligned}$$

In equation (2.10), X^m is the mth extension of the alphabet X, which has n^m symbols, $\sigma_1, \sigma_2, ..., \sigma_{n^m}$ and each σ_i corresponds to some sequence of $m\ x_k^{\prime}s$. One can define the r-th extension of an m-th order Markov source, where we group r symbols together to form one new 'super-symbol'. If we consider each of these 'super-symbols' as a symbol, our alphabet X becomes:

$$X = \{\sigma_1, \sigma_2, ..., \sigma_{n^r}\}$$

By grouping r symbols together, we have considered the correlation between r symbols, which can give us better estimate of the information content of a text. In reality, there could be long-range correlations between groups of symbols. To accurately calculate the average information, we actually need to consider an extremely long message and make the group as large as possible. Theoretically, the average information of a 'typical' stationary infinite text is given by the entropy rate $H(X)$, which is the limit of the joint entropy of n 'symbols' averaged over n:

$$H(X) = \lim_{n\to\infty} \frac{1}{n} H(X_1, X_2, ..., X_n) \tag{2.13}$$

We may also define the entropy rate, $H(S)$ using conditional probabilities:

$$H(S) = \lim_{n\to\infty} \frac{1}{n} H(X_n|X_{n-1}, X_{n-2}, ..., X_1) \tag{2.14}$$

One can show that the two quantities defined in (2.13) and (2.14) are basically equal (i.e. $H(S) = H(X)$).

What (2.14) tells us is that when reading a text, if we use a sufficiently large number of symbols to predict the forthcoming symbol, the accuracy of prediction reflects the average information of the text. If we can predict the next symbol very well, there is a lot of redundancy and the average information which is equal to the entropy rate is very small. Since n tends to infinity in (2.13) and (2.14), we have exhausted the search of any long-range correlations in the text.

2.4 Information of Text and Kolmogorov Complexity

In the previous section, we have discussed that the average information a text contains is given by its entropy rate. The problem of this approach is that entropy rate is defined using an infinite text of symbols. We have also discussed a model of information source and some of its properties. We are interested to know how closely the model and theories relate to the physical process of information generation in real life. In practice, every text is of finite length and we can only estimate its information content using predictions based on a finite number of preceding symbols. In some situations, such an estimate can be totally off. For instance, consider a simple experiment that uses the following program, **randtest.cpp** to generate 10 million bytes of data using a pseudo random number generator:

```
//randtest.cpp: Generates 10 million bytes of data
//Compile: g++ -o randtest randtest.cpp
#include <stdio.h>
#include <stdlib.h>
#include <math.h>

int main()
{
  int x;
  char *pc = (char *)&x;             //points to low byte of x
  FILE *fp;

  fp = fopen ( "randnums", "wb" );//open binary file "randnums"
                                // for write, no error checking
  for ( int i = 0; i < 10000000; ++i ){ //output 10 million bytes
    x = rand();                         //output only lowest byte
    putc ( (int) *pc, fp );             //output one byte
  }
  return 0;
}
```

The 10 millions bytes of data are saved in the file "randnums". Now let us use the common compression utility **gzip** to compress the data, saving the output data in the file "randnums.gz" and check the file sizes:

```
$ ./randtest
$ gzip -c randnums > randnums.gz
$ ls -l randnums*
  -rw-r--r-- 1 user user 10000000 2009-11-21 11:10 randnums
  -rw-r--r-- 1 user user 10001557 2009-11-21 11:10 randnums.gz
```

We see that the compressed file size is about the same as the original size. This implies that we were not able to compress the data and the average information of the file is 8 bits per symbol. If we calculate the entropy using Equation (2.12), we shall obtain a similar value. In other words, the file "randnums" contains about 80 million bits of information! If we need to transmit these data to a friend we need to transmit 80 million bits! We know that this could not be true because the data are generated from a simple program using a simple pseudo random number generator (**rand**()). We can simply send our friend the program along with the pseudo random number generator, which together may contain less than 1 Kbytes of data. Our friend can then use the program to reproduce all the 80 million bits of the file "randnums". Therefore, the information that the file "randnums" contains is actually much less than 80 million bits. Does this mean that the definition of entropy rate given in (2.13) or (2.14) is inconsistent with our experience of information of data? The main reason for the inconsistency is that we have only considered a finite number of symbols in the compression process. The utility program **gzip** is based on the Ziv-Lempel algorithm which uses a finite look-ahead buffer for searching a string that matches the string under consideration. Because of the limited buffer size, all characters appear random to the encoder and the text cannot be compressed. In practice, any pseudo random number generator (PRNG) has a a finite period, which means that the sequence repeats itself after a certain number. Within a period, the generated numbers appear random. In general, the period of a PRNG is very long for it to have practical use. If we have generated a sequence that is much longer than the period and our compression program has used a look-ahead buffer larger than the period, the huge file will be compressed to a very small one, which is consistent with our intuition that the sequence actually contains very little information. Therefore, in some situations entropy rate may not be a good estimate of the **average** information of data as it requires an infinite number of bits of data in the measurement to give the correct result.

A more fundamental approach to estimate the information of data or text is to consider the Kolmogorov complexity, also known as algorithmic entropy, which is a measure of the computational resources required to generate the text. For example, consider the following string of length 96:

go!go!go!go!go!go!go!go!go!go!go!go!go!go!go!go!
go!go!go!go!go!go!go!go!go!go!go!go!go!go!go!go!

The string can be described by a short English Language description like, "go! 32 times" which consists of only 12 characters.

More formally, the complexity of a string is the length of the string's shortest description in some fixed universal description language. One can show that the Kolmogorov complexity of a string cannot be too much larger than the length of the string itself. Suppose **P** is a program that outputs a string **x**, then **P** is a description of **x**. The length of the program, $\mathbf{l}(\mathbf{P})$ is essentially the complexity of the string **x**. We can now make a formal definition of Kolmogorov complexity.

Kolmogorov (algorithmic) complexity $K_u(x)$ of a string x with respect to a universal computer u is defined as

$$K_u(x) = \min_{P:u(P)=x} l(P) \tag{2.15}$$

the minimum length over all programs P that print x and halt.

One can show that if K_1 and K_2 are the complexity functions relative to description languages L_1 and L_2, then there exists a constant c, which depends only on languages L_1 and L_2, such that

$$|K_1(x) - K_2(x)| \leq c, \quad for\ all\ strings\ x \tag{2.16}$$

This implies that the effect of choosing a description language on K is bounded.

One can prove that Kolmogorov complexity is the minimum number of bits into which a string can be compressed without losing information. In other words, it is the information the string contains. Therefore, a string is incompressible if its length is equal to its Kolmogorov complexity. One can also show that when the string is sufficiently long, the entropy of the string converges to the Kolmogorov complexity. Therefore, the information contained in a fractal image or a set of pseudo random numbers is very small as the data can be generated by a simple program using an algorithm.

2.5 Data Reversibility

By now we know that data are different from information. We can use different amount of data to represent the same piece of information. In practice, a set of data may have a lot of redundancy and data compression is achieved by getting rid of the redundancy. There are two kinds of data compression, lossless and lossy. In lossless compression, no information is lost and the exact original data set can be recovered. In lossy compression, information is lost and the original data set cannot be recovered. In other words, in lossy compression, we throw away some information in order to achieve a higher compression ratio. *What kind of information do we want to throw away?* Naturally, we want to throw away the irrelevant information and retain the important information. Given a set of data, *how do we decide on which portion of data is more important than others*? In fact, separating the relevant and irrelevant information is the state of the art of lossy data compression. The following discussion gives a brief idea how this can be done.

Suppose we want to know about the age of the people in a country of a million. We would not want to remember the age of every individual. If we just want to remember one value concerning age, we would most likely remember the average age of the population; we don't care about the age of the president or the age of any 'great leader' of the country. The average value gives us a brief idea about the population of the country. Indeed, the average value of a data set is usually the most crucial value. On the other hand, we cannot reconstruct the whole set from its average value. In other words, when we average the values of a set of data, we lose information; the process is irreversible. This is also true in the physical world. For instance, consider the case that we put a drop of red ink in a glass of water. We will see that the ink spreads over and eventually the whole glass of water becomes red. However, no matter how long we continue to observe the glass of red water, we will never see the process reverses itself and the ink pigment forms a drop again. Microscopically, the process is reversible; when an ink pigment molecule interacts with a water molecule, there is nothing that forbids them to go in one direction or the other. From the point of view of information theory, the process is reversible because we have recorded the information of every single molecule. However, macroscopically, the entropy law of physics forbids the process to be reversible. This is because when we observe the glass of water macroscopically, we observe an unaccountable number of molecules simultaneously; we are observing the average behavior of the molecules. Because of the averaging effect, information is lost in the process and thus it is irreversible.

Chapter 3

Imaging Basics

3.1 Sampling and Quantization

Sampling is the process of examining the value of a continuous function at regular intervals. We might measure the voltage of an analog waveform every millisecond, or measure the brightness of a photograph every millimeter, horizontally and vertically. Sampling rate is the rate at which we make the measurements and can be defined as

$$\textit{Sampling rate} = \frac{1}{\textit{Sampling interval}} \; Hz$$

If sampling is performed in the time domain, Hz is $cycles/sec$.

In the case of image processing, we can treat an *image* as a two-dimensional light-intensity function $f(x, y)$ of spatial coordinates (x, y). Since light is a form of energy, $f(x, y)$ must be nonnegative. In order that we can store an *image* in a computer, which processes data in discrete form, the image function $f(x, y)$ must be digitized both spatially and in amplitude. Digitization of the spatial coordinates (x, y) is referred to as *image sampling* or *spatial sampling*, and digitization of the amplitude f is referred to as *quantization*. Moreover, for moving video images, we have to digitize the time component and this is called *temporal sampling*. Figure 3-1 shows the concept of spatial sampling.

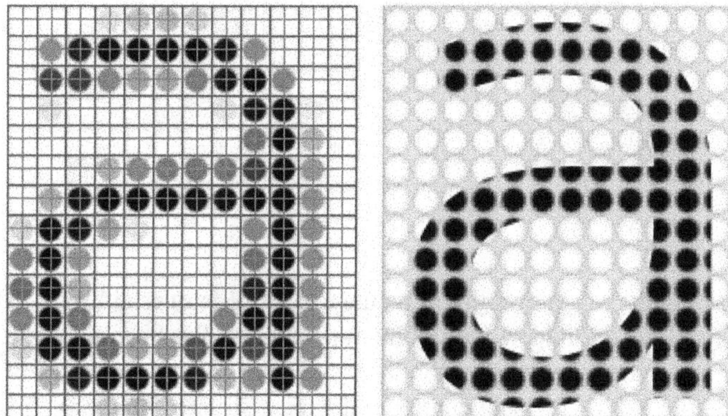

Figure 3-1 Spatial Sampling

Digital video is a representation of a real-world scene, sampled spatially and temporarily and with the light intensity value quantized at each spatial point. A scene is sampled at an instance of time to produce a *frame*, which consists of the complete visual scene at that instance, or a *field*, which consists of odd- or even-numbered lines of spatial samples. Figure 3-2 shows spatial and temporal sampling of videos.

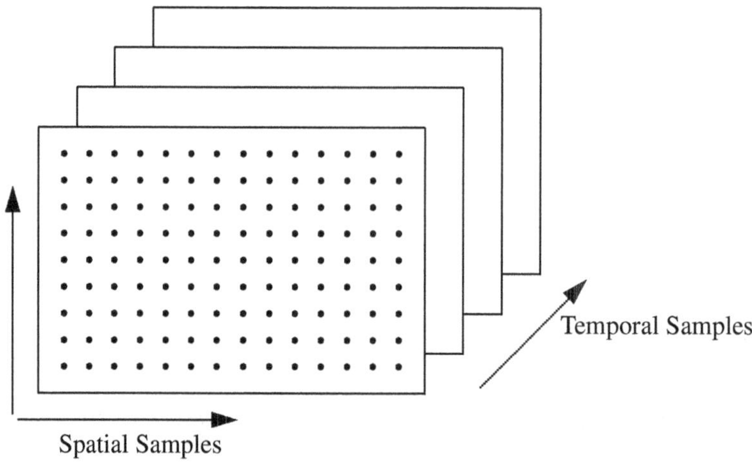

Figure 3-2 Temporal Sampling and Spatial Sampling

3.1.1 Spatial Sampling

Very often a two-dimensional (2D) sampled image is obtained by projecting a video scene onto a 2D sensor, such as an array of Charge Coupled Devices (CCD array) . For colour images, each colour component is filtered and projected onto an independent 2D CCD array. The CCD array outputs analogue signals representing the intensity levels of the colour component. Sampling the signal at an instance in time produces a sampled image or frame that has specified values at a set of spatial sampling points in the form of an $N \times M$ array as shown in the following equation.

$$f(x, y) \approx \begin{pmatrix} f(0,0) & f(0,1) & \ldots & f(0, M-1) \\ f(1,0) & f(1,1) & \ldots & f(1, M-1) \\ . & . & \ldots & . \\ . & . & \ldots & . \\ f(N-1,0) & f(N-1,1) & \ldots & f(N-1, M-1) \end{pmatrix} \tag{3.1}$$

The right image of Figure 3-1 shows that a rectangular grid is overlaid on a 2D image to obtain sampled values $f(x, y)$ at the intersection points of the grid. We may approximately reconstruct the sampled image by representing each sample as a square picture element (pixel) as shown on the left image of Figure 3-1. The visual quality of the reconstructed image is affected by the choice of the sampling points. The more sampling points we choose, the higher resolution the resulted sampled image will be. Of course, choosing more sampling points requires more computing power and storage.

3.1.2 Temporal Sampling

Temporal sampling of video images refers to the process of taking a rectangular 'snapshot' of the image signal at regular time intervals. The rate at which we take the the snapshots is the *sampling rate* and is defined as the *frame rate* or *field rate*. When we play back a sequence of frames obtained in this way at the same rate, an illusion of motion may be created. A higher frame rate produces apparently smoother motion but requires more computing resources to process the larger number of samples. Early silent films used anything between 16 and 24 frames per second (fps). Current television standards use sampling rate of 25 or 30 frames per second.

There are two commonly used temporal sampling techniques, *progressive* sampling and *interlaced* sampling. Progressive sampling is a frame-based sampling technique where a video signal is sampled as a series of complete frames. Film is a progressive sampling source for video. Interlaced sampling is a field-based sampling technique where the video is sampled periodically at two sample fields; half of the data in a frame (one field) are scanned at one time. To reconstruct the frame, a pair of sample fields are superimposed on each other (interlaced). In general, a field consists of either the odd-numbered or even-numbered scan lines within a frame as shown in Figure 3-3.

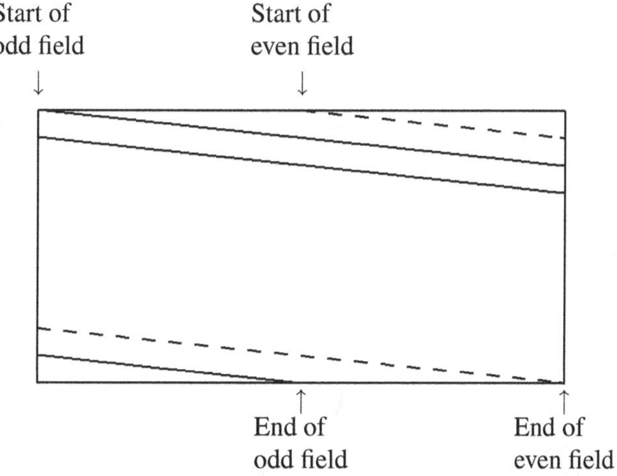

Figure 3-3 Interlaced Scanning

An interlaced video sequence contains a sequence of fields, each of which consists of half the data of a complete frame. The interlaced sampling technique can give the appearance of smoother motion as compared to the progressive sampling method when the data are sampled at the same rate. This is due to the "motion blur" effect of human eyes; the persistence of vision can cause images shown rapidly in sequence to appear as one. When we rapidly switch between two low quality fields, they appear like a single high quality image. Because of this advantage, most current video image formats, including several high-definition video standards, use interlaced techniques rather than progressive methods.

3.1.3 Quantization

Quantization is the procedure of constraining the value of a function at a sampling point to a predetermined finite set of discrete values. Note that the original function can be either continuous or discrete. For example, if we want to specify the temperature of Los Angels, ranging from 0^oC to 50^oC, up to a a precision of 0.1^oC, we must be able to represent 1001 possible values, which require 10 bits to represent one sample. On the other hand, if we only need a precision of 1^oC, we only have 51 possible values requiring 6 bits for the representation. For image processing, higher precision gives higher image quality but requires more bits in the representation of the samples. We will come back to this topic and discuss how to use quantization to achieve lossy image compression.

3.2 Color Spaces

To describe an image, we need a way to represent the color information. A gray-level image only requires one number to indicate the brightness or luminance of each spatial sample. In reality, our perception of light depends on the light frequency and other properties. When we view a source of light, our eyes respond to three main sensations. The first one is the **color**, which is the main frequencies of the light. The second one is the **intensity** (or brightness), which corresponds to the total energy and can be quantified as the luminance of the the light. The third one is the **purity** (or saturation) of the light, which describes how close a light appears to be a pure spectral color, such as green. Pale colors have low purity and they appear to be almost white. We use the term **chromaticity** to collectively refer to the two characteristics of light, color purity and dominant frequency (hue).

Very often, we employ a **color model** to precisely describe the color components or intensities. In general, a color model is any method for explaining the properties or behavior of color within some particular context. No single model can explain all aspects of color, so people make use of different models to help describe different color characteristics. Here, we consider a **color model** as an abstract mathematical model that describes how colors are presented as tuples of numbers, typically as three or four values or color components; the resulting set of colors that define how the components are to be interpreted is called a **color space**. The commonly used **RGB** color model naturally fits the representation of colors by computers. However, it is not a good model for studying the characteristics of an image.

3.3 RGB Color Model

X-ray, light, infrared radiation, microwave and radio waves are all electromagnetic (EM) waves with different wavelengths. Light waves lie in the visible spectrum with a narrow wavelength band from about 350 to 780 nm. The retina of a human eye can detect only EM waves lying within this visible spectrum but not anything outside. The eye contains two kinds of light-sensitive receptor cells, **cones** and **rods** that can detect light.

The **cones** are sensitive to colors and there are three types of cones, each responding to one of the three primary colors, red, green and blue. Scientists found that our perception of color is a result of our cones' relative response to the red, green and blue colors. Any color can be considered as a combination of these three colors with certain intensity values. The human eye can distinguish about 200 intensities of each of the red, green and blue colors. Therefore, it is natural that we represent each of these colors by a byte which can hold 256 values. In other words, 24 bits are enough to represent the 'true' color. More bits will not increase the quality of an image as human eyes cannot resolve the extra colors. Each eye has 6 to 7 million cones located near the center of the eye, allowing us to see the tiny details of an object.

On the other hand, the **rods** cannot distinguish colors but are sensitive to dim light. Each eye has 75 million to 150 millions rods located near its corner, allowing us to detect peripheral objects in an environment of near darkness.

We can characterize a visible color by a function $C(\lambda)$ where λ is the wavelength of the color in the visible spectrum. The value for a given wavelength λ gives the relative intensity of that wavelength in the color. This description is accurate when we measure the color with certain physical instrument. However, the human visual system (HVS) does not perceive color in this way. Our brains do not receive the entire distribution $C(\lambda)$ of the visible spectrum but rather three values – the **tristimulus values** – that are the responses of the three types (red, green and blue) of cones to a color. This human characteristics leads to the formulation of the trichromatic theory: *If two colors produce the same tristimulus values, they are visually indistinguishable.* A consequence of of this theory is that it is possible to match all of the colors in the visible spectrum by appropriate mixing of three primary colors. In other words, any color can be created by combining red, green, and blue in varying proportions. This leads to the development of the **RGB color model**.

The RGB (short for red, green, blue) color model decomposes a color into three components, Red (R), Green (G), and Blue (B); we can represent any color by three components R, G, B just like the case that a spatial vector is specified by three components x, y, z. If the color components R, G and B are confined to values between 0 and 1, all definable colors lie in a unit cube as shown in Figure 3-4. This color space is most natural for representing computer images, in which a color specification such as (0.1, 0.8, 0.23) can be directly translated into three positive integer values, each of which is represented by one byte.

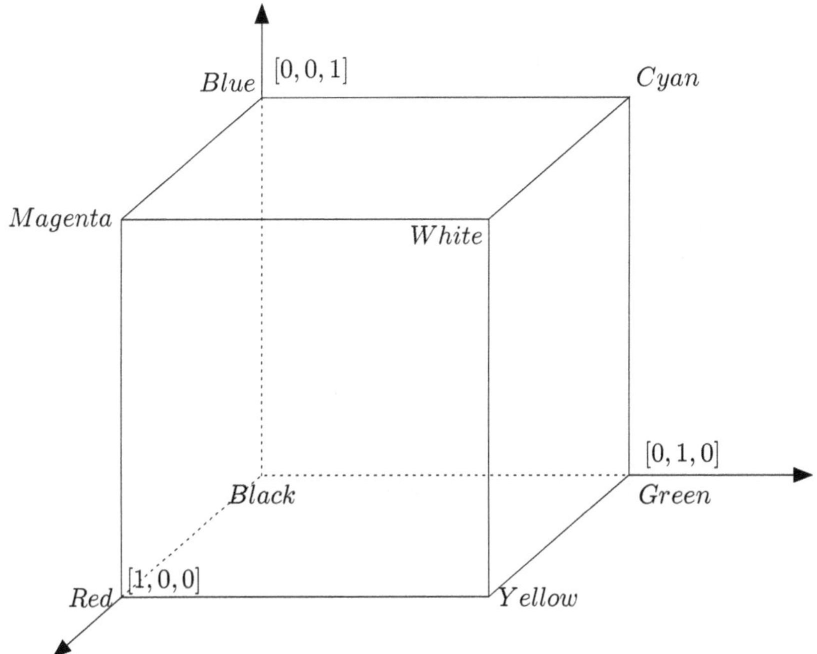

Figure 3-4 *RGB* Color Cube

In this model, we express a color C in the vector form,

$$C = \begin{pmatrix} R \\ G \\ B \end{pmatrix} \qquad 0 \le R, G, B \le 1 \tag{3.2}$$

In some other notations, the authors like to consider R, G, and B as three unit vectors like the three spatial unit vectors **i**, **j**, and **k**. Just as a spatial vector **V** can be expressed as $\mathbf{v} = x\mathbf{i} + y\mathbf{j} + z\mathbf{k}$, any color is expressed as $C = (rR + gG + bB)$, and the red, green, blue intensities are specified by the values of r, g, and b respectively. In our notation here, R, G, and B may represent the intensity values of the color components. The next few sections discuss in more detail the color representation of various standards.

Suppose we have two colors C_1 and C_2 given by

$$C_1 = \begin{pmatrix} R_1 \\ G_1 \\ B_1 \end{pmatrix}, \qquad C_2 = \begin{pmatrix} R_2 \\ G_2 \\ B_2 \end{pmatrix}$$

Does it make sense to add these two colors to produce a new color C? For instance, consider

$$C = C_1 + C_2 = \begin{pmatrix} R_1 + R_2 \\ G_1 + G_2 \\ B_1 + B_2 \end{pmatrix}$$

You may immediately notice that the sum of two components may give a value larger than 1, which lies outside the color cube and thus does not represent any color. Just like adding two points in space is illegitimate, we cannot arbitrarily combine two colors. A linear combination of colors makes sense only if the sum of the coefficients is equal to 1. Therefore, we can have

$$C = \alpha_1 C_1 + \alpha_2 C_2 \tag{3.3}$$

when

$$0 \leq \alpha_1, \alpha_2 \quad and \quad \alpha_1 + \alpha_2 = 1$$

In this way, we can guarantee that the resulted components will always lie within the color cube as each value will never exceed one. For example,

$$R = \alpha_1 R_1 + \alpha_2 R_2 \leq \alpha_1 \times 1 + \alpha_2 \times 1 = 1$$

which implies

$$R \leq 1$$

The linear combination of colors described by Equation (3.3) is called *color blending.*

3.4 Color Systems

In the RGB model described above, a given color is a point in a color cube as shown in Figure 3-4, and can be expressed as

$$C = \begin{pmatrix} R \\ G \\ B \end{pmatrix} \qquad 0 \leq R, G, B \leq 1$$

However, RGB systems do not produce identical perceptions and they vary significantly from one to another. For example, suppose we have a yellow color described by the triplet (0.9, 0.8, 0.0). If we feed these values to a CRT and a film image recorder, we shall see different colors, even though in both cases the red is 90 percent of the maximum, the green is 80 percent of the maximum, and there is no blue. The reason is that the CRT phosphors and the film dyes have different color distribution responses. Consequently, the range of displayable colors (or the color **gamut**) is different in each case.

Different organizations have different interests and emphasis on color models. For example, the graphics community is interested in device-independent graphics, and the real differences among display properties are not addressed by most graphics software APIs. Fortunately, this bas been addressed in colorimetery literature, and standards exist for many common color systems. For example, the National Television System Committee (NTSC) defines an RGB system which forms the basis for many CRT systems. We can view the differences in color systems as the differences between various coordinate system for representing the tristimulus values. If

$$C_1 = \begin{pmatrix} R_1 \\ G_1 \\ B_1 \end{pmatrix}, \quad \text{and} \quad C_2 = \begin{pmatrix} R_2 \\ G_2 \\ B_2 \end{pmatrix} \tag{3.4}$$

are the representations of the same color in two different systems, we can find a 3×3 color conversion matrix M such that

$$C_2 = MC_1 \tag{3.5}$$

Regardless of the way we find this matrix, it allows us to produce similar displays on different color systems.

However, this is not a good approach because the color gamuts of two systems may not be the same; even after the conversion of the color components from one system to another, the color may not be producible on the second system. Also, the printing and graphic arts industries use a four color subtractive system (CMYK) that includes black (K) as the fourth primary. Moreover, the linear color theory is only an approximation to human perception of colors. The distance between two points in the color cube does not necessarily measure how far apart the colors are perceptually. For example, humans are particularly sensitive to color shifts in blue.

The International Commission on Illumination, referred to as the CIE (Commission Internationale de l'Eclarage) defined in 1931 three standard primaries, which are actually imaginary colors. They are defined mathematically with positive color-matching functions shown in Figure 3-5. If the spectral power distribution (SPD) for a colored object is weighted by the curves of Figure 3-5, the CIE chromaticity coordinates can be calculated. This provides an international standard definition of all colors, and the CIE primaries eliminate negative-value color-matching and other problems related to the selection of a set of real primaries.

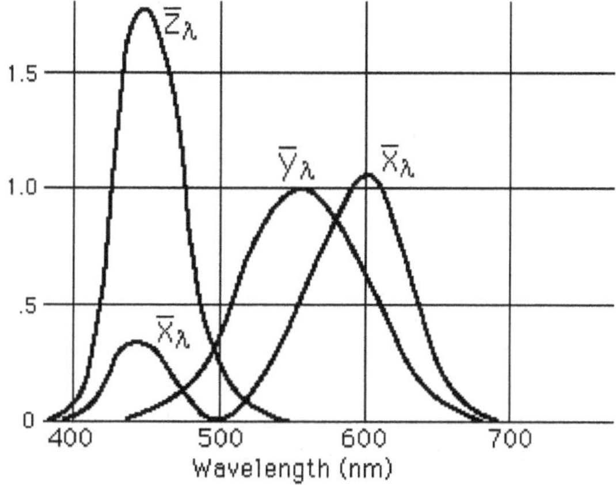

Figure 3-5 Matching functions of the three CIE primaries

3.4.1 The XYZ Color Model

The set of CIE primaries defines a color model that is in general referred to as the **XYZ color model**, where parameters X, Y, and Z represent the tristimulus values, the amount of each CIE primary required to produce a given color. The tristimulus values do not correspond to real colors, but they do have the property that any real color can be represented as a positive combination of them. Therefore, an RGB model describes a color in the same way as the XYZ model does. Actually, most color standards are based on this theoretical XYZ model. In this model, the Y primary is the luminance of the color and all colors can be represented by positive tristimulus values.

Due to the nature of the distribution of cones in the eye, the tristimulus values depend on the observer's field of view. To eliminate this variable, the CIE defined the standard (colorimetric) observer, which is characterized by three color matching functions. The color matching functions are the numerical description of the chromatic response of the observer. The three color-matching functions are referred to as $\overline{X}(\lambda), \overline{Y}(\lambda)$, and $\overline{Z}(\lambda)$, which can be thought of as the spectral sensitivity curves of three linear light detectors that yield the CIE XYZ tristimulus values X, Y, and Z. The tabulated numerical values of these functions are known collectively as the CIE standard observer.

The tristimulus values for a color with a spectral power distribution $I(\lambda)$ are given in terms of the standard observer by:

$$X = \int_0^\infty \overline{X}_\lambda I(\lambda) d\lambda$$

$$Y = \int_0^\infty \overline{Y}_\lambda I(\lambda) d\lambda \tag{3.6}$$

$$Z = \int_0^\infty \overline{Z}_\lambda I(\lambda) d\lambda$$

where λ is the wavelength of the equivalent monochromatic light.

A color can be specified by the tristimulus values, X, Y, and Z:

$$C = \begin{pmatrix} X \\ Y \\ Z \end{pmatrix} \tag{3.7}$$

We may also represent a color in the XYZ color space as an additive combination of the primaries using unit vectors $\mathbf{X}, \mathbf{Y}$, and $\mathbf{Z}$. Therefore, we can express Equation (3.7) as

$$C = X\mathbf{X} + Y\mathbf{Y} + Z\mathbf{Z} \tag{3.8}$$

We can use 3 × 3 matrices to convert from XYZ color representation to representations in other standard systems. Also, it is convenient to normalize the X, Y, and Z values against the sum $X + Y + Z$, which is the total light energy. The normalized values are usually referred to as the **chromaticity coordinates**:

$$x = \frac{X}{X+Y+Z}, \quad y = \frac{Y}{X+Y+Z}, \quad z = \frac{Z}{X+Y+Z} \tag{3.9}$$

As $x+y+z=1$, any color can be represented with just the x and y coordinates if the total energy is known. The parameters x and y depend only on hue and purity of the color and are called **chromaticity values**. Instead of using the total energy, people typically use the luminance Y and the chromaticity values x, and y to specify a color. The other two CIE values can be calculated as

$$X = \frac{x}{y}Y, \quad Z = \frac{z}{y}Y \tag{3.10}$$

where $z = 1 - x - y$. Using chromaticity coordinates (x, y), we can represent all colors on a two-dimensional diagram as shown in Figure 3-6.

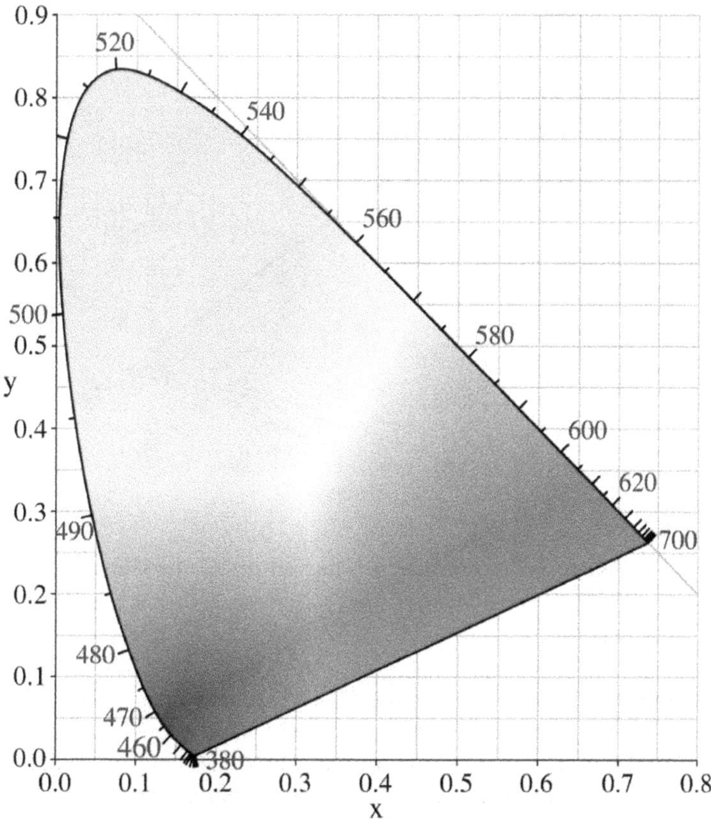

Figure 3-6 CIE Chromaticity Diagram

In Figure 3-6, we plot the normalized coordinates x and y for colors in the visible spectrum and obtain the horseshoe-shaped curve. Ticks along the curve are the spectral colors (pure colors). A tick number indicates the wavelength of the color in nm. For example, the wavelength of the red color is 700 nm and that of yellow is about 570 nm. The line connecting the endpoints of the horseshoe is known as the non-spectral *line of purples*, which is not part of the spectrum.

Lumninance values are not included in the chromaticity diagram; colors with different luminance but with the same chromaticity map to the same point in the diagram. The chromaticity diagram is useful for

- comparing color gamuts for different set of primaries,
- identifying complementary colors, and
- determining purity and dominant wavelength of a given color.

Color Gamuts

The gamut is the set of possible colors within a color system. No one system can reproduce all possible colors in the visible spectrum. It is not possible for a designer to create every color in the spectrum with either additive or subtractive colors. Both systems can reproduce a subset of all visible colors, and while those subsets generally overlap, there are colors which can be reproduced with additive color and not with subtractive color and vice versa.

We identify color gamuts on the chromaticity diagram as straight line segments or polygon regions. Figure 3-7 shows schematically the gamut of reproducible colors for the RGB primaries of a typical color CRT monitor, CMYK color printing, and for the NTSC television.

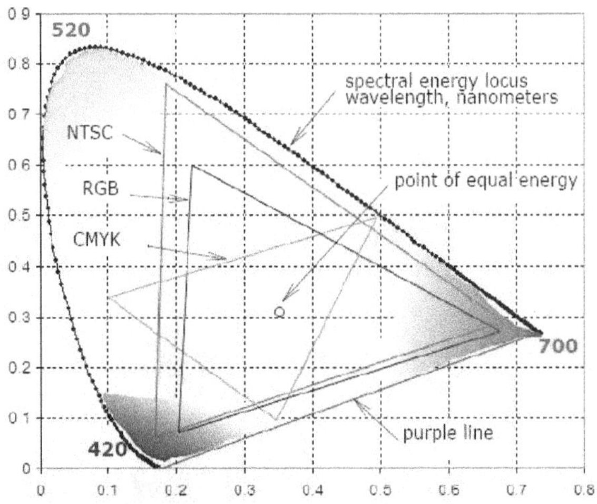

Figure 3-7 Chromaticity Diagram and Color Gamut

3.4.2 YUV Color Model

While the RGB color model is well-suited for displaying color images on a computer screen, it is not an effective model for image processing or video compression. This is because the human visual system (HVS) is more sensitive to luminance (brightness) than to colors. Therefore, it is more effective to represent a color image by separating the luminance from the color information and representing luma with a higher resolution than color.

The YUV color model, defined in the TV standards, is an efficient way of representing color images by separating brightness from color values. Historically, YUV color space was developed to provide compatibility between color and black /white analog television systems; it is not defined precisely in the technical and scientific literature. In this model, Y is the luminance (luma) component, which is the same as the Y component in the CIE XYZ color space, and U and V are the color differences known as chrominance or chroma, which is defined as the difference between a color and a reference white at the same luminance. The conversion from RGB to YUV is given by the following formulas:

$$\begin{aligned} Y &= k_r R + k_g G + k_b B \\ U &= B - Y \\ V &= R - Y \end{aligned} \tag{3.11}$$

with

$$\begin{aligned} &0 \leq k_r, k_b, k_g \\ &k_r + k_b + k_g = 1 \end{aligned} \tag{3.12}$$

Note that equations (3.11) and (3.12) imply that $0 \leq Y \leq 1$ if the R, G, B components lie within the unit color cube. However, U and V can be negative. Typically,

$$k_r = 0.299, k_g = 0.587, k_b = 0.114 \tag{3.13}$$

which are values used in some TV standards. For convenience, in the forthcoming discussions, we always assume that $0 \leq R, G, B \leq 1$ unless otherwise stated.

The complete description of an image is specified by Y (the luminance component) and the two color differences (chrominance) U and V. If the image is black-and-white, $U = V = 0$. Note that we do not need another difference ($G - Y$) for the green component because that would be redundant. We can consider (3.11) as three equations with three unknowns, R, G, and B, and thus we can always solve for the three unknowns and recover R, G, and B. A fourth equation is not necessary.

It seems that there is no advantage of using YUV over RGB to represent an image as both system requires three components to specify an image sample. However, as we mentioned earlier, human eyes are less sensitive to color than to luminance. Therefore, we can represent the U and V components with a lower resolution than Y and the reduction of the amount of data to represent chrominance components will not have an obvious effect on visual quality. Representing chroma with less number of bits than luma is a simple but effective way of compressing an image.

The conversion from RGB space to YUV space can be also expressed in matrix form:

$$\begin{pmatrix} Y \\ U \\ V \end{pmatrix} = \begin{pmatrix} 0.299 & 0.587 & 0.114 \\ -0.299 & -0.587 & 0.886 \\ 0.701 & -0.587 & -0.114 \end{pmatrix} \begin{pmatrix} R \\ G \\ B \end{pmatrix} \tag{3.14}$$

The conversion from YUV space to RGB space using matrix is accomplished with the inverse transformation of (3.14):

$$\begin{pmatrix} R \\ G \\ B \end{pmatrix} = \begin{pmatrix} 1 & 1 & 0 \\ 1 & 0 & 1 \\ 1 & -0.509 & -0.194 \end{pmatrix} \begin{pmatrix} Y \\ U \\ V \end{pmatrix} \tag{3.15}$$

3.4.3 YCbCr Color Model

The YCbCr color model defined in the standards of ITU (International Telecommunication Union) is closely related to YUV but with the chrominace components scaled and shifted to ensure that they lie within the range 0 and 1. It is sometimes abbreviated to YCC. It is also used in the JPEG and MPEG standards. In this model, an image sample is specified by a luminance (Y) component and two chrominance components (Cb, and Cr). The following equations convert an RGB image to one in YCbCr space.

$$\begin{aligned} Y &= k_r R + k_g G + k_b B \\ C_b &= \frac{B - Y}{2(1 - k_b)} + 0.5 \\ C_r &= \frac{(R - Y)}{2(1 - k_r)} + 0.5 \\ k_r &+ k_b + k_g = 1 \end{aligned} \tag{3.16}$$

An image may be captured in the RGB format and then converted to YCbCr to reduce storage or transmission requirements. Before displaying the image, it is usually necessary to convert the image back to RGB. The conversion from YCbCr to RGB can be done by solving for R, G, B in the equations of (3.16). The equations for converting from YCbCr to RGB are shown below:

$$\begin{aligned} R &= Y + (2C_r - 1)(1 - k_r) \\ B &= Y + (2C_b - 1)(1 - k_b) \\ G &= \frac{Y - k_r R - k_b B}{k_g} \\ &= Y - \frac{k_r(2C_r - 1)(1 - k_r) + k_b(2C_b - 1)(1 - k_b)}{k_g} \end{aligned} \tag{3.17}$$

If we use the ITU standard values $k_b = 0.114, k_r = 0.299, k_g = 1 - k_b - k_r = 0.587$ for (3.16) and (3.17), we will obtain the following commonly used conversion equations.

$$\begin{aligned} Y &= 0.299R + 0.587G + 0.114B \\ C_b &= 0.564(B - Y) + 0.5 \\ C_r &= 0.713(R - Y) + 0.5 \\ \\ R &= Y + 1.402C_r - 0.701 \\ G &= Y - 0.714C_r - 0.344C_b + 0.529 \\ B &= Y + 1.772C_b - 0.886 \end{aligned} \tag{3.18}$$

In equations (3.16), it is obvious that $0 \leq Y \leq 1$ as $0 \leq R, G, B \leq 1$. It turns out that the chrominance components C_b and C_r defined in (3.16) also always lie within the range [0, 1]. We prove this for the case of C_b. From (3.16), we have

$$\begin{aligned} C_b &= \frac{B - Y}{2(1 - k_b)} + \frac{1}{2} \\ &= \frac{B - k_r R - k_g G - k_b B + 1 - k_b}{2(1 - k_b)} \\ &= \frac{B}{2} + \frac{-k_r R - k_g G + 1 - k_b}{2(1 - k_b)} \\ &\geq \frac{B}{2} + \frac{-k_r \times 1 - k_g \times 1 + 1 - k_b}{2(1 - k_b)} \\ &= \frac{B}{2} \\ &\geq 0 \end{aligned}$$

Thus

$$C_b \geq 0 \tag{3.19}$$

Also,

$$\begin{aligned} C_b &= \frac{B - Y}{2(1 - k_b)} + \frac{1}{2} \\ &= \frac{B - k_r R - k_g G - k_b B}{2(1 - k_b)} + \frac{1}{2} \\ &\leq \frac{B - k_b B}{2(1 - k_b)} + \frac{1}{2} \\ &= \frac{B}{2} + \frac{1}{2} \\ &\leq \frac{1}{2} + \frac{1}{2} \\ &= 1 \end{aligned}$$

Thus

$$C_b \leq 1 \tag{3.20}$$

Combining (3.19) and (3.20), we have

$$0 \leq C_b \leq 1 \tag{3.21}$$

Similarly

$$0 \leq C_r \leq 1 \tag{3.22}$$

In summary, we have the following situation.

$$\begin{aligned} &\text{If} \quad 0 \leq R, G, B \leq 1 \\ &\text{then} \quad 0 \leq Y, C_b, C_r \leq 1 \end{aligned} \tag{3.23}$$

Note that the converse is not true. That is, if $0 \leq Y, C_b, C_r \leq 1$, it does **not** imply $0 \leq R, G, B \leq 1$. A knowledge of this helps us in the implementations of the conversion from RGB to YCbCr and vice versa. We mentioned earlier that the eye can only resolve about 200 different intensity levels of each of the RGB components. Therefore, we can quantize all the RGB components in the interval [0,1] to 256 values, from 0 to 255, which can be represented by one byte of storage without any loss of visual quality. In other words, one byte (or an 8-bit unsigned integer) is enough to represent all the values of each RGB component. When we convert from RGB to YCbCr, it only requires one 8-bit unsigned integer to represent each YCbCr component. This implicitly implies that all conversions can be done efficiently in integer arithmetic that we shall discuss below.

3.3 Conversions between RGB and YCbCr

It is straightforward to write a C/C++ program to convert RGB to YCbCr or from YCbCr to RGB. We discussed in the previous section that the implementation can be effectively done in integer arithmetic. However, for clarity of presentation, we shall first discuss a floating point implementation. The C/C++ programs presented in this book are mainly for illustration of concepts. In most cases, error checking is omitted and some variable values are hard-coded.

3.3.1 Floating Point Implementation

The program listed below shows the conversion between RGB and YCbCr using ITU standard coefficients. It is a direct implementation of equations (3.18). The R, G, and B values, which must lie between [0,1] are hard-coded and converted to Y, Cb, and Cr, which are then converted back to R, G, and B.

Listing 3-1 (rgbyccf.cpp) Conversions Between RGB and YCbCr

```
int main ()
{
  //0 <= R, G, B <= 1, sample values
  double R = 0.3, G = 0.7, B = 0.2, Y, Cb, Cr;

  printf("\nOriginal R, G, B:\t%f, %f, %f", R, G, B );

  Y  = 0.299 * R + 0.587 * G + 0.114 * B;
  Cb = 0.564 * (B - Y) + 0.5;
  Cr = 0.713 * (R - Y) + 0.5;

  printf("\nConverted Y, Cb, Cr:\t%f, %f, %f", Y, Cb, Cr );

  //recovering R, G, B
  R = Y + 1.402 * Cr - 0.701;
  G = Y - 0.714 * Cr - 0.344 * Cb  + 0.529;
  B = Y + 1.772 * Cb - 0.886;

  printf("\nRecovered R, G, B:\t%f, %f, %f\n\n", R, G, B );
  return 0;
}
```

The program generates the following outputs:

```
Original R, G, B:       0.300000, 0.700000, 0.200000
Converted Y, Cb, Cr:    0.523400, 0.317602, 0.340716
Recovered R, G, B:      0.300084, 0.699874, 0.200191
```

The recovered R, G, and B values differ slightly from the original ones due to rounding errors in computing and the representation of numbers in binary form.

3.3.2 Integer Implementation

The above program illustrates the conversion between RGB and YCbCr using floating-point calculations. However, such an implementation is not practical. Not only that rounding errors are introduced in the computations, floating-point arithmetic is very slow. When compressing an image, we need to apply the conversion to every pixel. Switching to integer-arithmetic in calculations can easily shorten the computing time by a factor of two to three. In RGB-YCbCr conversion, using integer-arithmetic is quite simple because we can always approximate a real number as a fraction between two integers. For example, the coefficients for calculating Y from RGB can be expressed as:

$$\begin{aligned} 0.299 &= 19595/2^{16} \\ 0.587 &= 38470/2^{16} \\ 0.114 &= 7471/2^{16} \end{aligned} \tag{3.24}$$

The integer-arithmetic expression for Y can be obtained by multiplying the equation

$$Y = 0.299R + 0.587G + 0.114B$$

by 2^{16}, which becomes

$$2^{16}Y = 19595R + 38470G + 7471B \tag{3.25}$$

At the same time, we quantize the R, G, and B values from [0, 1] to 0, 1, ..., 255 which can be done by multiplying the floating-point values by 255. We also need to quantize the shifting constants 0.5, 0.701, 0.529, and 0.886 of (3.18) using the same rule by multiplying them by 255, which will become

$$\begin{aligned} 0.5 \times 255 &= 128 \\ 0.701 \times 255 &= 179 \\ 0.529 \times 255 &= 135 \\ 0.886 \times 255 &= 226 \end{aligned} \tag{3.26}$$

Actually, representing a component of RGB with integer values 0 to 255 is the natural way that a modern computer handles color data. In practice, each pixel has three components (R, G, and B) and each component value is saved as an 8-bit unsigned number.

As shown in (3.18), in floating-point representation, the C_b component is given by

$$C_b = 0.564(B - Y) + 0.5$$

After quantization, it becomes

$$C_b = 0.564(B - Y) + 128 \tag{3.27}$$

Multiplying (3.27) by 2^{16}, we obtain

$$2^{16}C_b = 36962(B - Y) + 128 \times 2^{16} \tag{3.28}$$

The corresponding equation for C_r is:

$$2^{16}C_r = 46727(R - Y) + 128 \times 2^{16} \tag{3.29}$$

As R, G, and B have become integers, we can carry out the calculations using integer multiplications and then divide the results by 2^{16}. In binary calculations, dividing a value by 2^{16} is the same as shifting the value right by 16. Therefore, from (3.27), (3.28) and (3.29), the calculations of Y and C_b using integer-arithmetic can be carried out using the following code.

$$\begin{aligned} Y &= (19595 * R + 38470 * G + 7471 * B) >> 16; \\ Cb &= (36962 * (B - Y) >> 16) + 128; \\ Cr &= (46727 * (R - Y) >> 16) + 128; \end{aligned} \tag{3.30}$$

One should note that the sum of the coefficients in calculating Y is 2^{16} (i.e. $19595 + 38470 + 7471 = 65536 = 2^{16}$), corresponding to the requirement $k_r + k_g + k_b = 1$ in the floating-point representation.

The constraints of (3.23) and the requirement of $0 \leq R, G, B \leq 255$ imply that in our integer representation,

$$\begin{aligned} 0 \leq Y &\leq 255 \\ 0 \leq Cb &\leq 255 \\ 0 \leq Cr &\leq 255 \end{aligned} \tag{3.31}$$

In (3.9) the R component is obtained from Y and C_r:

$$R = Y + 1.402C_r - 0.701$$

In integer-arithmetic, this becomes

$$2^{16}R = 2^{16}Y + 91881C_r - 2^{16} \times 179 \tag{3.32}$$

The value of R is obtained by dividing (3.23) by 2^{16} as shown below in C/C++ code:

$$R = (Y + 91881 * Cr >> 16) - 179; \tag{3.33}$$

We can obtain similar equations for G and B. Combining all these, we can express equations of (3.18) in integer-arithmetic using C/C++ code like the following form:

$$\begin{aligned}
Y &= (19595 * R + 38470 * G + 7471 * B) >> 16;\\
Cb &= (36962 * (B - Y) >> 16) + 128;\\
Cr &= (46727 * (R - Y) >> 16) + 128;\\
\\
R &= Y + (91881 * Cr >> 16) - 179;\\
G &= Y - ((46793 * Cr + 22544 * Cb) >> 16) + 135;\\
B &= Y + (116129 * Cb >> 16) - 226;
\end{aligned} \tag{3.34}$$

Listing 3-2 (rgbycci.cpp) RGB-YCbCr Conversions Using Integer Arithmetic

```
----------------------------------------------------------------------
/* Note:
 *   2^16 = 65536
 *   kr = 0.299 = 19595 / 2^16
 *   kg = 0.587 = 38470 / 2^16
 *   Kb = 0.114 =  7471 / 2^16
 *   0.5 = 128 / 255
 *   0.564 = 36962 / 2^16
 *   0.713 = 46727 / 2^16
 *   1.402 = 91881 / 2^16
 *   0.701 = 135 / 255
 *   0.714 = 46793 / 2^16
 *   0.344 = 22544 / 2^16
 *   0.529 = 34668 / 2^16
 *   1.772 = 116129 / 2^16
 *   0.886 = 226 / 255
 */

int main ()
{
  unsigned char R, G, B; //RGB components
  unsigned char Y, Cb, Cr; //YCbCr components

  //some sample values for demo
   R = 252; G = 120; B = 3;

  //convert from RGB to YCbcr
  Y = (unsigned char)((19595 * R + 38470 * G + 7471 * B ) >> 16);
  Cb = (unsigned char)( (36962 * ( B - Y )  >> 16) + 128 );
```

```
  Cr = (unsigned char) ( (46727 * ( R - Y )  >> 16) + 128 );

  printf("\nOriginal RGB and corresponding YCbCr values:");
  printf("\n\tR = %6d, G  = %6d, B  = %6d", R, G, B );
  printf("\n\tY = %6d, Cb = %6d, Cr = %6d", Y, Cb, Cr );

  //convert from YCbCr to RGB
  R = ( unsigned char ) (Y + (91881 * Cr  >> 16) - 179 );
  G = ( unsigned char ) (Y - ((22544 * Cb + 46793 * Cr) >> 16) + 135);
  B = ( unsigned char ) (Y  + (116129 * Cb  >> 16) - 226 );

  printf("\n\nRecovered RGB values:");
  printf("\n\tR = %6d, G  = %6d, B  = %6d\n\n", R, G, B );

  return 0;
}
```

In (3.34), it is obvious that a 32-bit integer is large enough to hold any intermediate calculations. Program Listing 3-2 above shows its implementation. The program generates the outputs shown below.

Outputs of Program Listing 3-2

```
Original RGB & corresponding YCbCr values:
        R =    252, G  =     120, B  =      3
        Y =    146, Cb =      47, Cr =    203

Recovered RGB values:
        R =    251, G  =     120, B  =      3
```

Again, some precision has been lost when we recover R, G, and B from the converted Y, Cb, and Cr values. This is due to the right shifts in the calculations, which are essentially truncate operations. Because of rounding or truncating errors, the recovered R, G, and B values may not lie within the range [0, 255]. To remedy this, we can have a function that check the recovered value; if the value is smaller than 0, we set it to 0 and if it is larger than 255, we set it to 255. The check should be done in the intermediate steps or we can represent R, G, and B with a signed-number having more than 8 bits. For example,

```
if ( R < 0 )
  R = 0;
else if ( R > 255 )
  R = 255;
```

However, this check is not necessary when we convert from RGB to YCbCr. This is because from (3.23), we know that we always have $0 \leq Y, C_b, C_r \leq 1$. For any positive real number, a and $0 \leq a \leq 1$ and any positive integer I,

$$0 \leq Round(aI) \leq Round(I) = I \quad \text{and similarly} \quad 0 \leq Truncate(aI) \leq I$$

This implies that after quantization and rounding, we always have $0 \leq Y, C_b, C_r \leq 255$.

3.4 YCbCr Sampling Formats

We mentioned earlier that we may represent the C_r and C_b components with less bits than Y without much effect on visual quality as our eyes are less sensitive to color than to luminance.

This is a simple way of compressing an image. In general, people consider four adjacent pixels of an image at a time and this leads to the standards 4:4:4, 4:2:2, and 4:2:0 sampling formats, which are supported by video standards MPEG-4 and H.264.

4:4:4 YCbCr Sampling Formats

4:4:4 YCbCr sampling means that for every four luma samples there are four C_b and four C_r samples and hence the three components, Y, C_b, and C_r have the same resolution. The numbers indicate the relative sampling rate of each component in the horizontal direction. So at every pixel position in the horizontal direction, a sample of each component of (Y, C_b, C_r) exists. The 4:4:4 YCbCr format requires as many bits as the RGB format and thus preserves the full fidelity of the chrominance components.

4:2:2 YCbCr Sampling Formats (High Quality Color Reproduction)

4:2:2 YCbCr sampling means that the chrominance components have the same vertical resolution as the luma but half the horizontal resolution. Therefore, for every four luma samples there are two C_b and two C_r samples. Sometimes this format is referred to as YUY2.

4:2:0 YCbCr Sampling Formats (Digital Television and DVD Storage)

4:2:0 YCbCr sampling means that each of the chrominance components has half the horizontal and vertical resolution of the luma component. That is, for every four luma samples (Y) there are one C_b and one C_r samples. It is sometimes known as YV12 and is widely used in video conferencing, digital television and digital versatile disk (DVD) storage. The term "4:2:0" is rather confusing as the numbers do not reflect relative resolutions between the components and apparently have been chosen due to historical reasons to distinguish it from the 4:4:4 and 4:2:2 formats.

Figure 3-8 shows the sampling format of 4:2:0; progressive sampling is used.

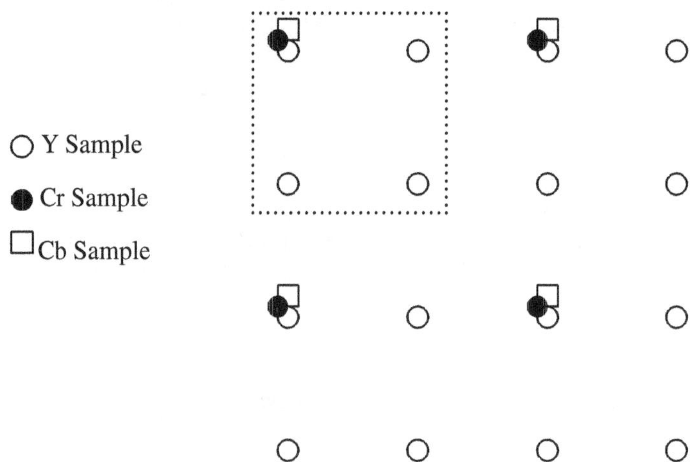

Figure 3-8 4:2:0 Sampling Patterns

Example 3-1

```
Image resolution: 1024 x 768 pixels

4:4:4 Y, Cb, Cr resolution: 1024 x 768 samples
Total number of bits: 1024x768x8x3 = 18874368 bits

4:2:0 Y resolution: 1024 x 768 samples
4:2:0 Cb, Cr resolution: 512x384 samples (8 bits for samples)
Total number of bits: (1024 x 768 x 8) + (512 x 384 x 8 x 2)
                     = 9437184 bits

The 4:2:0 format requires half as many bits as the 4:4:4
format and the RGB format.
```

3.5 Measuring Video Quality

It is important to have some agreed upon methods to measure the quality of video so that we can evaluate and compare various video images presented to the viewer. However, this is a difficult and often an imprecise process and inherently subjective as there are so many factors that can influence the measurement. In general, there are two classes of methods that people use to measure video quality: *subjective tests*, where human subjects are asked to assess or rank the images, and *objective tests*, which compute the distortions between the original and processed video sequences.

3.5.1 Subjective Quality Measurement

Subjective quality measurement asks human subjects to rank the quality of a video based on their own perception and understanding of quality. For example, a viewer can be asked to rate the quality on a 5-point scale, with quality ratings ranging from bad to excellent as shwon in Figure 3-9.

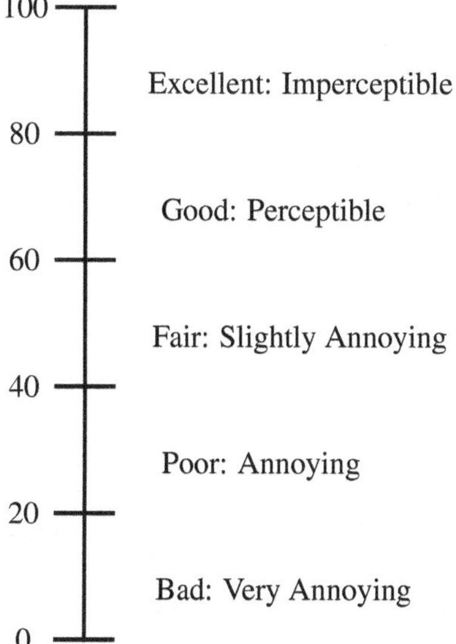

Figure 3-9 Example of video quality assessment scale used in subjective tests

Very often, a viewer's perception on a video is affected by many factors like the viewing environment, the lighting conditions, display size and resolution, the viewing distance, the state of mind of the viewer, whether the material is interesting to the viewer and how the viewer interacts with the visual scene. It is not uncommon that the same viewer who observes the same video at different times under different environments may give significantly different evaluations on the quality of the video. For example, it has been shown that subjective quality ratings of the same video sequence are usually higher when accompanied by good quality sound, which may lower the evaluators' ability to detect impairments. Also, viewers tend to give higher ratings to images with higher contrast or more colorful scenes even though objective tests show that they have larger distortions in comparison to the originals.

Nevertheless, subjective quality assessment still remains the most reliable methods of measuring video quality. It is also the most efficient method to test the performance of components, like video codecs, human vision models and objective quality assessment metrics.

3.5.1.1 ITUR BT.500

The ITU-R Recommendation BT-500-11 formalizes video subjective tests by recommending various experiment parameters like viewing distance, room lighting, display features, selection of subjects and test material, assessment and data analysis methods. There are three most commonly used procedures from the standard: *Double Stimulus Continuous Quality Scale (DSCQS), Double Stimulus Impairment Scale (DSIS) and Single Stimulus Continuous Quality Evaluation (SSCQE).*

Double Stimulus Continuous Quality Scale (DSCQS)

In the DSCQS method, a viewer is presented with a pair of images or short sequences X and Y, one after the other. The viewer is asked to rank X and Y by marking on a continuous line with five intervals ranging from 'Bad' to 'Excellent', which has an equivalent numerical scale from 0 to 100, like the one shown in Figure 3-9. The reference and test sequences are shown to the viewer twice in alternating fashion, the order chosen in random. The accessor does not know in advance which is the reference sequence and which is the test sequence. Figure 3-10 shows an experimental set-up that can be used for testing a video coder-decoder (CODEC); it is randomly assigned which sequence is X and which sequence is Y.

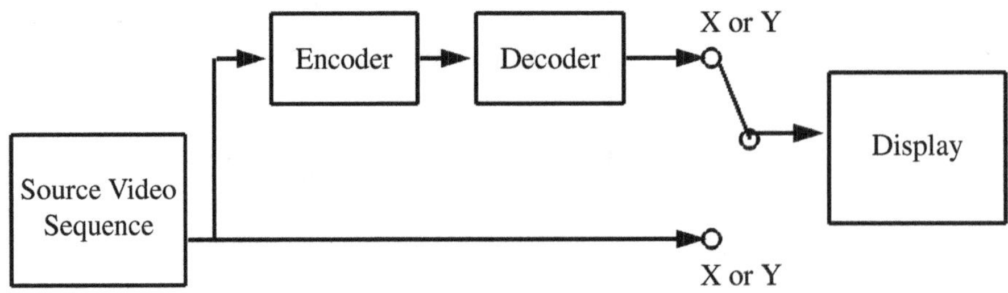

Figure 3-10 DSCQS Testing System

Double Stimulus Impairment Scale (DSIS)

In the DSIS method the reference sequence is always presented before the test sequence, and it is not necessary to show the pair twice. Viewers are asked to rate the sequences on a 5-point scale, ranging from "very annoying" to "imperceptible" like the one shown in Figure 3-9. This method is more effective for evaluating clearly visible impairments, such as noticeable artifacts caused by encoding or transmission.

Both the DSCQS and DSIS methods use short sequences (8 - 10 sec) in the test and this becomes a problem when we want to evaluate video sequences with long duration and quality varies significantly over time like those distributed via the Internet.

Single Stimulus Continuous Quality Evaluation (SSCQE)

SSCQE is designed to evaluate video sequences with significant temporal variations of quality. In this method, longer sequences (20 - 30 minutes) are presented to the viewers without any reference sequence. The accessors evaluate instantaneously the perceived quality by continuously adjusting a side slider on the DSCQS scale, ranging from "bad" to "excellent". The slider value is periodically sampled every 1 - 2 seconds. Using this method, differences between alternative transmission configurations can be analyzed in a more informative manner. However, as the accessor has to adjust the slider from time to time, she may be distracted and thus the rating may be compromised. Also, because of the 'recency or memory effect', it is quite difficult for the accessor to consistently detect momentary changes in quality, leading to stability and reliability problems of the results.

3.5.2 Objective Quality Measurement

Though subjective measurements are the most reliable method to evaluate video qualities, they are complex and expensive as human subjects are required to do the evaluation. It is a lot more convenient and cost-effective to automatically measure quality using an algorithm. Indeed, video processing system developers rely heavily on objective (algorithmic) measurement to access video qualities. The simplest and most widely used form of measuring the quality is Peak Signal to Noise Ratio (PSNR), which calculates the distortion at the pixel level. Peak Signal to Noise Ratio (PSNR) measures the mean squared error (MSE) between the reference and test sequences on a logarithmic scale, relative to the square of the highest possible signal value in the image, $(2^n - 1)^2$, where n is the number of bits per image sample. It is described by Equation (3.35):

$$PSNR_{db} = 10log_{10}\frac{(2^n - 1)^2}{MSE} \tag{3.35}$$

The mean squared error, MSE of two $M \times N$ images X and Y where one of the images is considered to be a noisy approximation of the other with sample values X_{ij} and Y_{ij} respectively can be calculated using the following equation:

$$MSE = \frac{1}{M \times N}\sum_{i=0}^{M-1}\sum_{j=0}^{N-1}(X_{ij} - Y_{ij})^2 \tag{3.36}$$

Though PSNR is a straightforward metric to calculate, it cannot describe distortions perceived by a complex and multi-dimensional system like the human visual system (HVS), and thus fails to give good evaluations in many cases. For example, a viewer may be interested in an object of an image but not its background. If the background is largely distorted, the viewer would still rate that the image is of high quality; however, PSNR measure would indicate that the image is of poor quality. The limitations of this metric have led to recent research in image processing that has focused on developing metrics that resembles the response of real human viewers. Many approaches have been proposed but none of them can be accepted as a standard to be used as an alternative to subjective evaluation. The search of a good acceptable objective test for images will remain a research topic for some time.

Chapter 4

Image and Video Storage Formats

There are a lot of proprietary image and video file formats, each with clear strengths and weaknesses. The file formats are generally not a user-defined option and many of the features are specified by the vendors. This book is about video compression programming and we are not interested in exploring various file formats. However, we do need to know a few formats in order that we can carry out experiments on image or video compression using files downloaded from the Internet. Therefore, we shall discuss a couple of simple standard formats and some related tools that we will use later in this book.

4.1 Portable Pixel Map (PPM)

The Portable Pixel Map (PPM) file format is a lowest and simplest common denominator color image format. A PPM file contains very little information about the image besides basic colors and thus it is easy to write programs to process the file, which is the purpose of this format. A PPM file consists of a sequence of one or more PPM images. There are no data, delimiters, or padding before, after, or between images. The PPM format closely relates to two other bitmap formats, the PBM format, which stands for Portable Bitmap (a monochrome bitmap), and PGM format, which stands for Portable Gray Map (a gray scale bitmap). All these formats are not compressed and consequently the files stored in these formats are usually quite large. In addition, the PNM format means any of the three bitmap formats. You may use the unix manual command **man** to learn the details of the PPM format:

$man ppm

The three bitmap formats can be stored in two possible representations:

1. an ASCII text representation (which is extremely verbose), and
2. a binary representation (which is comparatively smaller).

Each PPM image consists of the following (taken from unix ppm manual):

1. A "magic number" for identifying the file type. A ppm image's magic number is the two characters "P6".
2. Whitespace (blanks, TABs, CRs, LFs).
3. A width, formatted as ASCII characters in decimal.
4. Whitespace.
5. A height, again in ASCII decimal.
6. Whitespace.

7. The maximum color value (*Maxval*), again in ASCII decimal. Must be less than 65536 and more than zero.
8. Newline or other single whitespace character.
9. A raster of *Height* rows, in order from top to bottom. Each row consists of *Width* pixels, in order from left to right. Each pixel is a triplet of red, green, and blue samples, in that order. Each sample is represented in pure binary by either 1 or 2 bytes. If the *Maxval* is less than 256, it is 1 byte. Otherwise, it is 2 bytes. The most significant byte is first. A row of an image is horizontal. A column is vertical. The pixels in the image are square and contiguous.
10. In the raster, the sample values are "nonlinear". They are proportional to the intensity of the ITU-R Recommendation BT.709 red, green, and blue.

In summary, a PPM file has a header and a body, which may be created using a text editor. The header is very small with the following properties:

1. The first line contains the magic identifier "P3" or "P6".
2. The second line contains the *width* and *height* of the image in ascii code.
3. The last part of the header is the maximum color intensity integer value.
4. Comments are preceded by the symbol #.

Here are some header examples:

<u>Header example 1</u>

```
P6 1024 788 255
```

<u>Header example 2</u>

```
P6
1024 788
# A comment
255
```

<u>Header example 3</u>

```
P3
1024   # the image width
788    # the image height
       # A comment
1023
```

The following is an example of a PPM file in P3 format.

```
P3
# feep.ppm
4 4
15
0  0  0    0  0  0    0  0  0   15  0 15
0  0  0    0 15  7    0  0  0    0  0  0
0  0  0    0  0  0    0 15  7    0  0  0
15  0 15    0  0  0    0  0  0    0  0  0
```

You can simply use a text editor to create it; for example, copy-and-paste the content into a file named "feep.ppm" with the header "P3" aligned to the leftmost margin; it then becomes a PPM file and can be viewed by a browser or the unix utility **display** by ImageMagick. When you execute the command,

$ **display feep.ppm**

you should see a tiny image appear on the upper left corner of your screen.

4.2 The Convert Utility

Once we obtain an image in PPM format, we can easily convert it to other popular formats such as PNG, JPG, or GIF using the **convert** utility, which is a member of the ImageMagick suite of tools. Conversely, if you obtain an image from other sources in another format, you may also use **convert** to convert it to the PPM format. Besides making conversion between image formats, the utility can also resize an image, blur, crop, despeckle, dither, draw on, flip, join, re-sample, and do much more. It can even create an image from text. We use the unix manual command to see the details of its usage:

$ **man convert**

We can also run 'convert -help' to get a summary of its command options. The following are some simple examples of its usage.

```
$convert feep.ppm  feep.png
$convert house.jpg house.ppm
$convert house.jpg -resize 60% house.png
$convert -size 128x32 xc:transparent -font \
    Bookman-DemiItalic -pointsize 28 -channel RGBA \
    -gaussian 0x4 -fill lightgreen -stroke green \
    -draw "text 0,20 'Freedom'" freedom.png
```

The last command creates a PNG (Portable Network Graphics) file named "freedom.png" from the text "Freedom". Figure 4-1 shows the image thus created.

Figure 4-1 Image Created by **convert**

If you want to convert a PDF file to PPM, you may use the utility **pdftoppm**. You may run **"pdftoppm –help"** to find out the details of its usage.

4.3 Read and Write PPM Files

To process any PPM and related graphics file, you may use the the **netpbm** library *http://netpbm.sourceforge.net*, which can be downloaded from the Internet. However, for the purpose of this book, we just need something very simple to read or write a PPM file. In this section, we present a simple C program that shows how to read or write a PPM file.

The C/C++ program shown in **Listing 4-1** briefly demonstrates the reading and writing of PPM files; the file names and some parameters are hard-coded; the class **CImage** with public members *red, green*, and *blue* is used to save the color data of one pixel. In a C++ program, a public **class** is the same as a C **struct**.

Program Listing 4-1 Read and Write PPM Files

```
-------------------------------------------------------------------------
/* ppmdemo.cpp
 * Demostrate read and write of PPM files.
```

```
 * Compile: g++ -o ppmdemo ppmdemo.cpp
 * Execute: ./ppmdemo
 */
#include <stdio.h>
#include <stdlib.h>
#include <string.h>

//A public class is the same as a 'struct'
class CImage {
public:
  unsigned char red;
  unsigned char green;
  unsigned char blue;
};

// Create PPM header from image width and height. "P6" format used.
// PPM header returned in integer array ppmh[].
void make_ppm_header ( int ppmh[], int width, int height )
{
  //standard header data, 'P' = 0x50, '6' = 0x36, '\n' = 0x0A
  int ca[] = {0x50, 0x36, 0x0A,                              //"P6"
      //image width=260, height = 288
      0x33, 0x36, 0x30, 0x20, 0x32, 0x38,
              //color levels / pixel = 256
              0x38, 0x0A, 0x32, 0x35, 0x35, 0x0A };

  //only have to change width and height
  char temp[10], k;

  sprintf(temp, "%3d", width );                 //width in ascii code
  k = 0;
  for ( int i = 3; i <= 5; ++i )                //replace width
    ca[i] = temp[k++];

  sprintf(temp, "%3d", height );                //height in ascii code
  k = 0;
  for ( int i = 7; i <=9; ++i )                 //replace height
    ca[i] = temp[k++];

  for ( int i = 0; i < 15; ++i )                //form header
    ppmh[i] = ca[i];
}

void save_ppmdata (FILE *fp, CImage *ip, int width, int height)
{
  int size = width * height;
  for ( int i = 0; i < size; ++i ){
    putc ( ip[i].red, fp );
    putc ( ip[i].green, fp );
    putc ( ip[i].blue, fp );
  }
}

void ppm_read_comments ( FILE *fp )
{
```

```
  int c;
  while ( (c = getc ( fp ) )  == '#' ) {
    while ( getc( fp ) != '\n' )
        ;
  }
  ungetc ( c, fp );
}

class ppm_error
{
  public:
    ppm_error() {
      printf("\nIncorrect PPM format!\n");
      exit ( 1 );
    }
};

int main()
{
  int ppmh[20];                          //PPM header
  int width = 32, height = 32;           //image width and height
  make_ppm_header ( ppmh, width, height );
  //PPM file for testing read
  FILE *input = fopen("testread.ppm", "rb");
  //PPM file for testing write
  FILE *output = fopen ("testwrite.ppm", "wb");

  //write demo
  for ( int i = 0; i < 15; ++i )         //save PPM header
    putc ( ppmh[i], output );

  CImage image[width][height];
  for ( int i = 0; i < height; ++i ) {   //create a red rectangle
    for ( int j = 0; j < width; ++j ) {
        image[i][j].red = 255;           //red component
        image[i][j].green = 0;           //green component
        image[i][j].blue = 0;            //blue component
    }
  }
  save_ppmdata ( output, (CImage*) image, width, height );
  printf("\nPPM file testwrite.ppm created!\n");
  fclose ( output );

  //read demo
  ppm_read_comments ( input );           //read comments
  char temp[100];
  fscanf ( input, "%2s", temp );
  temp[3] = 0;
  if ( strncmp ( temp, "P6", 2 ) )
    throw ppm_error();
  ppm_read_comments ( input );
  fscanf ( input, "%d", &width );
  ppm_read_comments ( input );
  fscanf ( input, "%d", &height );
  ppm_read_comments ( input );
```

```
  int colorlevels;
  fscanf ( input, "%d", &colorlevels );
  printf("\n%s PPM file: ", temp );
  printf(" \n\twidth=%d\theight=%d\tcolorlevles=%d\n",
              width,height,colorlevels+1 );
  ppm_read_comments ( input );
  while (( c = getc ( input )) == '\n'); //get rid of extra returns
  ungetc ( c ,input );

  //save the data in another file
  CImage ibuf[width][height];
  fread ( ibuf,  3, width * height, input );
  output = fopen("test.ppm", "wb"); //to save PPM data in "test.ppm"
  make_ppm_header ( ppmh, width, height );
  for ( int i = 0; i < 15; ++i )     //save PPM header
    putc ( ppmh[i], output );
  save_ppmdata (output, (CImage*) ibuf, width, height);//save data
  printf("\nPPM file test.ppm created!\n");

  fclose ( input );  fclose ( output );
  return 0;
}
```

When you execute the program **ppmdemo**, you should see messages similar to the following displayed.

```
PPM file testwrite.ppm created!

P6 PPM file:
        width=200        height=300        colorlevles=256

PPM file test.ppm created!
```

The program first creates a PPM file named "testwrite.ppm" whose data form a red square. If you view the file with the command **display testwrite.ppm**, you should see a small red square image. The program then reads in the data from the PPM file "testread.ppm" in the *data* directory and prints out its width, height and color levels. Finally, it writes the information to another file named "test.ppm". Again, you can view the image using the command **display test.ppm**.

4.4 Common Intermediate Format (CIF)

There exists a wide variety of 'standard' video formats which would lay a heavy burden on a developer to study and understand them for encoding or decoding data saved in their formats. In practice, it is common for a party to use a utility program to capture or convert the data to a set of standard 'intermediate formats' before compressing or transmitting the data. The **Common Intermediate Format** (**CIF**), first proposed in the H.261 standard, is designed for the purpose of standardizing the horizontal and vertical resolutions in pixels of YCbCr video data. CIF allows easy conversions to standard television systems of PAL (Phase Alternating Line) and NTSC (the National Television System Committee). CIF is also known as **FCIF** (Full Common Intermediate Format); it defines a video sequence with a luminance resolution of 352×288 and a frame rate of $30000/1001 (\approx 29.97)$ fps with color encoding using YCbCr 4:2:0. Note that a CIF-image (352×288) consists of 22×18 macroblocks, each of which is a 16×16 pixel block that we shall discuss in Chapter 5. **QCIF**, meaning "Quarter CIF" defines a resolution with frame width and height halved as compared to that of CIF. Similarly, **SQCIF** (Sub Quarter CIF), **4CIF** ($4 \times$ CIF

) and **16CIF** define various resolutions with CIF as the basis. Table 4-1 below summarizes these formats.

Table 4-1 Common Intermediate Format

Format	Luminance Resolution (horizontal × vertical)	Bits / Frame (4:2:0, 8 bits/Sample)
CIF	352 × 288	1216512
QCIF	176 × 144	304128
SQCIF	128 × 96	147456
4CIF	704 × 576	4866048
16CIF	1408 × 1152	14598144

The CIF formats do not use square pixels. Rather, they specify a pixel to have a native aspect ratio of approximately 1.222:1 because on older television systems, a pixel aspect ratio of 1.2:1 was the standard for 525-line systems. As computer systems use square-pixel, a CIF raster has to be rescaled horizontally by about 109% in order to avoid a "stretched" appearance.

The choice of a particular CIF format depends on the application and available resources like storage and transmission capacity. For example, video conferencing requires real-time transmission of data and its applications commonly use CIF and QCIF that give fairly good resolution but do not give an overwhelming amount of data. As standard-definition-television has higher transmission bandwidth and DVD-videos are recorded off-line, 4CIF is an appropriate format. For mobile multimedia applications, QCIF or SQCIF are appropriate as the display resolution and transmission bandwidth are limited. Column 3 of Table 4-1 shows the number of bits required to represent one uncompressed frame for each CIF format, where YCbCr 4:2:0 format and 8 bits per luma and chroma sample are used.

Chapter 5

Macroblocks

5.1 Introduction

A PC image or a frame with moderate size usually consists of many pixels and requires a large amount of storage space and computing power to process it. For example, an image of size 240 x 240 has 57600 pixels and requires $\frac{3}{2} \times 57600 = 86,400$ bytes of storage space if **4:2:0** format is used. It is difficult and inconvenient to process all of these data simultaneously. In order to make things more manageable, an image is decomposed into **macroblocks**. A macroblock is a 16 x 16 pixel-region, which is the basic unit for processing a frame and is used in video compression standards like MPEG, H.261, H.263, and H.264. A macroblock has a total of $16 \times 16 = 256$ pixels.

In our coding, we shall also process an image in the units of macroblocks. For simplicity and the convenience of discussion, we assume that each of our frames consists of an integral number of macroblocks. That is, both the width and height of an image are divisible by 16. The Common Intermediate Format (CIF) discussed in Chapter 4 also has a resolution of 352×288 that corresponds to 22×18 macroblocks. In addition, we shall use the **4:2:0** YCbCr format; a macroblock then consists of a 16×16 Y sample block, an 8×8 Cb sample block and an 8×8 Cr sample block. To better organize the data, we further divide the 16×16 Y sample block into four 8×8 sample blocks. Therefore, a **4:2:0** macroblock has a total of six 8×8 sample blocks; we label these blocks from 0 to 5 as shown in Figure 5-1:

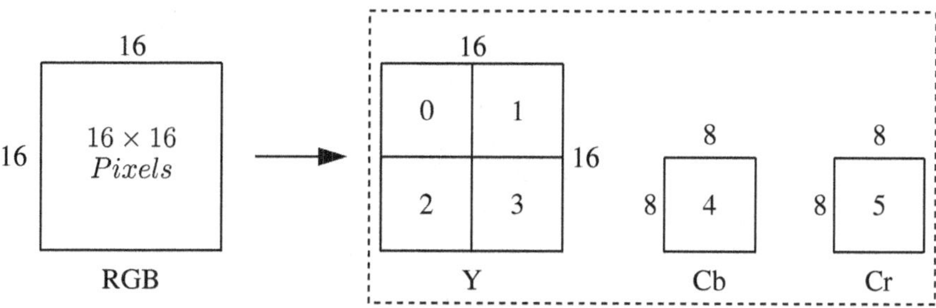

Figure 5-1. Macroblock of 4:2:0

5.2 Implementing RGB and 4:2:0 YCbCr Transformation for Video Frames

When implementing the conversion of RGB to YCbCr, we process the data in units of macroblocks; a macroblock has four 8×8 Y sample blocks and one 8×8 sample block for each of Cb and Cr samples. We also assume that a frame has an integral number of macroblocks. In the **4:2:0** YCbCr format, for each RGB pixel, we make a conversion for Y but we only make a conversion for Cb and Cr for every four RGB pixels (see Figure 3-8). Each group is formed by grouping 4 neighbouring pixels. For simplicity, when calculating the Cb, and Cr components, we simply use the upper left pixel of the four and ignore the other three. (Alternatively, one can take the average value of the four RGB pixel values when calculating the Cb and Cr values.) For convenience of programming, we define three **structs**: struct **RGB** holds the RGB values of a pixel, struct **YCbCr** holds the Ycbcr values of a pixel, and **YCbCr_MACRO** holds the YCbCr sample values of a macroblock of (16×16 *pixels*) of Figure 5-1. In C++, a **structs** is a **class** with public data members only. We put all these definitions in the header file "common.h", which is listed in Figure 5-2.

```
//common.h
//defines an RGB pixel
class RGB {
public:
  unsigned char R;                //0 - 255
  unsigned char G;                //0 - 255
  unsigned char B;                //0 - 255
};

class YCbCr {
public:
  unsigned char Y;                //0 - 255
  unsigned char Cb;               //0 - 255
  unsigned char Cr;               //0 - 255
};

//4:2:0 YCbCr Macroblock
class YCbCr_MACRO {
public:
  unsigned char Y[256];           //16x16 ( four 8x8 samples )
  unsigned char Cb[64];           //8x8
  unsigned char Cr[64];           //8x8
};

class RGBImage {
public:
  short width;                    //image width
  short height;                   //image height
  unsigned char *ibuf;            //pointer to buffer
                                  //  holding image data
};
```

Figure 5-2 Public classes (structs) for Processing Macro Blocks

We have learned in Chapter 3 how to convert an RGB pixel to YCbCr values using integer arithmetic. We define a function named **rgb2ycbcr** (RGB &a, YCbCr &b) to convert an RGB pixel a to a YCbCr pixel b and a function named **rgb2y**(RGB &a, unsigned char &y) to convert an RGB pixel a to a Y component y. Now, we need a function to convert an entire RGB macroblock to a

4:2:0 YCbCr macroblock, which consists of four 8×8 Y sample blocks, one 8×8 Cb sample block and one 8×8 Cr sample block. The following function **macroblock2ycbcr()**, listed in Figure 5-3 does the job; the input of it can be considered as a 16×16 two dimensional array, *macro16x16*[][] holding 16×16 RGB pixels; the output is a pointer to a **YCbCr_MACRO** struct defined in Figure 5-2, which holds the converted Y, Cb, Cr sample values with array Y[] holding the four Y sample blocks, and arrays Cb[] and Cr[] holding the sample blocks Cb and Cr respectively.

```
/*
  Convert an RGB macro block ( 16x16 ) to 4:2:0 YCbCr sample blocks
  (six 8x8 blocks).
*/
void macroblock2ycbcr( RGB *macro16x16,  YCbCr_MACRO *ycbcr_macro )
{
  int i, j, k, r;
  YCbCr ycb;

  r = k = 0;
  for ( i = 0; i < 16; ++i ) {
    for ( j = 0; j < 16; ++j ) {
      if ( !( i & 1 ) && !( j & 1 ) ) {  //1 Cb,Cr for 4 pixels
        rgb2ycbcr(macro16x16[r], ycb);//convert to Y,Cb,Cr values
        ycbcr_macro->Y[r] = ycb.Y;
        ycbcr_macro->Cb[k] = ycb.Cb;
        ycbcr_macro->Cr[k] = ycb.Cr;
        k++;
      } else {                       //only need Y for other 3 pixels
        rgb2y ( macro16x16[r], ycbcr_macro->Y[r] );
      }
      r++;                           //convert every pixel for Y
    }
  }
}
```

Figure 5-3 Function for converting an RGB macroblock to 4:2:0 YCbCr Sample Blocks

In Figure 5-3, the statement "*if (!(i & 1) && !(j & 1)) {* " is true only when both *i* and *j* are even. This implies that it selects one pixel for a group of four neighbouring pixels as shown in Figure 3-8, and makes a conversion to Y, Cb, Cr; it makes a conversion of only the Y component for the other 3 pixels as we have considered the 4:2:0 YCbCr format. For example, the statement is true when

$(i, j) = (0, 0), (0, 2), ..., (2, 0), (2, 2), ..., (14, 14).$

We can similarly define a function, **ycbcr2macroblock()** to convert a YCbCr macroblock to an RGB macroblock. The following program, **rgb_ycc.cpp** of Listing 5-1 contains all the functions we need to convert video frames from RGB to YCbCr and back. It can be compiled to object code **rgb_ycc.o** by the command "g++ -c rgb_ycc.cpp".

Program Listing 5-1 (rgb_ycc.cpp) RGB-YCbCr Conversions

```
----------------------------------------------------------------------
/*
  Convert from RGB to YCbCr using  ITU-R recommendation BT.601.
     Y = 0.299R + 0.587G + 0.114B
    Cb = 0.564(B - Y ) + 0.5
    Cr = 0.713(R - Y ) + 0.5

  Integer arithmetic is used to speed up calculations.
```

```
  Note:
       2^16 = 65536
       kr = 0.299 = 19595 / 2^16
       kg = 0.587 = 38470 / 2^16
       Kb = 0.114 =  7471 / 2^16
       0.5 = 128 / 255
       0.564 = 36962 / 2^16
       .......
  Input: an RGB pixel
  Output: a YCbCr "pixel".
*/

void rgb2ycbcr( RGB &rgb, YCbCr &ycc )
{
  //coefs summed to 65536(1<<16), so Y is always within [0, 255]

  ycc.Y = (unsigned char)((19595 * rgb.R + 38470 * rgb.G +
              7471 * rgb.B ) >> 16);
  ycc.Cb = (unsigned char)((36962*(rgb.B - ycc.Y ) >> 16) + 128);
  ycc.Cr = (unsigned char)((46727*(rgb.R - ycc.Y ) >> 16) + 128);
}

//just convert an RGB pixel to Y component
void rgb2y( RGB &rgb, unsigned char  &y )
{
  y = (short)((19595*rgb.R + 38470*rgb.G + 7471*rgb.B ) >> 16);
}

//limit value to lie within [0,255]
void chop ( int & r, int &g, int &b )
{
    if ( r < 0 ) r = 0;
    else if ( r > 255 ) r = 255;
    if ( g < 0 ) g = 0;
    else if ( g > 255 ) g = 255;
    if ( b < 0 ) b = 0;
    else if ( b > 255 ) b = 255;
}

/*
  Convert from YCbCr to RGB domain. Using ITU-R standard:
     R = Y + 1.402Cr - 0.701
     G = Y - 0.714Cr - 0.344Cb + 0.529
     B = Y + 1.772Cb - 0.886
  Integer arithmetic is used to speed up calculations.
*/
void ycbcr2rgb( YCbCr &ycc, RGB &rgb )
{ int r, g, b;

  r = ( ycc.Y           + ( 91881 * ycc.Cr   >> 16 ) - 179 );
  g = ( ycc.Y  - (( 22544 * ycc.Cb + 46793 * ycc.Cr ) >> 16) + 135);
  b =  ( ycc.Y  + (116129 * ycc.Cb   >> 16 ) - 226 );
  chop ( r, g, b );            //enforce values to lie within [0,255]
  rgb.R = ( unsigned char ) r;
  rgb.G = ( unsigned char ) g;
```

```
  rgb.B = ( unsigned char ) b;
}

/*
  Convert an RGB macro block ( 16x16 ) to 4:2:0 YCbCr sample blocks
  ( six 8x8 blocks ).
*/
void macroblock2ycbcr ( RGB *macro16x16,  YCbCr_MACRO *ycbcr_macro )
{
  int i, j, k, r;
  YCbCr ycb;

  r = k = 0;
  for ( i = 0; i < 16; ++i ) {
    for ( j = 0; j < 16; ++j ) {
      if (!( i & 1 ) && !( j & 1 )){//one Cb, Cr for every 4 pixels
        rgb2ycbcr(macro16x16[r], ycb);//convert to Y, Cb, Cr values
        ycbcr_macro->Y[r] = ycb.Y;
        ycbcr_macro->Cb[k] = ycb.Cb;
        ycbcr_macro->Cr[k] = ycb.Cr;
        k++;
      } else {        //only need the Y component for other 3 pixels
        rgb2y ( macro16x16[r], ycbcr_macro->Y[r] );
      }
      r++;            //convert every pixel for Y
    }
  }
}

/*
  Convert the six 8x8 YCbCr sample blocks to RGB macroblock(16x16).
*/
void ycbcr2macroblock( YCbCr_MACRO *ycbcr_macro, RGB *macro16x16 )
{
  int i, j, k, r;
  short y;
  YCbCr ycb;
  r = k = 0;
  for ( i = 0; i < 16; ++i ) {
    for ( j = 0; j < 16; ++j ) {
      //one Cb, Cr has been saved for every 4 pixels
      if ( !( i & 1 ) && !( j & 1 ) ) {
        ycb.Y = ycbcr_macro->Y[r];
        ycb.Cb = ycbcr_macro->Cb[k];
        ycb.Cr = ycbcr_macro->Cr[k];
        ycbcr2rgb ( ycb, macro16x16[r]);
        k++;
      } else {
        ycb.Y = ycbcr_macro->Y[r];
        ycbcr2rgb( ycb, macro16x16[r] );
      }
      r++;
    }
  }
}
```

After we have implemented the functions to convert an RGB macroblock to a YCbCr macroblock and vice versa, we can utilize these functions to convert an image frame from RGB to YCbCr and save the data. As 4:2:0 format is used, the saved YCbCr data are only half as much as the original RGB data. In our discussions, the four Y sample blocks of a YCbCr macroblock is stored in the linear array Y[256] (Figure 5-2). In some cases, it is more convenient to separate the 256 Y samples into four sample blocks, each with size 64 (8×8). The relation between the indexes of the linear array and the four sample blocks, labeled 0, 1, 2, and 3 is shown in Figure 5-4 and the code that divides the 256 samples into four arrays is shown in the figure below.

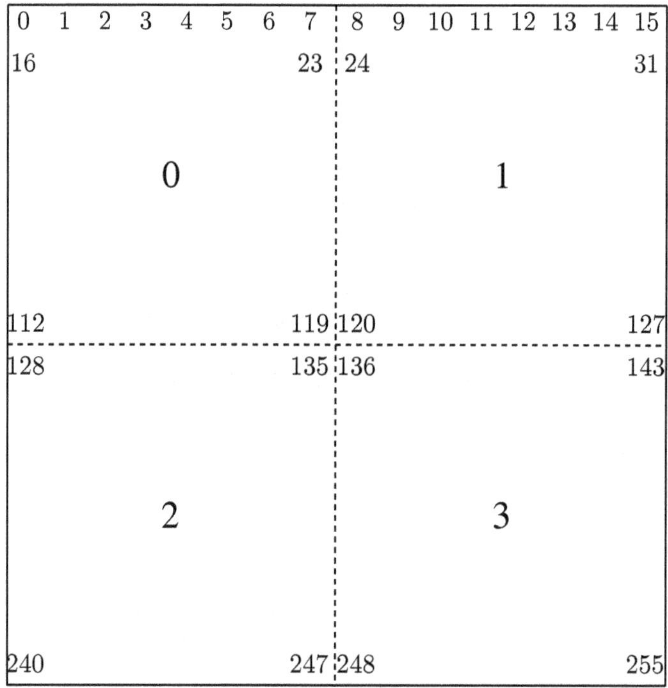

Figure 5-4. Y Sample Block Indexes

The following code shows how to separate a Y block of Figure 5-4 to four sublocks.

```
YCbCr_MACRO ycbcr_macro;
....
unsigned char Y4[4][64];
int start, k, r;

//start always points the beginning of a block
for(int b=0; b < 4; b++){
  if ( b < 2 )
    start = 8 * b;
  else
    start = 128 + 8 * ( b - 2 );
  k = start;
  r = 0
  for (int i = 0; i < 8; i++){ //one sample block
    for(int j=0; j < 8; j++)
      Y4[b][r++] = ycbcr_macro.Y[k+j];
    k += 16;                  //next row
  }
```

The program **encode.cpp**, shown in Listing 5-2 uses a similar code to save Y samples as four 8×8 blocks.

Program Listing 5-2

```
------------------------------------------------------------------------
/*
  encode.cpp
  Contains functions to convert an RGB frame to YCbCr and to save
  the converted data.
  Compile: g++ -c encode.cpp
*/
#include <stdio.h>
#include <stdlib.h>
#include "common.h"
#include "rgb_ycc.h"

//save one YCbCr macroblock.
void save_yccblocks( YCbCr_MACRO *ycbcr_macro, FILE *fpo )
{
  short block, i, j, k;
  unsigned char *py;

  //save four 8x8 Y sample blocks
  for ( block = 0; block < 4; block++ ) {
    if ( block < 2 )
      //points to beginning of block
      py = ( unsigned char * ) &ycbcr_macro->Y + 8*block;
    else
      py =(unsigned char *)&ycbcr_macro->Y+128+8*(block-2);
    for ( i = 0; i < 8; i++ ) { //one sample-block
      if ( i > 0 ) py += 16;     //advance py by 16( one row )
      for ( j = 0; j < 8; j++ ) {
        putc ( ( int )  *(py+j),fpo);    //save one byte of data
      }
    }
  }

  //save one 8x8 Cb block
  k = 0;
  for ( i = 0; i < 8; ++i ) {
    for ( j = 0; j < 8; ++j ) {
      putc( ( int ) ycbcr_macro->Cb[k++], fpo );
    }
  }

  //save one 8x8 Cr block
  k = 0;
  for ( i = 0; i < 8; ++i ) {
    for ( j = 0; j < 8; ++j ) {
      putc( ( int ) ycbcr_macro->Cr[k++], fpo );
    }
  }
}
```

```
/*
  Convert RGB to YCbCr and save the converted data.
*/
void encode ( RGBImage *image, FILE *fpo )
{
  short row, col, i, j, r;
  RGB macro16x16[256];     //16x16 pixel macroblock;24-bit RGB pixel
  YCbCr_MACRO ycbcr_macro;//macroblock for YCbCr samples
  RGB *p;                  //pointer to an RGB pixel
  static int nframe = 0;

  for ( row = 0; row < image->height; row += 16 ) {
    for ( col = 0; col < image->width; col += 16 ) {
      //points to beginning of macroblock
      p=(RGB *)image->ibuf+(row*image->width + col);
      r = 0;                      //note pointer arithmetic
      for ( i = 0; i < 16; ++i ) {
        for ( j = 0; j < 16; ++j ) {
          macro16x16[r++] = (RGB) *p++;
        }
        p += (image->width-16); //points to next row within macroblock
      }
      macroblock2ycbcr ( macro16x16,  &ycbcr_macro );//RGB to YCbCr
      save_yccblocks( &ycbcr_macro, fpo );  //save one YCbCr macroblock
    } //for col
  } //for row
}
-----------------------------------------------------------------------
```

In **encode.cpp** of Listing 5-2, the function **save_yccblocks()** saves one YCbCr macroblock in a file pointed by the the file pointer *fpo*; the function **encode()** makes use of **macroblock2ycbcr()** and **save_yccblocks()** to convert an RGB image or frame to YCbCr and saves the converted data in a file. Note that the standard C function putc() saves only the lower 8-bit of an integer and this is what we want; we can use getc() to read the byte back.

The corresponding code that converts a file of YCbCr data to RGB data is shown in **decode.cpp** of Listing 5-3.

Program Listing 5-3

```
-----------------------------------------------------------------------
/*
  decode.cpp
  Contains functions to read YCbCr data from a file and convert
  from YCbCr to RGB.
  Compile: g++ -c decode.cpp
*/
#include <stdio.h>
#include <stdlib.h>
#include "common.h"
#include "rgb_ycc.h"

/*
  Get YCbCr data from file pointed by fpi. Put the four 8x8 Y sample
  blocks, one 8x8 Cb sample block and one 8x8 Cr sample block into a
  struct ( class object) of YCbCr_MACRO.
```

```
  Return: number of bytes read from file and put in
          YCbCr_MACRO struct.
*/
int get_yccblocks( YCbCr_MACRO *ycbcr_macro, FILE *fpi )
{
  short r, row, col, i, j, k, n, block;
  short c;
  unsigned char *py;

  n = 0;
  //read data from file and put them in four 8x8 Y sample blocks
  for ( block = 0; block < 4; block++ ) {
    if ( block < 2 )
      //points to beginning of block
      py = ( unsigned char * ) &ycbcr_macro->Y + 8*block;
    else
      py = (unsigned char *)&ycbcr_macro->Y+128+8*(block-2);
    for ( i = 0; i < 8; i++ ) {       //one sample-block
      if ( i > 0 ) py += 16;          //advance py by 16 (one row)
      for ( j = 0; j < 8; j++ ) {
        if ( ( c = getc ( fpi ))  == EOF) //read one byte
              break;
        *(py + j) = (unsigned char) c; //save in YCbCr_MACRO struct
         n++;
      } //for j
    } //for i
  } //for block
  //now do that for 8x8 Cb block
  k = 0;
  for ( i = 0; i < 8; ++i ) {
    for ( j = 0; j < 8; ++j ) {
      if ( ( c = getc ( fpi )) == EOF )
        break;
        ycbcr_macro->Cb[k++] = (unsigned char )c;
        n++;
    }
  }

  //now do that for 8x8 Cr block
  k = 0;
  for ( i = 0; i < 8; ++i ) {
    for ( j = 0; j < 8; ++j ) {
      if ( ( c = getc ( fpi )) == EOF )
        break;
      ycbcr_macro->Cr[k++] = (unsigned char) c;
      n++;
    }
  }
  return n;                                 //number of bytes read
}

/*
 *   Convert a YCbCr frame to an RGB frame.
 */
int decode_yccFrame ( RGBImage &image, FILE *fpi )
```

```
{
  short r, row, col, i, j, k, block;
  int n = 0;
  RGB macro16x16[256];      //16x16 pixel macroblock; 24-bit RGB pixel
  YCbCr_MACRO ycbcr_macro;//macroblock for YCbCr samples
  RGB *rgbp;                //pointer to an RGB pixel
  for ( row = 0; row < image.height; row += 16 ) {
    for ( col = 0; col < image.width; col += 16 ) {
      int m = get_yccblocks( &ycbcr_macro, fpi );
      if ( m <= 0 ) { printf("\nout of data\n"); return m;}
      n += m;
      ycbcr2macroblock( &ycbcr_macro, macro16x16 );
      //points to beginning of macroblock
      rgbp = ( RGB *)(image.ibuf)+(row*image.width+col);
      r = 0;
      for ( i = 0; i < 16; ++i ) {
        for ( j = 0; j < 16; ++j ) {
          *rgbp++ =  macro16x16[r++];
        }
        rgbp += (image.width - 16);//next row within macroblock
      }
    } //for col
  }  //for row
  return n;
}
```

In **decode.cpp** of Listing 5-3, the function **get_yccblocks()** gets YCbCr data from a file pointed by file pointer *fpi*; the data are organized in macroblocks, consisting of four 8x8 Y sample blocks, one 8x8 Cb sample block and one 8x8 Cr sample block. The function saves the data into a struct (class object) of YCbCr_MACRO. The function **decode_yccFrame()** uses **get_yccblocks()** to convert the YCbCr data of an image or frame saved in a file to RGB and stores the RGB data in the buffer of a class object of RGBImage.

5.3 Testing Implementation Using PPM Image

We can test the implementation presented in section 5.2 using a PPM image, the format of which has been discussed in Chapter 4. It is the simplest portable format that one can have and does not have any compression. As pointed out before, the implementation of section 5.2 only works for images with height and width divisible by 16. If you obtain a PPM image with dimensions non-divisible by 16, you need to use the "convert" utility with the "-resize" option to change its dimensions before doing the test.

Again, we simplify our code by hard-coding the file names used for testing. We put the testing files in the directory "../data/", a child directory of the parent of the directory the testing programs reside. Suppose the testing file is called "beach.ppm". All we want to do is to read the RGB data of "beach.ppm", convert them to YCbCr and save the YCbCr macroblocks in the file "beach.ycc". In saving the YCbCr macroblocks, we also need to save the image dimensions for decoding. We employ a very simple format for our ".ycc" file; the first 8 bytes contain the header text, "YCbCr420"; the next two bytes contain the image width followed by another two bytes of image height; data start from the thirteenth byte. We then read the YCbCr macroblocks back from "beach.ycc" into a buffer and convert the YCbCr data to RGB. We save the recovered RGB data in the file "beach1.ppm". The testing program **test_encode_ppm.cpp** that performs these tasks is listed in Listing 5-4.

Program Listing 5-4

```
-------------------------------------------------------------------------
/*
 * test_encode_ppm.cpp
 * Program to test integer implementations of RGB-YCbCr conversions
 * and the use of macroblocks to compress data. PPM files are used
 * for testing. It reads "../data/beach.ppm" RGB data, converts
 * them to 4:2:0 YCbCr macroblocks which will be saved in file
 * "../data/beach.ycc"; it then reads back the YCbCr macroblocks
 * from "../data/beach.ycc", converts them to RGB data and save
 * the data in "../data/beach1.ppm".  PPM files can be viewed using
 * "xview".
 * Compile: g++ -o test_encode_ppm test_encode_ppm.cpp rgb_ycc.o \
 *                    encode.o decode.o
 * Execute: ./test_encode_ppm
 */

#include <stdio.h>
#include <stdlib.h>
#include <string.h>
#include "common.h"

//A public class is the same as a 'struct'
class CImage {
public:
  unsigned char red;
  unsigned char green;
  unsigned char blue;
};

void encode ( RGBImage *image, FILE *fpo );
int decode_yccFrame ( RGBImage &image, FILE *fpi );

/*
 * Create PPM header from image width and height. "P6" format used.
 * PPM header returned in integer array ppmh[].
 */
void make_ppm_header ( int ppmh[], int width, int height )
{
  //standard header data, 'P' = 0x50, '6' = 0x36, '\n' = 0x0A
  int ca[] = {0x50, 0x36, 0x0A,                          //"P6"
      //image width=260,height=288
      0x33, 0x36, 0x30, 0x20, 0x32, 0x38, 0x38, 0x0A,
      0x32, 0x35, 0x35, 0x0A }; //color levels/pixel=256
  //only have to change width and height
  char temp[10], k;
  sprintf(temp, "%3d", width );          //width in ascii code
  k = 0;
  for ( int i = 3; i <= 5; ++i )         //replace width
    ca[i] = temp[k++];
  sprintf(temp, "%3d", height );         //height in ascii code
  k = 0;
  for ( int i = 7; i <=9; ++i )          //replace height
    ca[i] = temp[k++];
```

```
  for ( int i = 0; i < 15; ++i )          //form header
    ppmh[i] = ca[i];
}

void save_ppmdata ( RGBImage &image, FILE *fp )
{
  int size = 3 * image.width * image.height;

  for ( int i = 0; i < size; ++i )
    putc ( image.ibuf[i], fp ) ;
}

void ppm_read_comments ( FILE *fp )
{
  int c;
  while ( (c = getc ( fp ) )  == '#' ) {
    while ( getc( fp ) != '\n' )
;
  }
  ungetc ( c, fp );
}

class ppm_error
{
  public:
    ppm_error() {
      printf("\nIncorrect PPM format!\n");
      exit ( 1 );
    }
};

void write_ycc_header( short width, short height, FILE *fpo )
{
  char header[] = { 'Y', 'C', 'b', 'C', 'r', '4', '2', '0' };
  for ( int i = 0; i < 8; ++i )
    putc ( header[i], fpo );
  char *p;
  p = ( char *) &width;      //points to lower byte of width
  putc ( *p++,  fpo );       //save lower byte of width
  putc ( *p,  fpo );         //save upper byte of width
  p = ( char *) &height;     //points to lower byte of height
  putc ( *p++,  fpo );       //save lower byte of height
  putc ( *p,  fpo );         //save upper byte of height
}

int read_ycc_header( short &width, short &height, FILE *fpi )
{
  char header[9];
  for ( int i = 0; i < 8; ++i )
    header[i] = (char) getc ( fpi );
  if ( strncmp ( header, "YCbCr420", 8 ) )
    return -1;
  char *p;
  p = ( char *) &width;       //read the width
```

```
  *p++ = getc ( fpi );
  *p = getc ( fpi );
  p = ( char *) &height;      //read the height
  *p++ = getc ( fpi );
  *p = getc ( fpi );

  return 1;
}

int main()
{
  FILE *fp;
  int c;
  fp = fopen ("../data/beach.ppm", "rb");//PPM file for testing
  RGBImage image;

  ppm_read_comments ( fp );               //read comments
  char temp[100];
  fscanf ( fp, "%2s", temp );
  temp[3] = 0;
  if ( strncmp ( temp, "P6", 2 ) )
    throw ppm_error();
  ppm_read_comments ( fp );
  fscanf ( fp, "%d", &image.width );
  ppm_read_comments ( fp );
  fscanf ( fp, "%d", &image.height );
  ppm_read_comments ( fp );
  int colorlevels;
  fscanf ( fp, "%d", &colorlevels );
  ppm_read_comments ( fp );
  while ((c = getc ( fp )) == '\n');//get rid of extra line returns
  ungetc ( c ,fp );

  if ( image.width % 16 != 0 || image.height % 16 != 0 ) {
    printf("\nProgram only works for image dimensions divisible \
           by 16.\n \
           Use 'convert' utility to change image dimension!\n");
    return 1;
  }

  int isize;
  isize = image.width * image.height;
  //allocate memory to hold RGB data
  image.ibuf = (unsigned char *)malloc (3*isize);
  fread ( image.ibuf,  3, isize, fp );
  fclose ( fp );

  //encode RGB data in YCbCr 4:2:0 format and save in "beach.ycc"
  fp = fopen ( "../data/beach.ycc", "wb" );
  write_ycc_header ( image.width, image.height, fp );
  encode ( &image, fp );
  delete image.ibuf;                 //remove the image buffer
  fclose ( fp );

  //read the YCbCr data back from "beach.ycc" and convert to RGB
```

```
  fp = fopen ( "../data/beach.ycc", "rb" );
  if ( read_ycc_header ( image.width, image.height, fp ) == -1 ){
    printf("\nNot YCC File\n");
    return 1;
  }
  isize = image.width * image.height;
  printf("\nImage width:%d, height:%d\n",image.width,image.height);
  //allocate memory to hold image
  image.ibuf = ( unsigned char *) malloc ( 3 * isize );
  decode_yccFrame ( image, fp );
  fclose ( fp );

  //now save the decoded data in ppm again
  fp=fopen("../data/beach1.ppm","wb");//output PPM file for testing
  int ppmh[20];                        //PPM header*
  make_ppm_header ( ppmh, image.width, image.height );
  for ( int i = 0; i < 15; ++i )       //save PPM header
    putc ( ppmh[i], fp );
  save_ppmdata ( image, fp );          //save RGB data
  fclose ( fp );
  delete image.ibuf;                   //deallocate memory

  return 0;
}
------------------------------------------------------------------------
```

To generate an executable, we have to link this file to the object files discussed in section 5.2 using a command similar to the following:

```
$g++ -o test_encode_ppm test_encode_ppm.cpp rgb_ycc.o encode.o decode.o
```

The program "test_encode_ppm" uses some of the functions discussed in Chapter 4 to read and write PPM files. When it is executed, it does the following:

1. reads RGB data from "../data/beach.ppm",
2. saves YCbCr data in "../data/beach.ycc", and
3. saves reconstructed RGB data in "../data/beach1.ppm".

You can view the PPM files using "xview"; the command "xview ../data/beach.ppm" displays the original RGB image and the command "xview ../data/beach1.ppm" displays the recovered RGB image.

You should find that the two images almost look identical to each other even though we have compressed "beach.ppm" to "beach.ycc" by a factor of two. If you want to find out the file sizes, you can issue the command "ls -l ../data/beach*". Upon executing this command, you should see a display similar to the following:

```
73743   ../data/beach1.ppm
73743   ../data/beach.ppm
36876   ../data/beach.ycc
```

The first column indicates the file sizes in bytes. As you can see, files "beach.ppm" and "beach1.ppm" have identical size but the file "beach.ycc" that contains YCbCr data is only half the size of the file "beach.ppm" that contains RGB data. You can examine the image using the command like **display ../data/beach1.ppm**.

Figure 5 presents the images we have used and generated in our experiment; the original RGB image (beach.ppm) is shown in Figure 5-5a and the restored RGB image (beach1.ppm) is shown in Figure 5-5b.

a) Original b) Recovered

Figure 5-5 Original and Recovered Images in 4:2:0 Transformations

Chapter 6

Discrete Cosine Transform (DCT)

6.1 Time, Space and Frequency Domains

Data compression techniques can be classified as *lossless* or *lossy*. In lossless compression, we can reverse the process and recover the exact original data. This technique works by exploiting and removing redundancy of data and no information is lost in the process. Typically, lossless compression is used to compress text and binary programs and compression ratios achieved are usually not very high.

In lossy compression, we throw away some information carried by the data and thus the process is not reversible. The technique can give us much higher compression ratios. *Given a set of data, what kind of information should we throw away?* It turns out that choosing the portion of information to throw away is the state-of-the-art of lossy compression. Note that in technical terms, we can have redundant data but **not** redundant information. However, we can have irrelevant information and usually this is the part of the information want to throw away. For example, when we write a story about a marathon runner, we may usually omit the part that tells the time she sleeps, the time she gets up and the time she eats without affecting the story. Given an image, we want to determine which components are not as relevant as other components and discard the less relevant components. In previous chapters, we discussed that by transforming the representation of an image from RGB to 4:2:0 YCbCr format, which separates the intensity from color components, we can easily compress an image by a factor of two without much down grading of the image quality. The underlying principles in this stage of compression is that human eyes are more sensitive to brightness than to color and in practice, we do not need to retain as much information of the color components as we need in presenting an image. However, even after this change in format, we still represent the image in the spatial domain, where a sample value depends on the positon of the two-dimensional space. That is, it is a function of the coordinates (x, y) of a two-dimensional plane. Our eyes do not have any crucial discrimination of a point at any special position in space and thus it is difficult for us to further pick the irrelevant information and throw it away if we need to. On the other hand, if we could represent the image in the frequency domain, we know that our eyes are not very sensitive to high frequency components and if we have to get rid of any information, we would like to get rid of those components first.

It turns out that in nature, any wave can be expressed as a superposition of sine and cosine waves. In other words, any periodic signals can be decomposed into a series of sine and cosine waves with frequencies that are integer multiples of a certain frequency. This is the well-known **Fourier Theorem**, which is one of the most important discoveries in the history of science and technology. It is the foundation of many science and engineer applications. Lossy image compression is one of the many applications that utilize a transform built upon the theorem.

6.2 Discrete Cosine Transform (DCT)

Numerous research has been conducted on transforms for image and video compression. There are a few methods that are practical and popularly used. For static image compression, the Discrete Wavelet Transform (DWT) is the most popular method and can yield good results; it has been incorporated in the JPEG standard. Other popular methods that require less memory to operate include Karhunen-Loeve Transform (KLT), Singular Value Decomposition (SVD), and Discrete Cosine Transform (DCT). For video compression, DCT tends to give very good performance and has been incorporated in the MPEG standard. In this book, DCT will be the only significant transform that we shall discuss. DCT closely relates to Discrete Fourier Transform (DFT). Figure 6-1 shows the operation of two dimensional DCT on a block of $N \times M$ pixels.

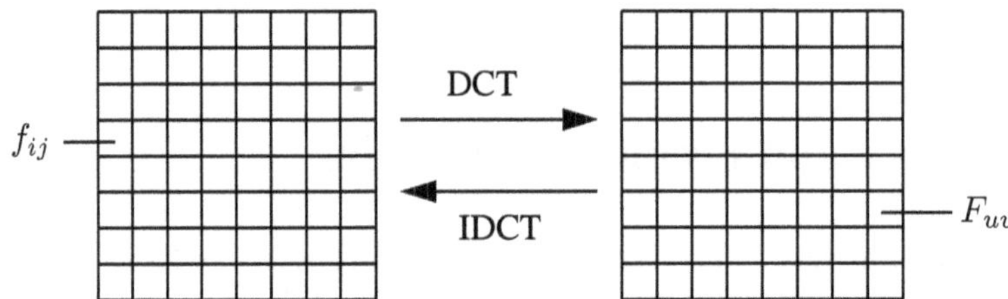

Figure 6-1. DCT and Inverse DCT (IDCT)

In the figure, f_{ij} are the pixel values and F_{uv} are the transformed values. The transform is reversible meaning that if we discount the rounding errors occurred in arithmetic calculations, we can recover the original pixel values by reversing the transformation. The reversed transformation is known as Inverse DCT or IDCT, which is also shown in **Figure 6-1**.

The general equation for a 2D **DCT** of a block of $N \times M$ pixels with values f_{ij}s is defined by the following equation:

$$F_{uv} = N_u M_v \sum_{i=0}^{N-1} \sum_{j=0}^{M-1} f_{ij} cos\frac{(2j+1)v\pi}{2M} cos\frac{(2i+1)u\pi}{2N} \tag{6.1}$$

where

$$K_r = \begin{cases} \sqrt{\frac{1}{K}} & \text{if } r = 0 \\ \sqrt{\frac{2}{K}} & \text{if } r > 0 \end{cases} \tag{6.2}$$

and K is M or N in (6.1).

The corresponding IDCT is given by the following equation:

$$f_{ij} = \sum_{u=0}^{N-1} \sum_{v=0}^{M-1} N_u M_v F_{uv} cos\frac{(2j+1)v\pi}{2M} cos\frac{(2i+1)u\pi}{2N} \tag{6.3}$$

In many applications, $N = M$ and equations (6.1) and (6.2) can be expressed in matrix forms. If **f** and **F** denote the matrices (f_{ij}) and (F_{uv}) respectively, equation (6.1) can be rewritten in the following matrix form:

$$\mathbf{F} = \mathbf{R}\,\mathbf{f}\,\mathbf{R}^{\mathbf{T}} \tag{6.4}$$

where $\mathbf{R}^{\mathbf{T}}$ is the transpose of the transform matrix **R**. The matrix elements of **R** are

$$R_{ij} = N_i cos\frac{(2j+1)i\pi}{2N} \tag{6.5}$$

where N_i is defined in (6.2). It turns out that the inverse of **R** is the same as its transpose, i.e. $\mathbf{R}^{-1} = \mathbf{R}^{\mathbf{T}}$. Therefore, the inverse transformation, IDCT can be found by:

$$\mathbf{f} = \mathbf{R}^{\mathbf{T}} \, \mathbf{F} \, \mathbf{R} \tag{6.6}$$

Example

Consider N = M = 4. The DCT transform matrix **R** is a 4×4 matrix. Using the fact that $cos(\pi - \theta) = -cos\theta$, $cos(\pi + \theta) = -cos\theta$ and $cos(2\pi + \theta) = cos\theta$, we obtain the following matrix:

$$\mathbf{R} = \begin{pmatrix} a & a & a & a \\ b & c & -b & -c \\ a & -a & -a & a \\ c & -b & -b & c \end{pmatrix} \quad where \quad \begin{array}{rl} a = & \frac{1}{2} \\ b = & \sqrt{\frac{1}{2}} cos\frac{\pi}{8} \\ c = & \sqrt{\frac{1}{2}} cos\frac{3\pi}{8} \end{array} \tag{6.7}$$

Evaluating the cosines, we have

$$\mathbf{R} = \begin{pmatrix} 0.5 & 0.5 & 0.5 & 0.5 \\ 0.653 & 0.271 & -0.271 & -0.653 \\ 0.5 & -0.5 & -0.5 & 0.5 \\ 0.271 & -0.653 & -0.653 & 0.271 \end{pmatrix} \tag{6.8}$$

Sometimes DCT is referred to as Forward DCT (FDCT) in order to distinguish it from Inverse DCT (IDCT).

6.3 Floating-point Implementation of DCT and IDCT

A direct floating-point implementation of DCT and IDCT of an $N \times N$ block is straight forward and simple. All we need to do is to use two for-loops to do summations. Program Listing 6-1 shows the implementation. In the program, the functions **dct_direct**() and **idct_direct**() do the actual work of DCT, and IDCT respectively; they use floating point (double) in calculations. The functions **dct**() and **idct**() simply cast short values to double and call **dct_direct**() or **idct_direct**() to do the transformations. In the functions, the values of *(f+i*N+j) and *(F+u*N+v) refer to the values of f[i][j] and F[u][v], corresponding to f_{ij} and F_{uv} in equations (6.1) and (6.3) respectively; a[u] and a[v] correspond to N_u and N_v.

Program Listing 6-1 Floating Point Implementation of DCT and IDCT

```
--------------------------------------------------------------------
/*
  dct_direct.cpp
  A straight forward implementation of DCT and IDCT for the purpose
  of learning and testing. Floating-point arithmetic is used.  Such
  an implementation should not be used in practical applications.

  Compile: g++ -o dct_direct dct_direct.cpp -lm
  Execute: ./dct_direct
*/
#include <stdio.h>
#include <stdlib.h>
#include <math.h>
```

```
using namespace std;
#define PI 3.141592653589

//input: f, N; output: F
short dct_direct( short N, double *f, double *F )
{
  double a[32], sum, coef;
  short i, j, u, v;

  if ( N > 32 || N <= 0 ) {
    printf ("\ninappropriate N\n");
    return -1;
  }
  a[0] = sqrt ( 1.0 / N );
  for ( i = 1; i < N; ++i ) {
    a[i] = sqrt ( 2.0 / N );
  }
  for ( u = 0; u < N; ++u ) {
    for ( v = 0; v < N; ++v ) {
      sum = 0.0;
      for ( i = 0; i < N; ++i ) {
        for ( j = 0; j < N; ++j ) {
          coef = cos((2*i+1)*u*PI/(2*N))*cos((2*j+1)*v*PI/(2*N));
          sum += *(f+i*N+j) * coef;            //f[i][j] * coef
        } //for j
        *(F+u*N+v) = a[u] * a[v] * sum;
      } //for i
    } //for u
  } //for v

  return 1;
}

//input: N, F; output f
short idct_direct( short N, double *F, double *f )
{
  double a[32], sum, coef;
  short i, j, u, v;

  if ( N > 32 || N <= 0 ) {
    printf ("\ninappropriate N\n");
    return -1;
  }
  a[0] = sqrt ( 1.0 / N );
  for ( i = 1; i < N; ++i ) {
    a[i] = sqrt ( 2.0 / N );
  }
  for ( i = 0; i < N; ++i ) {
    for ( j = 0; j < N; ++j ) {
      sum = 0.0;
      for ( u = 0; u < N; ++u ) {
        for ( v = 0; v < N; ++v ) {
          coef =  cos((2*j+1)*v*PI/(2*N))*cos ((2*i+1)*u*PI/(2*N));
          sum+=a[u]*a[v]*(*(F+u*N+v))*coef;//a[u]*a[v]*F[u][v]*coef
```

```
        } //for j
        *(f+i*N+j) =  sum;
      } //for i
    } //for u
  } //for v

  return 1;
}

/*
  change values from short to double and vice versa.
*/
short dct ( short N, short *f, short *F )
{
  double  tempx[1024], tempy[1024];
  int  total, i;

  if ( N > 32 || N <= 0 ) {
    printf ("\ninappropriate N\n");
    return -1;
  }
  total = N * N;
  for ( i = 0; i < total; ++i ) {
    tempx[i] = (double) *(f+i);
  }
  dct_direct  ( N, tempx, tempy );                //DCT operation
  for ( i = 0; i < total; ++i ) {
    *(F+i) = (short ) ( floor (tempy[i]+0.5) ); //rounding
  }

  return 1;
}

/*
  change values from short to doulbe, and vice versa.
*/
short idct ( short N, short *F, short *f )
{
  double  tempx[1024], tempy[1024];
  int  total, i;

  if ( N > 32 || N <= 0 ) {
    printf ("\ninappropriate N\n");
    return -1;
  }
  total = N * N;
  for ( i = 0; i < total; ++i ) {
    tempy[i] = (double) *(F+i);
  }
  idct_direct ( N, tempy, tempx );                //IDCT operation
  for ( i = 0; i < total; ++i ) {
    *(f+i) = (short ) ( floor (tempx[i]+0.5) ); //rounding
  }

  return 1;
```

```
}

void print_elements ( short N,  short *f )
{
  short i, j;

  for ( i = 0; i < N; ++i ){
    printf("\n");
    for ( j = 0; j < N; ++j ) {
      printf ("%4d, ", *(f+N*i+j) );
    }
  }
}

int main()
{
  short f[8][8], F[8][8];
  int i, j, N;
  char temp[8][8];
  N = 8;

  //try some values for testing
  for ( i = 0; i < N; ++i ) {
    for ( j = 0; j < N; ++j ) {
        f[i][j] = i + j;
    }
  }

  printf("\nOriginal sample values");
  print_elements ( N, &f[0][0] );
  printf("\n--------------------\n");

  dct ( N, &f[0][0], &F[0][0] );                    //performing DCT
  printf("\nCoefficients of DCT:");
  print_elements ( N, &F[0][0] );
  printf("\n--------------------\n");

  idct ( N, &F[0][0], &f[0][0] );                   //performing IDCT
  printf("\nValues recovered by IDCT:");
  print_elements ( N, &f[0][0] );
  printf("\n");
}
```

The implementation shown in Listing 6-1 is inefficient and impractical in image and video compression, which requires numerous operations of DCT and IDCT. Also, it is not a good programming practice to print out messages inside a function which is designed for other purposes. However, this program can be used for checking purposes when we later implement DCT and IDCT using more efficient methods. When the program is executed, it prints the following outputs, where $N = 8$ has been considered.

```
---------------------------------------------------------------------------
Original sample values
   0,    1,    2,    3,    4,    5,    6,    7,
   1,    2,    3,    4,    5,    6,    7,    8,
```

```
  2,     3,     4,     5,     6,     7,     8,     9,
  3,     4,     5,     6,     7,     8,     9,    10,
  4,     5,     6,     7,     8,     9,    10,    11,
  5,     6,     7,     8,     9,    10,    11,    12,
  6,     7,     8,     9,    10,    11,    12,    13,
  7,     8,     9,    10,    11,    12,    13,    14,
-------------------

Coefficients of DCT:
 56,   -18,     0,    -2,     0,    -1,     0,     0,
-18,     0,     0,     0,     0,     0,     0,     0,
  0,     0,     0,     0,     0,     0,     0,     0,
 -2,     0,     0,     0,     0,     0,     0,     0,
  0,     0,     0,     0,     0,     0,     0,     0,
 -1,     0,     0,     0,     0,     0,     0,     0,
  0,     0,     0,     0,     0,     0,     0,     0,
  0,     0,     0,     0,     0,     0,     0,     0,
-------------------

Values recovered by IDCT:
  0,     1,     2,     3,     4,     5,     6,     7,
  1,     2,     3,     4,     5,     6,     7,     8,
  2,     3,     4,     5,     6,     7,     8,     9,
  3,     4,     5,     6,     7,     8,     9,    10,
  4,     5,     6,     7,     8,     9,    10,    11,
  5,     6,     7,     8,     9,    10,    11,    12,
  6,     7,     8,     9,    10,    11,    12,    13,
  7,     8,     9,    10,    11,    12,    13,    14,
-----------------------------------------------------------------
```

We can see from the output that there are only a few nonzero coefficient values after DCT and they are clustered at the upper left corner. So after DCT, it becomes clear to us that the sample block **f** actually does not contain as much information as it appears and it is a lot easier to carry out data compression in the transformed domain.

The value of the DCT coefficient F(0, 0) at position (0, 0) is in general referred to as the DC value and others are referred to as AC values. This is because F(0, 0) is essentially a scaled average of all the sample values. We can easily see this if we write down the formula for calculating its value by setting $u = 0, v = 0$, and $N = M$ in Equation (6.1). That is,

$$F_{00} = \frac{1}{N} \sum_{i=0}^{N-1} \sum_{j=0}^{N-1} f_{ij} \tag{6.9}$$

where we have used the fact that $N_0 N_0 = \sqrt{\frac{1}{N}}\sqrt{\frac{1}{N}} = \frac{1}{N}$, and $cos(0) = 1$. (F_{00}/N is the exact average of all the values.) In Chapter 2, we discussed that the average of a set of values could give us the most crucial information of the set if we are only allowed to know one single value. Therefore, the DC value of the DCT coefficients of a block of samples is the most important single value and we want to retain its value.

6.4 Fast DCT

As DCT is so important in signal processing, a lot of research has been done to speed up its calculations. One main idea behind speeding up DCT is to break down the summation into stages and in each stage, intermediate sums of two quantities are formed. The intermediate sums will be used in later stages to obtain the final sum. In this way, the number of calculations grows with $NlogN$ rather than N^2 as in the case of direct DCT for an $N \times N$ sample block. This kind of DCT is referred to as Fast DCT. In this section, we only discuss the speeding up of Forward DCT. The techniques also apply to Inverse DCT that we shall discuss later.

If we consider only small values of N in the form of $N = 2^n$, it is not difficult to understand how the stage break-down is done. For instance, consider $N = 8$, which is what we need in our video compression. (In Chapter 5, we discussed that a macroblock consists of 8×8 sample blocks.) We can rewrite (6.1) as follows.

$$F_{uv} = a_u a_v \sum_{i=0}^{7} \sum_{j=0}^{7} f_{ij} cos \frac{(2j+1)v\pi}{16} cos \frac{(2i+1)u\pi}{16} \tag{6.10}$$

with

$$\begin{aligned} a_0 &= \sqrt{\frac{1}{8}} = \frac{1}{2\sqrt{2}} \\ a_k &= \sqrt{\frac{2}{8}} = \frac{1}{2} \qquad \text{for } k > 0 \end{aligned} \tag{6.11}$$

Equation (6.10) implies that we can express a two dimensional (2D) DCT as two one-dimensional (1D) DCT. Equation (6.10) can be rewritten as follows.

$$F_{uv} = a_u a_v \sum_{i=0}^{7} \overline{F}_{iv} cos \frac{(2i+1)u\pi}{16} \tag{6.12}$$

where

$$\overline{F}_{iv} = \sum_{j=0}^{7} f_{ij} cos \frac{(2j+1)v\pi}{16} \tag{6.13}$$

Aside from a multiplicative constant, Equation (6.13) can be interpreted as a 1D DCT or the DCT of one row (the i-th row) of samples of an 8×8 sample block. For convenience of writing, we shall suppress writing the index i; it is understood that we consider one row of samples. Also, we let

$$\begin{aligned} x_j &= f_{ij} \\ y_v &= \overline{F}_{iv} \end{aligned} \tag{6.14}$$

Equation (6.13) becomes

$$y_k = \sum_{j=0}^{7} x_j cos \frac{(2j+1)k\pi}{16}, \qquad k = 0, 1, ..., 7 \tag{6.15}$$

If we let $\theta = \frac{\pi}{16}$, we can list all the coefficients of y_k (k = 0, 1, .. 7) in a table as shown below.

	x_0	x_1	x_2	x_3	x_4	x_5	x_6	x_7
y_0	1	1	1	1	1	1	1	1
y_1	$cos(1\theta)$	$cos(3\theta)$	$cos(5\theta)$	$cos(9\theta)$	$cos(11\theta)$	$cos(13\theta)$	$cos(15\theta)$	$cos(15\theta)$
y_2	$cos(2\theta)$	$cos(6\theta)$	$cos(10\theta)$	$cos(14\theta)$	$cos(18\theta)$	$cos(22\theta)$	$cos(26\theta)$	$cos(30\theta)$
y_3	$cos(3\theta)$	$cos(9\theta)$	$cos(15\theta)$	$cos(21\theta)$	$cos(27\theta)$	$cos(33\theta)$	$cos(39\theta)$	$cos(45\theta)$
y_4	$cos(4\theta)$	$cos(12\theta)$	$cos(20\theta)$	$cos(28\theta)$	$cos(36\theta)$	$cos(44\theta)$	$cos(52\theta)$	$cos(60\theta)$
y_5	$cos(5\theta)$	$cos(15\theta)$	$cos(25\theta)$	$cos(35\theta)$	$cos(45\theta)$	$cos(55\theta)$	$cos(65\theta)$	$cos(75\theta)$
y_6	$cos(6\theta)$	$cos(18\theta)$	$cos(30\theta)$	$cos(42\theta)$	$cos(54\theta)$	$cos(66\theta)$	$cos(78\theta)$	$cos(90\theta)$
y_7	$cos(7\theta)$	$cos(21\theta)$	$cos(35\theta)$	$cos(49\theta)$	$cos(63\theta)$	$cos(77\theta)$	$cos(91\theta)$	$cos(105\theta)$

Table 6-1

Since $\theta = \frac{\pi}{16}$, we have $16\theta = \pi$. We can simplify the above table by making use of some basic cosine properties such as

$$\begin{aligned} cos(\pi - \alpha) &= -cos(\alpha) \\ cos(2\pi - \alpha) &= cos(\alpha) \end{aligned} \tag{6.16}$$

Using (6.16), we can reduce $cos(n\theta)$ with $n \leq 8$ to a form of $\pm cos(k\theta)$ with $k \leq 7$. For example,

$$\begin{aligned} cos(9\theta) &= cos(16\theta - 7\theta) &= cos(\pi - 7\theta) &= -cos(7\theta) \\ cos(35\theta) &= cos(32\theta + 3\theta) &= cos(2\pi + 3\theta) &= cos(3\theta) \end{aligned}$$

Applying these, we can simplify Table 6-1 to Table 6-2 as shown below, where cs represents $cosine$:

	x_0	x_1	x_2	x_3	x_4	x_5	x_6	x_7
y_0	1	1	1	1	1	1	1	1
y_1	$cs(1\theta)$	$cs(3\theta)$	$cs(5\theta)$	$cs(7\theta)$	$-cs(7\theta)$	$-cs(5\theta)$	$-cs(3\theta)$	$-cs(1\theta)$
y_2	$cs(2\theta)$	$cs(6\theta)$	$-cs(6\theta)$	$-cs(2\theta)$	$-cs(2\theta)$	$-cs(6\theta)$	$cs(6\theta)$	$cs(2\theta)$
y_3	$cs(3\theta)$	$-cs(7\theta)$	$-cs(1\theta)$	$-cs(5\theta)$	$cs(5\theta)$	$cs(1\theta)$	$cs(7\theta)$	$-cs(3\theta)$
y_4	$cs(4\theta)$	$-cs(4\theta)$	$-cs(4\theta)$	$cs(4\theta)$	$cs(4\theta)$	$-cs(4\theta)$	$-cs(4\theta)$	$cs(4\theta)$
y_5	$cs(5\theta)$	$-cs(1\theta)$	$cs(7\theta)$	$cs(3\theta)$	$-cs(3\theta)$	$-cs(7\theta)$	$cs(1\theta)$	$-cs(5\theta)$
y_6	$cs(6\theta)$	$-cs(2\theta)$	$cs(2\theta)$	$-cs(6\theta)$	$-cs(6\theta)$	$cs(2\theta)$	$-cs(2\theta)$	$cs(6\theta)$
y_7	$cs(7\theta)$	$-cs(5\theta)$	$cs(3\theta)$	$-cs(1\theta)$	$cs(1\theta)$	$-cs(3\theta)$	$cs(5\theta)$	$-cs(7\theta)$

Table 6-2

In Table 6-2, each y_i is equal to the sum over k of x_k times the coefficient at column k and row i. We observe that the columns possess certain symmetries; besides the first row, whenever $cos(k\theta)$ appears in an i-th column, it also appears in another j-th column when $i + j = 7$. This implies that we can always group the i-th and j-th columns together in our summing operations to compute $(x_i \pm x_j)cos(k\theta)$ provided $i + j = 7$. For example, we can rewrite y_0 and y_2 as follows:

$$\begin{aligned} y_0 &= (x_0 + x_7) + (x_1 + x_6) + (x_2 + x_5) + (x_3 + x_4) \\ y_2 &= (x_0 + x_7)c_2 + (x_1 + x_6)c_6 - (x_2 + x_5)c_6 - (x_3 + x_4)c_2 \end{aligned} \tag{6.17}$$

where

$$c_k = cos(k\theta)$$

Once we have computed $(x_i + x_j)$ with $i + j = 7$, we can use this intermediate result in the calculations of both of y_0 and y_2. Moreover, we can continue this process recursively until we obtain the final values. For instance, let

$$\begin{aligned} x'_i &= (x_i + x_j), & i + j &= 7 \\ x'_j &= (x_i - x_j), & i + j &= 7 \\ x''_i &= (x'_i + x'_j), & i + j &= 7/2 = 3 \\ x''_j &= (x'_i - x'_j), & i + j &= 7/2 = 3 \end{aligned} \tag{6.18}$$

We can rewrite y_0 and y_2 in (6.17) as follows:

$$\begin{aligned} y_0 = & \; (x'_0 + x'_3) + (x'_1 + x'_2) &= (x''_0 + x''_1) \\ y_2 = & \; (x'_0 - x'_3)c_2 + (x'_1 - x'_2)c_6 &= x''_3 c_2 + x''_2 c_6 \end{aligned} \tag{6.19}$$

We can decompose y_4 and y_6 in a similar way as y_4 only uses c_4 and y_6 uses only c_2 and c_6 of the cosine functions in the calculations. Equations of (6.20) shows the decomposition of y_4 and y_6:

$$\begin{aligned} y_4 = &\ (x'_0 + x'_3)c_4 - (x'_1 + x'_2)c_4 = &\ (x''_0 - x''_1)c_4 \\ y_6 = &\ (x'_0 - x'_3)c_6 + (x'_2 - x'_1)c_2 = &\ x''_3 c_6 - x''_1 c_2 \end{aligned} \tag{6.20}$$

The calucation of the other $y'_k s(y_1, y_3, y_5,$ and $y_7)$ involves four cosine functions $(c_1, c_3, c_5$ and $c_7)$ and they appear to be more difficult to decompose. It turns out that these cosine functions can be expressed in terms of each other by making use of some basic cosine properties like those expressed in (6.21):

$$\begin{aligned} &cos(\alpha - \beta) = cos(\alpha)cos(\beta) + sin(\alpha)sin(\beta) \\ &8\theta = \frac{8\pi}{16} = \frac{\pi}{2} \\ &c_4 = cos(4\theta) = sin(4\theta) = cos(\frac{\pi}{4}) = sin(\frac{\pi}{4}) = \frac{1}{\sqrt{2}} \\ &c_1 = cos(1\theta) = cos(8\theta - 7\theta) = cos(\frac{\pi}{2} - 7\theta) = sin(7\theta) \\ &c_3 = cos(3\theta) = cos(7\theta - 4\theta) = cos(7\theta)cos(4\theta) + sin(7\theta)sin(4\theta) = \frac{c_7 + c_1}{\sqrt{2}} \\ &c_5 = cos(5\theta) = cos(1\theta + 4\theta) = cos(1\theta)cos(4\theta) - sin(1\theta)sin(4\theta) = \frac{c_1 - c_7}{\sqrt{2}} \end{aligned} \tag{6.21}$$

Making use of the identities of (6.21), we can apply the decomposition steps to all the $y'_i s$. For example, we can express y_1 as

$$\begin{aligned} y_1 &= (x_0 - x_7)c_1 + (x_1 - x_6)c_3 + (x_2 - x_5)c_5 + (x_3 - x_4)c_7 \\ &= x'_7 c_1 + x'_6 c_3 + x'_5 c_5 + x'_4 c_7 \\ &= x'_7 c_1 + \frac{x'_6(c_1 + c_7)}{\sqrt{2}} + \frac{x'_5(c_1 - c_7)}{\sqrt{2}} + x'_4 c_7 \\ &= [x'_7 + \frac{x'_6 + x'_5}{\sqrt{2}}]c_1 + [x'_4 + \frac{x'_6 - x'_5}{\sqrt{2}}]c_7 \\ &= [x'_7 + x''_6]c_1 + [x'_4 + x''_5]c_7 \\ &= x'''_7 c_1 + x'''_4 c_7 \end{aligned} \tag{6.22}$$

In (6.22), the subscripts in the third and fourth recursive stages are not well-defined but their meanings should be clear. We observe that in the calculations, we often have expressions in the the following form:

$$\begin{aligned} c &= (a + b) \\ d &= (a - b) \end{aligned} \tag{6.23}$$

The computations of (6.23) can be represented by a diagram shown in Figure 6-2, which is referred to as a butterfly computation because of its appearance. It is also a simple flow graph.

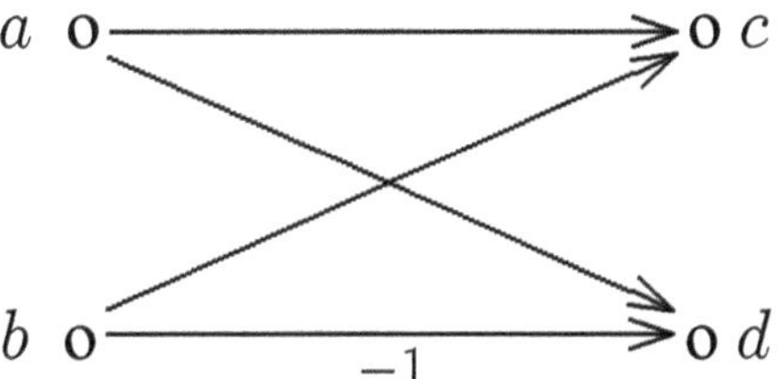

Figure 6-2. Flow Graph of Butterfly Computation

If we include the constants a_k in our calculation of y_k and let

$$C_k = c_k a_k = \frac{c_k}{2} = \frac{cos(\theta)}{2} \quad k \geq 1, \ and$$
$$C_0 = \frac{1}{\sqrt{2}}$$

we arrive at the following flow graph. (Note that $a_0 = \frac{1}{2\sqrt{2}} = C_4$.)

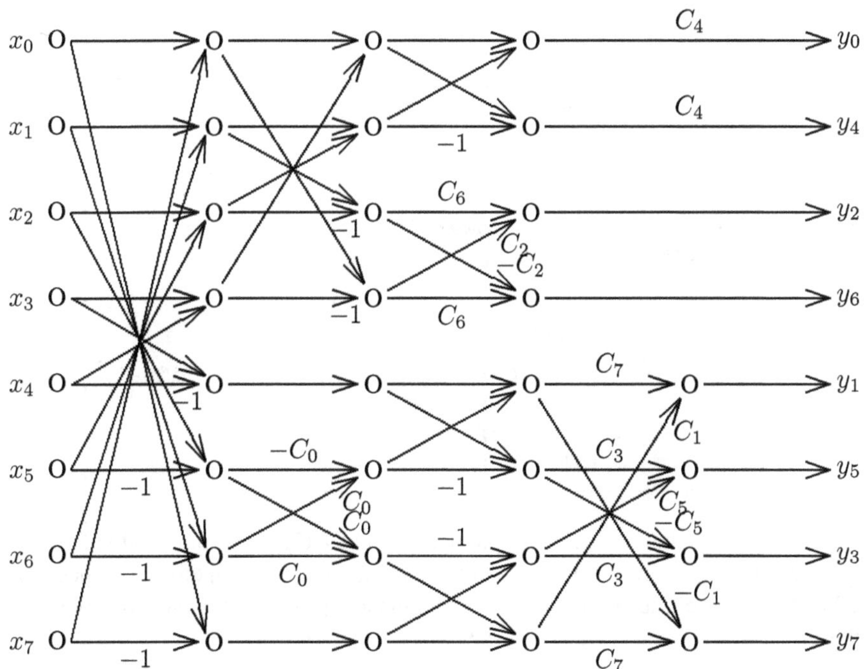

Figure 6-3. Flow Graph of 8×8 DCT using Butterfly Computation

We can obtain y_k by tracing the paths of getting to it. For example, y_2 is given by

$$
\begin{aligned}
y_2 &= x''_2 C_6 + x''_3 C_2 \\
&= [x'_1 - x'_2] C_6 + [x'_0 - x'_3] C_2 \\
&= [(x_1 + x_6) - (x_2 + x_5] C_6 + [(x_0 + x_7) - (x_3 + x_4)] C_2
\end{aligned}
$$

The following piece of C/C++ code shows how we can compute $y'_k s$ from $x'_k s$. The first for-loop does the butterfly computations ($x_i \pm x_j$), which are the first stage operations of the flow graph shown in Figure 6-3. It then performs the eight operations of the second stage of Figure 6-3. Next, the code does the calculations of the upper-half third stage, which is also the final stage of the upper-half flow graph. The lower-half has a total of four stages; the remaining code carries out the transforms of the third and fourth stages of the lower-half flow graph of Figure 6-3:

```
-----------------------------------------------------------------------
for (j = 0; j < 4; j++) {  //1st stage transform, see flow-graph
      j1 = 7 - j;
      x1[j] = x[j] + x[j1];
      x1[j1] = x[j] - x[j1];
}
x[0] = x1[0] + x1[3];         //second stage transform
x[1] = x1[1] + x1[2];
x[2] = x1[1] - x1[2];
x[3] = x1[0] - x1[3];
x[4] = x1[4];
x[5] = ( x1[6] - x1[5] ) * C0;
x[6] = ( x1[6] + x1[5]) * C0
x[7] = x1[7];

y[0] = ( x[0] + x[1] )*C4; //upper-half of 3rd (final) stage,
y[4] = ( x[0] - x[1] )*C4; //  see flow-graph
y[2] = x[2] * C6 + x[3] * C2;
y[6] = x[3] * C6 - x[2] * C2;

x1[4] = x[4] + x[5];          //lower-half of third stage
x1[5] = x[4] - x[5];
x1[6] = x[7] - x[6];
x1[7] = x[7] + x[6];

y[1] = x1[4] * C7 + x1[7] * C1;//lower-half of 4th (final) stage
y[7] = x1[7] * C7 - x1[4] * C1;
y[5] = x1[5] * C3 + x1[6] * C5;
y[3] = x1[6] * C3 - x1[5] * C5;
-----------------------------------------------------------------------
```

This code works a lot faster than the direct implementation of DCT; most practical video coders use a similar implementation. However, for the coder to be commercially competitive, we need to go one step further. We have to use integer-arithmetic, which makes further significant speed improvement of the calculations.

6.5 Integer Arithmetic

In practice, we use integer arithmetic to implement a Fast DCT. To see how this works, without loss of generality, let us consider 16-bit integers and consider a simple example with a number $x = 2.75$.

We cannot express this number as an integer directly, but we can imagine that there is a binary point at the right side of bit 0 of a 16-bit integer. In this imaginary format, x can be represented as a bit vector with imaginary digits (i.e. $2.75 = 2^1 + 2^{-1} + 2^{-2}$):

$$\begin{array}{lcccccccccccccccccc} \textit{bit position}: & 15 & & & & & & 9 & 8 & 7 & 6 & 5 & 4 & 3 & 2 & 1 & 0 & & \\ x = & 0 & 0 & 0 & 0 & 0 & 0 & 0 & 0 & 0 & 0 & 0 & 0 & 0 & 0 & 1 & 0 & . & 1 \; 1 \end{array} \tag{6.24}$$

In (6.24), the 16-bit integer does not contain the two '1' bits to the right of the binary point, which is the fractional part of x. To retain the information of the fractional part, we can shift the whole number left by 8 bits. Shifting a number left by 8 bits is the same as multiplying it by $2^8 (= 256)$. After this shift, the binary point will be at the position between bit 8 and bit 7; the number $x (= 2.75)$ becomes an integer x' as shown below:

$$\begin{array}{lccccccccccccccccc} \textit{bit position}: & 15 & & & & & & 9 & 8 & & 7 & 6 & 5 & 4 & 3 & 2 & 1 & 0 \\ x' = & 0 & 0 & 0 & 0 & 0 & 0 & 1 & 0 & . & 1 & 1 & 0 & 0 & 0 & 0 & 0 & 0 \end{array} \tag{6.25}$$

The value of x now becomes

$$x' = 2^9 + 2^7 + 2^6 = 704$$

which is the same as $2.75 \times 256 = 704$. If we now divide x' by 256, or right-shift it by 8 bits, we obtain the integer 2; that is, we have truncated the fraction part of 2.75. In many cases, we would prefer a round operation than a truncate. Rounding 2.75 gives us 3. The rounding result can be achieved by first adding 0.5 to 2.75 before the truncation. If we express 0.5 in our imaginary format and left-shift it by 8 bits, we obtain the value $128 (= 2^7)$. So adding 0.5 to x corresponds to the operation of adding 2^7 to x'. This is illustrated in the following equations, where $x'' = x' + 0.5 \times 2^7$:

$$\begin{array}{lcccccccccccccccccc} \textit{bit position} & : & 15 & & & & & & 9 & 8 & & 7 & 6 & 5 & 4 & 3 & 2 & 1 & 0 \\ x' & = & 0 & 0 & 0 & 0 & 0 & 0 & 1 & 0 & . & 1 & 1 & 0 & 0 & 0 & 0 & 0 & 0 \\ +0.5 \times 2^7 & = & 0 & 0 & 0 & 0 & 0 & 0 & 0 & 0 & . & 1 & 0 & 0 & 0 & 0 & 0 & 0 & 0 \\ x'' & = & 0 & 0 & 0 & 0 & 0 & 0 & 1 & 1 & . & 0 & 1 & 0 & 0 & 0 & 0 & 0 & 0 \end{array} \tag{6.26}$$

Obviously, when we right-shift x'' by 8 bits, we obtain our desired value 3. In general, we can transform real positive numbers to integers by multiplying the real numbers by 2^n; rounding effect is achieved by adding the value 2^{n-1} to the results before shifting them right n bits. This is true for positive numbers but *will it be also true for negative numbers? Should we still add 0.5 to the negative number or should we subtract 0.5 from it before the truncation?* The following example sheds light on what we should do.

Most modern-day computers use two's complement to represent negative numbers. Binary numbers that can have negative values are referred to as signed numbers, otherwise they are referred to as unsigned numbers. In two's complement representation, if we right-shift an unsigned number one bit, a 0 is always shifted into the leftmost bit position. However, if we right-shift a negative signed-number, a 1 is shifted in. For example, consider the following piece of code:

```
--------------------------------------------------------------------------
int main()
{
  char sc = 0x82;          //8-bit signed number
```

```
  unsigned uc = 0x82;     //8-bit unsigned number

  sc >>= 1;               //right-shift one bit
  uc >>= 1;               //right-shift one bit

  printf("\nsigned shift:   0x%x", sc );
  printf("\nunsigned shift: 0x%x", uc );
}
```

When executed, the program will produce the following outputs:

```
signed shift:   0xc1
unsigned shift: 0x41
```

The outputs show that a 1 has been shifted into *sc* (signed char) and a 0 has been shifted into *uc* (unsigned char). Because of this property, in C/C++ programming, integer-division of a negative signed-number by 2^n is different from right-shifting it by n bits. For example,

$$-1/2 = 0 \qquad but \;\; -1 >> 1 \;\; yields \;\; -1$$

$$-3/2 = -1 \qquad but \;\; -3 >> 1 \;\; yields \;\; -2$$

Now consider the negative signed-number $y = -2.75$. Its 2s complement representation can be obtained by complementing all bits of the corresponding positive number (2.75) shown in (6.24) and adding 1 to the rightmost bit of the complemented number. Thus it has the following binary form.

$$\begin{array}{lcccccccccccccccccc} bit\ position: & 15 & & & & & & 9 & 8 & 7 & 6 & 5 & 4 & 3 & 2 & 1 & 0 & & \\ y = & 1 & 1 & 1 & 1 & 1 & 1 & 1 & 1 & 1 & 1 & 1 & 1 & 1 & 0 & 1 & . & 0 & 1 \end{array} \tag{6.27}$$

When we round -2.75, we would like to obtain a value of -3 rather than -2 as the former is closer to its real value. Suppose we perform the same operations that we did to positive numbers discussed above, shifting it left 8 bits, adding 0.5×2^7 and then right shifting 8 bits. This situation is illustrated by following equations where $y'' = y' + 0.5 \times 2^7$.

$$\begin{array}{lcccccccccccccccccc} bit\ position & : & 15 & & & & & & 9 & 8 & & 7 & 6 & 5 & 4 & 3 & 2 & 1 & 0 \\ y' & = & 1 & 1 & 1 & 1 & 1 & 1 & 0 & 1 & . & 0 & 1 & 0 & 0 & 0 & 0 & 0 & 0 \\ +0.5 \times 2^7 & = & 0 & 0 & 0 & 0 & 0 & 0 & 0 & 0 & . & 1 & 0 & 0 & 0 & 0 & 0 & 0 & 0 \\ y'' & = & 1 & 1 & 1 & 1 & 1 & 1 & 0 & 1 & . & 1 & 1 & 0 & 0 & 0 & 0 & 0 & 0 \end{array} \tag{6.28}$$

When we right-shift y'' 8 bits, we obtain the following.

$$\begin{array}{lccccccccccccccccccc} bit\ position & : & 15 & & & & & & 9 & 8 & 7 & 6 & 5 & 4 & 3 & 2 & 1 & 0 & & \\ y'' >> 8 & = & 1 & 1 & 1 & 1 & 1 & 1 & 1 & 1 & 1 & 1 & 1 & 1 & 1 & 0 & 1 & . & 1 & 1 \end{array} \tag{6.29}$$

In (6.29), $y'' >> 8$ has a value of -3 (in 2s complement representation) and is what we want. Therefore, we conclude that to obtain the rounding effect, we always add 0.5 (= 0.1 in binary) to the number before truncating (right-shifting) for both positive and negative numbers.

When we add two numbers using integer arithmetic, we must align the binary points of the two numbers before addition. If the first number has been left-shifted by n bits, the second one must also be shifted by the same amount. In our implementation of Fast DCT, we use 32-bit integers; all the coefficients C_i are pre-multiplied by $1024(= 2^{10})$. After the calculations, we right-shift the integers by the same number of bits to obtain the final results. The code of the implementation of Fast DCT is listed below:

Program Listing 6-2 . Integer-arithmetic Implementation of Fast DCT

```
---------------------------------------------------------------------------
#include <string.h>
#include <stdio.h>
#include <math.h>

#define PI 3.141592653589
const short shift = 10; //10 bits precision: fixed-point arithmetic
const short shift1 = 2*shift;//at final stage,values shifted twice
const int fac = 1 << shift;  //multiply all constants by 2^10(=1024)
const int delta = 1 << (shift-1);//rounding adjustment ~ 0.5x2^10
const int delta1=1<<(shift1-1);//final rounding adjustment~0.5x2^20
const double a = PI / 16.0;    //angle theta

//DCT constants; use integer-arithmetic.
const int c0 = (int) ( 1 / sqrt ( 2 ) * fac );
const int c1 = (int) ( cos ( a ) / 2 * fac );
const int c2 = (int) ( cos ( 2*a ) / 2 * fac );
const int c3 = (int) ( cos ( 3*a ) / 2 * fac );
const int c4 = (int) ( cos ( 4*a ) / 2 * fac );
const int c5 = (int) ( cos ( 5*a ) / 2 * fac );
const int c6 = (int) ( cos ( 6*a ) / 2 * fac );
const int c7 = (int) ( cos ( 7*a ) / 2 * fac );

/*
  DCT function.
  Input: X, array of 8x8, containing data with values in [0, 255].
  Ouput: Y, array of 8x8 DCT coefficients.
*/
void dct(int *X, int *Y)
{
   int   i, j, j1, k;
   int x[8], x1[8], m[8][8];


   /*
     Row transform
     i-th row, k-th element
   */
   for (i = 0, k = 0; i < 8; i++, k += 8) {
      for (j = 0; j < 8; j++)
        x[j] = X[k+j];        //data for one row

      for (j=0; j < 4; j++){//first stage transform, see flow-graph
        j1 = 7 - j;
        x1[j]  = x[j] + x[j1];
        x1[j1] = x[j] - x[j1];
```

```
    }
    x[0] = x1[0] + x1[3]; //second stage transform
    x[1] = x1[1] + x1[2];
    x[2] = x1[1] - x1[2];
    x[3] = x1[0] - x1[3];
    x[4] = x1[4];   //after multiplication,add delta for rounding
    //shift-right to undo 'x fac' to line up binary
    //  points of all x[i]
    x[5] = ((x1[6] - x1[5]) * c0 + delta) >> shift;
    x[6] = ((x1[6] + x1[5]) * c0 + delta ) >> shift;
    x[7] = x1[7];

    m[i][0] = (x[0] + x[1])*c4;//upper-half of 3rd (final) stage,
    m[i][4] = (x[0] - x[1]) * c4;    //  see flow-graph
    m[i][2] = x[2] * c6 + x[3] * c2;
    m[i][6] = x[3] * c6 - x[2] * c2;

    x1[4] = x[4] + x[5];              //lower-half of 3rd stage
    x1[5] = x[4] - x[5];
    x1[6] = x[7] - x[6];
    x1[7] = x[7] + x[6];

    m[i][1] = x1[4] * c7 + x1[7] * c1;//lower-half of 4th stage
    m[i][7] = x1[7] * c7 - x1[4] * c1;
    m[i][5] = x1[5] * c3 + x1[6] * c5;
    m[i][3] = x1[6] * c3 - x1[5] * c5;
} //for i

/*
    At this point, coefficients of each row (m[i][j]) has been
    multiplied by 2^10. We can undo the multiplication by <<10
    here before doing the column transform. However, as we are
    using int variables, which are 32-bit to do multiplications,
    we can tolerate another multiplication of 2^10. So we delay
    our undoing until the end of the vertical transform and we
    undo all left-shift operations by shifting the results right
    20 bits ( i.e. << 2 * 10 ).
*/
// Column transform
for (i = 0; i < 8; i++) {                //eight columns

    //consider one column
    for (j = 0; j < 4; j++) {            //first-stage operation
      j1 = 7 - j;
      x1[j] = m[j][i] + m[j1][i];
      x1[j1] = m[j][i] - m[j1][i];
    }
                                         //second-stage operation
    x[0] = x1[0] + x1[3];
    x[1] = x1[1] + x1[2];
    x[2] = x1[1] - x1[2];
    x[3] = x1[0] - x1[3];
    x[4] = x1[4];
    //undo one shift for x[5], x[6] to avoid overflow
    x1[5] = (x1[5] + delta) >> shift;
```

```
      x1[6] = (x1[6] + delta) >> shift;

      x[5] = (x1[6] - x1[5]) * c0;
      x[6] = (x1[6] + x1[5]) * c0;
      x[7] = x1[7];

      m[0][i] = (x[0] + x[1])*c4;//upper-half of 3rd (final) stage
      m[4][i] = (x[0] - x[1])*c4;//  see flow-graph
      m[2][i] = ( x[2] * c6 + x[3] * c2 );
      m[6][i] = ( x[3] * c6 - x[2] * c2 );

      x1[4] = x[4] + x[5];          //lower-half of third stage
      x1[7] = x[7] + x[6];
      x1[5] = x[4] - x[5];
      x1[6] = x[7] - x[6];

      m[1][i] = x1[4] * c7 + x1[7] * c1;//lower-half of 4th stage
      m[5][i] = x1[5] * c3 + x1[6] * c5;
      m[3][i] = x1[6] * c3 - x1[5] * c5;
      m[7][i] = x1[7] * c7 - x1[4] * c1;
   } // for i

  //we have left-shift (multiplying constants) twice
  for ( i = 0; i < 8; ++i ) {
    for ( j = 0; j < 8; ++j ) {
      *Y++ =  (m[i][j] + delta1) >> shift1;//round by adding delta
    }
  }
}
-------------------------------------------------------------------------
```

In Listing 6-2, constant *shift* has value 10 and *shift1* has value 20 which are used for shifting values. Constant *fac* is obtained by left-shift 1 by 10 and thus has a value of 1024. Integer constants $c0, c1, c2, c3, c4, c5, c6, c7$ correspond to coefficients $C'_k s$ in (6.23) multiplied by 1024. Constants *delta* and *delta1* are used for rounding adjustments as explained above. In the second stage transform, in calculating $x[5]$ and $x[6]$, we have multiplied $x1[5]$ and $x1[6]$ by $c0$. However, no multiplication of any ci is involved in other $x[i]$'s. Therefore, to line up the binary point of all $x[i]$'s including $x[5]$ and $x[6]$, we have to right-shift the intermediate results of $x[5]$ and $x[6]$ by 10 bits, i.e.

$$\begin{aligned} x1[5] &= (x1[5] + delta) >> shift; \\ x1[6] &= (x1[6] + delta) >> shift; \end{aligned} \tag{6.30}$$

At the end, because we have multiplied the constants ci's twice in the intermediate calculations, we must undo the corresponding shifting operations by right-shifting the intermediate results by $shift1$ (= 20). Shifting an integer 20 bits is equivalent to shifting it 10 bits twice.

The code in Listing 6-2 can be used to do Fast DCT of a practical video compression application.

6.6 Inverse DCT (IDCT) Implementation

Once we have written the code for DCT, the implementation of IDCT becomes easy. We just need to reverse the steps in the DCT program. In the flow graph shown in Figure 6-3, when we traverse from left to right, we obtain the DCT; if we traverse from right to left, we obtain the IDCT. To understand why this is so, lets examine a butterfly computation, where we obtain (c, d) from (a, b). If we reverse the direction of the butterfly flow-graph, going from right to left, we recover (a, b) from (c, d) by

$$
\begin{aligned}
a &= (c + d)/2 \\
b &= (c - d)/2
\end{aligned}
\tag{6.31}
$$

Figure 6-4 shows the reversed butterfly except that we have suppressed writing the constant $\frac{1}{2}$ in the diagram.

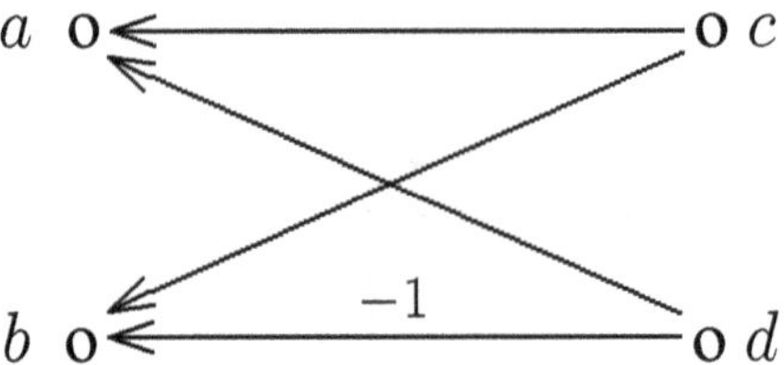

Figure 6-4. Flow Graph of Reversed Butterfly Computation

Basically, (6.23) and (6.31) have the same form. If we had multiplied the right side of (6.23) by $\frac{1}{\sqrt{2}}$ and solved for c, and d to obtain (6.31), then the forms of (6.23) and (6.31) would become identical; there's no difference in going forward (from left to right) and going backward (from right to left) in the flow graph.

Another case shown in the flow graph of Figure 6-3 is of the form

$$
\begin{aligned}
c &= aC_i - bC_j \\
d &= aC_j + bC_i
\end{aligned}
\tag{6.32}
$$

where $C_k = cos(k\theta)$, and $\theta = \frac{\pi}{16}$. (If the "minus" operation occurs in the second rather than the first equation of (6.32), we can simply interchange the roles of c and d to make it look the same as (6.32).) It turns out that in (6.32) we always have $i + j = 8$. Therefore,

$$C_j = cos(j\theta) = cos(\frac{j\pi}{16}) = cos(\frac{(8-i)\pi}{16}) = cos(\frac{\pi}{2} - i\theta) = sin(i\theta) \tag{6.33}$$

and we can express the equations of (6.32) in a matrix form as shown below.

$$
\begin{pmatrix} c \\ d \end{pmatrix} = \begin{pmatrix} cos(i\theta) - sin(i\theta) \\ sin(i\theta) + cos(i\theta) \end{pmatrix} \begin{pmatrix} a \\ b \end{pmatrix}
\tag{6.34}
$$

You may now recognize that the equations in (6.34) represent a rotation of $i\theta$ on a plane about the origin, which rotates the point (a, b) to the point (c, d). The inverse of such a transformation is a rotation of $-i\theta$ which will bring the point (c, d) back to (a, b). That is,

$$\begin{pmatrix} a \\ \\ b \end{pmatrix} = \begin{pmatrix} cos(i\theta) + sin(i\theta) \\ \\ -sin(i\theta) + cos(i\theta) \end{pmatrix} \begin{pmatrix} c \\ \\ d \end{pmatrix} \tag{6.35}$$

where we have applied $sin(-i\theta) = -sin(i\theta)$ and $cos(-i\theta) = cos(i\theta)$ in the evaluation. Thus, we can obtain the inverse of (6.32) by simply changing the sign of C_j. That is, we replace any $-C_j$ by C_j and the corresponding C_j by $-C_j$. So the inverse of (6.32) is given by

$$\begin{aligned} a &= cC_i + dC_j \\ d &= -cC_j + dC_i \end{aligned} \tag{6.36}$$

By doing this substitution for all $-C_j's$ in Figure 6-3, we can obtain the flow graph for IDCT. Correspondingly, in developing the IDCT program, we start with the DCT code, starting from the bottom of the DCT function, and working our way up with the replacing strategy; the resulted code is the IDCT function. We list the complete program, **dct_video.cpp** that implements both DCT and IDCT below; they are straightforward implementations of what we have discussed. The functions are ready for use for video compression.

Program Listing 6-3 DCT and IDCT Integer Implementation

```
------------------------------------------------------------------------
/*
  dct_video.cpp
  An implementation of 8x8 DCT and IDCT for video compression.
  32-bit integer-arithmetic is assumed.
  For DCT operation:
     dct ( int *X, int *Y );
     X is the input pointing to an 8x8 array of samples; values
       must be within [0, 255]
     Y is the output pointing to an 8x8 array of DCT coefficients.
  For IDCT operation:
     idct ( int *Y, int *X );
     Y is the input pointing to an 8x8 array of DCT coefficients.
     X is the output pointing to an 8x8 array of sample values.

  compile: g++ -c dct_video.cpp
  To use them, include the the following header statements in your
  application.
      void dct(int *X, int *Y);
      void idct(int *Y, int *X);
*/

#include <string.h>
#include <stdio.h>
#include <math.h>

#define PI 3.141592653589
const short shift = 10;              //10 bits precision
//at the final stage,values have been shifted twice
const short shift1 = 2 * shift;
const int fac = 1 << shift ;     //multiply all constants by 2^10
```

```
const int delta = 1 << (shift-1);//for rounding adjustment~0.5x2^10
const int delta1 = 1 << (shift1-1);//final rounding adjust~0.5x2^20
const double a = PI / 16.0;        //angle theta

//DCT constants; use integer-arithmetic.
const int c0 = (int) ( 1 / sqrt ( 2 ) * fac );
const int c1 = (int) ( cos ( a ) / 2 * fac );
const int c2 = (int) ( cos ( 2*a ) / 2 * fac );
const int c3 = (int) ( cos ( 3*a ) / 2 * fac );
const int c4 = (int) ( cos ( 4*a ) / 2 * fac );
const int c5 = (int) ( cos ( 5*a ) / 2 * fac );
const int c6 = (int) ( cos ( 6*a ) / 2 * fac );
const int c7 = (int) ( cos ( 7*a ) / 2 * fac );

/*
  DCT function.
  Input: X, array of 8x8, containing data with values in [0, 255].
  Ouput: Y, array of 8x8 DCT coefficients.
*/
void dct(int *X, int *Y)
{
   int   i, j, j1, k;
   int x[8], x1[8], m[8][8];

   /*
     Row transform
     i-th row, k-th element
   */
   for (i = 0, k = 0; i < 8; i++, k += 8) {
      for (j = 0; j < 8; j++)
        x[j] = X[k+j];                       //data for one row

      for (j = 0; j < 4; j++) {              //first stage transform
        j1 = 7 - j;
        x1[j] = x[j] + x[j1];
        x1[j1] = x[j] - x[j1];
      }
      x[0] = x1[0] + x1[3];                  //second stage transform
      x[1] = x1[1] + x1[2];
      x[2] = x1[1] - x1[2];
      x[3] = x1[0] - x1[3];
      x[4] = x1[4];  //after multiplication,add delta for rounding
      //shift to line up binary points
      x[5] = ((x1[6] - x1[5]) * c0 + delta ) >> shift;
      x[6] = ((x1[6] + x1[5]) * c0 + delta ) >> shift;
      x[7] = x1[7];

      m[i][0] = (x[0] + x[1])*c4; //upper-half of 3rd (final) stage
      m[i][4] = (x[0] - x[1]) * c4;
      m[i][2] = x[2] * c6 + x[3] * c2;
      m[i][6] = x[3] * c6 - x[2] * c2;

      x1[4] = x[4] + x[5];         //lower-half of third stage
      x1[5] = x[4] - x[5];
      x1[6] = x[7] - x[6];
```

```
    x1[7] = x[7] + x[6];

    m[i][1] = x1[4] * c7 + x1[7] * c1; //lower-half of 4th stage
    m[i][7] = x1[7] * c7 - x1[4] * c1;
    m[i][5] = x1[5] * c3 + x1[6] * c5;
    m[i][3] = x1[6] * c3 - x1[5] * c5;
  } //for i

  /*
    At this point, coefficients of each row ( m[i][j] ) has
    been multiplied by 2^10. We can undo the multiplication
    by << 10 here before doing the vertical transform. However,
    as we are using int variables, which are 32-bit to do
    multiplications, we can tolerate another multiplication of
    2^10. So we delay our undoing until the end of the vertical
    transform and we undo all left-shift operations by shifting
    the results right 20 bits ( i.e. << 2 * 10 ).
  */
  // Column transform
  for (i = 0; i < 8; i++) {                  //eight columns

    //consider one column
    for (j = 0; j < 4; j++) {                //first-stage operation
      j1 = 7 - j;
      x1[j] = m[j][i] + m[j1][i];
      x1[j1] = m[j][i] - m[j1][i];
    }
                                             //second-stage operation
    x[0] = x1[0] + x1[3];
    x[1] = x1[1] + x1[2];
    x[2] = x1[1] - x1[2];
    x[3] = x1[0] - x1[3];
    x[4] = x1[4];
    //undo one shift for x[5], x[6] to avoid overflow
    x1[5] = (x1[5] + delta) >> shift;
    x1[6] = (x1[6] + delta) >> shift;

    x[5] = (x1[6] - x1[5]) * c0;
    x[6] = (x1[6] + x1[5]) * c0;
    x[7] = x1[7];

    m[0][i] = (x[0] + x[1])*c4;//upper-half of 3rd (final) stage,
    m[4][i] = (x[0] - x[1])*c4;// see flow-graph
    m[2][i] = ( x[2] * c6 + x[3] * c2 );
    m[6][i] = ( x[3] * c6 - x[2] * c2 );

    x1[4] = x[4] + x[5];           //lower-half of third stage
    x1[7] = x[7] + x[6];
    x1[5] = x[4] - x[5];
    x1[6] = x[7] - x[6];

    m[1][i] = x1[4] * c7 + x1[7] * c1;//lower-half of 4th stage
    m[5][i] = x1[5] * c3 + x1[6] * c5;
    m[3][i] = x1[6] * c3 - x1[5] * c5;
    m[7][i] = x1[7] * c7 - x1[4] * c1;
```

```
    } // for i

   //we have left-shift (multiplying constants) twice
   for ( i = 0; i < 8; ++i ) {
     for ( j = 0; j < 8; ++j ) {
       *Y++ = (m[i][j] + delta1) >> shift1;//round by adding delta
     }
   }
}

/*
  Implementation of idct() is to reverse the operations of dct().
  We first do vertical transform and then horizontal;this is easier
  for debugging as the operations are just the reverse of those in
  dct(); of course, it works just as well if you do the horizontal
  transform first. So in this implementation, the first stage of
  idct() is the final stage of dct() and the final stage of idct()
  is the first stage of dct().
*/

void idct(int *Y, int *X)
{
   int   j1, i, j, k;
   int x[8], x1[8], m[8][8], y[8];
   k = i = 0;

  //column transform
  for ( i = 0; i < 8; ++i ) {
    for (j = 0; j < 8; j++)
        y[j] = Y[i+8*j];

    x1[4] = y[1] * c7 - y[7] * c1;  //lower-half final stage of dct
    x1[7] = y[1] * c1 + y[7] * c7;
    x1[6] = y[3] * c3 + y[5] * c5;
    x1[5] = -y[3] * c5 + y[5] * c3;

    x[4] = ( x1[4] + x1[5] );      //lower-half of 3rd stage of dct
    x[5] = ( x1[4] - x1[5] );
    x[6] = ( x1[7] - x1[6] );
    x[7] = ( x1[7] + x1[6] );

    x1[0]=(y[0] + y[4])*c4;//upper-half of 3rd (final) stage of dct
    x1[1] = ( y[0] - y[4] ) * c4;
    x1[2] = y[2] * c6 - y[6] * c2;
    x1[3] = y[2] * c2 + y[6] * c6;


    x[0] = ( x1[0] + x1[3] );              //second stage of dct
    x[1] = ( x1[1] + x1[2] );
    x[2] = ( x1[1] - x1[2] );
    x[3] = ( x1[0] - x1[3] );


    //x[4], x[7] no change
    //after multiplication, add delta for rounding
```

```
    // shift-right to undo 'x fac'  to line up x[]s
    x1[5] = ((x[6] - x[5]) * c0 + delta ) >> shift;
    x1[6] = ((x[6] + x[5]) * c0 + delta ) >> shift;
    x[5] = x1[5];
    x[6] = x1[6];

    for (j = 0; j < 4; j++) {     //first stage transform of dct
        j1 = 7 - j;
        m[j][i] = (x[j] + x[j1] );
        m[j1][i] = (x[j] - x[j1] );
    }
  } //for i

   //row transform
  for ( i = 0; i < 8; i++ ) {
    for (j = 0; j < 8; j++)
        y[j] = m[i][j] ;          //data for one row

    x1[4] = y[1] * c7 - y[7] * c1;
    x1[7] = y[1] * c1 + y[7] * c7;
    x1[6] = y[3] * c3 + y[5] * c5;
    x1[5] = -y[3] * c5 + y[5] * c3;

    x[4] = ( x1[4] + x1[5] );     //lower-half of third stage
    x[5] = ( x1[4] - x1[5] );
    x[6] = ( x1[7] - x1[6] );
    x[7] = ( x1[7] + x1[6] );

    x1[0] = ( y[0] + y[4] ) * c4;
    x1[1] = ( y[0] - y[4] ) * c4;
    x1[2] = y[2] * c6 - y[6] * c2;
    x1[3] = y[2] * c2 + y[6] * c6;

    //undo one shift for x[5], x[6] to avoid overflow
    x1[5] = (x[5] + delta) >> shift;
    x1[6] = (x[6] + delta) >> shift;
    x[5] = (x1[6] - x1[5]) * c0;
    x[6] = (x1[6] + x1[5]) * c0;
      //x[4], x[7] no change
    x[0] = ( x1[0] + x1[3] );     //second stage transform
    x[1] = ( x1[1] + x1[2] );
    x[2] = ( x1[1] - x1[2] );
    x[3] = ( x1[0] - x1[3] );

    for (j = 0; j < 4; j++) {     //first stage transform
        j1 = 7 - j;
        m[i][j] = (x[j] + x[j1]);
        m[i][j1] = (x[j] - x[j1]);
      }
    }
    //we have left-shift (multiplying constants) twice
    for ( i = 0; i < 8; ++i ) {
      for ( j = 0; j < 8; ++j ) {
        *X++ = (m[i][j] + delta1) >> shift1;//round by adding delta
      }
```

```
    }
}
---------------------------------------------------------------------
```

We can compile **dct_video.cpp** of Listing 6-3 using the command,

```
g++ -c dct_video.cpp
```

which generates the object module **dct_video.o** that can be linked to an application. We provide **test_dct.cpp** that can be downloaded from the web site of this book for you to test the DCT and IDCT routines of **dct_video.cpp**. Note that the sample values used in testing must be within the range [0, 255].

The following command links **dct_video.o** with **test_dct.o**, the object module of **test_dct.cpp** to generate the executable **test_dct**; the option "-lm" means to link with the standard maths library.

```
g++ -o test_dct dct_video.o test_dct.cpp -lm
```

The following is what will be displayed when we execute **test_dct**.

```
---------------------------------------------------------------------
Original Data:
------------------
1, 2, 3, 4, 5, 6, 7, 8,
1, 5, 9, 13, 17, 21, 25, 29,
1, 8, 15, 22, 29, 36, 43, 50,
1, 11, 21, 31, 41, 51, 61, 71,
1, 14, 27, 40, 53, 66, 79, 92,
1, 17, 33, 49, 65, 81, 97, 113,
1, 20, 39, 58, 77, 96, 115, 134,
1, 23, 45, 67, 89, 111, 133, 155,

Data after dct:
330, -210, 0, -22, 0, -6, 0, -2,
-191, 124, 0, 13, 0, 4, 0, 1,
0, 0, 0, 0, 0, 0, 0, 0,
-20, 13, 0, 1, 0, 0, 0, 0,
0, 0, 0, 0, 0, 0, 0, 0,
-6, 4, 0, 1, 0, 0, 0, 0,
0, 0, 0, 0, 0, 0, 0, 0,
-1, 1, 0, 1, 0, 0, 0, 0,

Data recovered by idct:
------------------
1, 2, 3, 4, 5, 6, 7, 8,
1, 5, 9, 13, 17, 21, 25, 29,
1, 8, 15, 22, 29, 36, 43, 50,
1, 11, 21, 31, 41, 51, 61, 71,
1, 14, 27, 40, 53, 66, 79, 92,
1, 17, 33, 49, 65, 81, 97, 113,
1, 20, 39, 58, 77, 96, 115, 134,
1, 23, 45, 67, 89, 111, 133, 155,
---------------------------------------------------------------------
```

6.7 Applying DCT and IDCT to YCbCr Macroblocks

In Chapter 5, we have discussed the down sampling of an RGB image to 4:2:0 YCbCr macroblocks. A 4:2:0 YCbCr macroblock conists of four 8x8 Y sample blocks , one 8x8 Cb sample block and one 8x8 Cr sample block. It is natural to apply the Fast DCT with N = 8 discussed above to each of these sample blocks. In Chapter 5, we developed a test program ("test_encode_ppm.cpp") that reads an RGB image in PPM format, decomposes and converts it to 4:2:0 YCbCr macroblocks, and saves the YCbCr data in a ".ycc" file. Here, we go one step further. We want to develop a test program that reads the RGB data from a PPM file, converts them to YCbCr macroblocks, applies DCT to the sample blocks, and saves the DCT coefficients in a file with extension ".dct". Our ".dct" file has a format similar to that of a ".ycc" file; the first 8 bytes consists of the header text "DCT4:2:0"; the next two bytes contains the image width followed by another two bytes of image height; data start from the thirteenth byte. The test program can also reverse the process. The reversed process consists of reading a ".dct" file, applying IDCT to the data to recover the YCbCr macroblocks, converting YCbCr back to RGB and saving the RGB data in a PPM file.

To accomplish these, we need to add a few more functions in the programs **encode.cpp** and **decode.cpp** discussed in Chapter 5. Suppose we have put all functions that read and write ".ppm" and ".ycc" files presented in "test_encode_ppm.cpp" in the file "ppm-ycc.cpp" and their prototypes in "ppm-ycc.h". The following functions are added to **encode.cpp**:

```
void save_one_dctblock ( int *Y, FILE *fpo );
void save_dct_yccblocks( YCbCr_MACRO *ycbcr_macro, FILE *fpo );
void encode_dct ( RGBImage *image, FILE *fpo );
```

These functions are shown in Listing 6-4. Their meanings are self-explained by the code.

Program Listing 6-4 Encoding an RGB Frame to DCT Coefficients

```
----------------------------------------------------------------------
/*
  encode.cpp
  Contains functions to convert an RGB frame to YCbCr and from YCbCr
  to 16-bit DCT coefficients. It also contains functions to save
  the converted data.
  Compile: g++ -c encode.cpp
*/
#include <stdio.h>
#include <stdlib.h>
#include "../5/common.h"
#include "../5/rgb_ycc.h"

void dct(int *X, int *Y);
void idct(int *Y, int *X);

void print_dct_block ( int Y[] )
{

   for ( int i = 0; i < 64; ++i ){
      if ( i % 8 == 0 ) printf("\n");
      printf("%d,\t", Y[i] );
  }
  printf("\n-----------------");
```

```
}

void save_one_dctblock ( int Y[], FILE *fpo )
{
    short Ys[64];

    for ( int i = 0; i < 64; ++i ) //change to short for saving
      Ys[i] = ( short ) Y[i];
    fwrite ( Ys, 2, 64, fpo );     //save DCT coefficients of the
                                    //  block
}

/*
 * Apply DCT to six 8x8 sample blocks of a 4:2:0 YCbCr macroblock
 * and save the coefficients in a file pointed by fpo
 */
void save_dct_yccblocks( YCbCr_MACRO *ycbcr_macro, FILE *fpo )
{
  short block, i, j, k;
  unsigned char *py;
  int  X[64], Y[64];                //for dct transform

  //save DCT of Y
  for ( block = 0; block < 4; block++){//Y has 4 8x8 sample blocks
    if ( block < 2 )
      py=(unsigned char *)&ycbcr_macro->Y+8*block;//begin of block
    else //points to beginning of block
      py = (unsigned char *)&ycbcr_macro->Y+128+8*(block-2);
    k = 0;
    for ( i = 0; i < 8; i++ ) {     //one sample-block
      if ( i > 0 ) py += 16;        //multiply i by 16(one row)
      for ( j = 0; j < 8; j++ ) {
        X[k++] = ( int ) *( py + j );
      }
    }
    dct (  X, Y );                  //DCT transform of 8x8 block
    save_one_dctblock ( Y, fpo );   //save DCT coeffs of 8x8 block
  }
  k = 0;
  for ( i = 0; i < 8; ++i ) {
    for ( j = 0; j < 8; ++j ) {
      X[k] = ycbcr_macro->Cb[k];
      k++;
    }
  }
  dct (  X, Y );                    //DCT of Cb 8x8 sample block
  save_one_dctblock( Y, fpo );
  k = 0;
  for ( i = 0; i < 8; ++i ) {
    for ( j = 0; j < 8; ++j ) {
      X[k] = ycbcr_macro->Cr[k];
      k++;
    }
  }
  dct ( X, Y );                     //DCT of Cr 8x8 sample block
```

```
  save_one_dctblock ( Y, fpo );
}

/*
 * Convert RGB  data to YCbCr, then to DCT coeffs and
 * save DCT coeffs.
 */
void encode_dct ( RGBImage *image, FILE *fpo )
{
  short row, col, i, j, r;
  RGB *p;                        //pointer to a pixel
  RGB macro16x16[256];           //16x16 macroblock;24-bit RGB pixel
  YCbCr_MACRO ycbcr_macro;       //macroblock for YCbCr samples
  static int nframe = 0;

  for ( row = 0; row < image->height; row += 16 ) {
    for ( col = 0; col < image->width; col += 16 ) {
      //points to beginning of macroblock
      p = (RGB *)image->ibuf+(row * image->width + col);
      r = 0;                     //note pointer arithmetic
      for ( i = 0; i < 16; ++i ) {
        for ( j = 0; j < 16; ++j ) {
          macro16x16[r++] = (RGB) *p++;
        }
        p += (image->width-16); //next row within macroblock
      }
      macroblock2ycbcr ( macro16x16,  &ycbcr_macro );
      save_dct_yccblocks( &ycbcr_macro, fpo );
    } //for col
  } //for row
}
.......
( Functions already presented in Listing 5-2 are omitted here. )
---------------------------------------------------------------------
```

In Listing 6-4, the function **encode_dct**() declares *p* as a pointer variable pointing to an RGB object (i.e., RGB *p), which contains the red, green, blue values of one pixel for a total of 3 bytes. This pointer is used to access the pixels of a 16 × 16 macroblock. Since the image width and height are divisible by 16, the starting position of each macroblock at row *row* and column *col* is given by:

$$\text{macroblock address} = imageAddress + row \times imagewidth + col$$

The 'address' is counted relative to the 'imageAddress' in terms of pixels. It is not measured in bytes. Therefore, when we increment *p* (i.e. ++p), it automatically advances 3 bytes (or one pixel) and points to the next pixel.

The corresponding functions we need to add to **decode.cpp** of Listing 5-2 of Chapter 5 include the following:

```
int get_one_dctblock ( int *Y, FILE *fpi );
int get_dct_yccblocks( YCbCr_MACRO *ycbcr_macro, FILE *fpi );
int decode_dct ( RGBImage &image, FILE *fpi );
```

These functions are shown in Listing 6-5. Again, their meanings are self-explained by the code.

Program Listing 6-5 Decoding DCT Coefficients to an RGB Frame

```
------------------------------------------------------------------------
/*
  decode.cpp
  Contains functions to:
     read DCT data from a file,
     carries out IDCT to obtain YCbCr macroblocks from
       DCT coefficients,
     convert YCbCr data to RGB, and
     read YCbCr data from a file
  Compile: g++ -c decode.cpp
*/
#include <stdio.h>
#include <stdlib.h>
#include "../5/common.h"
#include "../5/rgb_ycc.h" //header developed in Chapter 5

void dct(int *X, int *Y);
void idct(int *Y, int *X);

int get_one_dctblock ( int Y[], FILE *fpi )
{
  short Ys[64];
  if ( !fread ( Ys, 2, 64, fpi ) )
        return 0;
  for ( int i = 0; i < 64; ++i )
    Y[i] = Ys[i];
  return 1;
}

/*
 * Get DCT coefficients from file, apply IDCT to obtain the
 * YCbCr macroblocks.
 */
int get_dct_yccblocks( YCbCr_MACRO *ycbcr_macro, FILE *fpi )
{
  short r, row, col, i, j, k, n, block;
  short c;
  unsigned char *py;
  int Y[64], X[64];

  n = 0;
  //read data from file and put them in four 8x8 Y sample blocks
  for ( block = 0; block < 4; block++ ) {
    if ( !get_one_dctblock( Y, fpi ) )
      return 0;
    idct ( Y, X );
    k = 0;
    if ( block < 2 )
      py = ( unsigned char * ) &ycbcr_macro->Y + 8*block;
    else
      py = (unsigned char *)&ycbcr_macro->Y + 128 + 8*(block-2);
    for ( i = 0; i < 8; i++ ){//one sample-block
      if ( i > 0 )py+=16;  //advance py by 16 (1 row of macroblock)
```

```
      for ( j = 0; j < 8; j++ ) {
        *( py + j ) = X[k++];
         n++;
      } //for j
    } //for i
  } //for block
  //now do that for 8x8 Cb block
  k = 0;
  if ( !get_one_dctblock( Y, fpi ) )
    return 0;
  idct ( Y, X );
  for ( i = 0; i < 8; ++i ) {
    for ( j = 0; j < 8; ++j ) {
       ycbcr_macro->Cb[k] = X[k];
       k++;    n++;
    }
  }

  //now do that for 8x8 Cr block
  k = 0;
  if ( !get_one_dctblock( Y, fpi ) )
    return 0;
  idct ( Y, X );
  for ( i = 0; i < 8; ++i ) {
    for ( j = 0; j < 8; ++j ) {
      ycbcr_macro->Cr[k] = X[k];
      k++;    n++;
    }
  }

  return n;                           //number of bytes read
}

/*
 *   Decode DCT coeffs to a YCbCr frame and then to RGB.
 */
int decode_dct ( RGBImage &image, FILE *fpi )
{
  short r, row, col, i, j, k, block;
  int n = 0;
  RGB macro16x16[256];      //16x16 macroblock; 24-bit RGB pixel
  YCbCr_MACRO ycbcr_macro; //macroblock for YCbCr samples
  RGB *rgbp;                //pointer to an RGB pixel
  int fpos = ftell ( fpi );
  for ( row = 0; row < image.height; row += 16 ) {
    for ( col = 0; col < image.width; col += 16 ) {
      int m = get_dct_yccblocks( &ycbcr_macro, fpi );
      if ( m <= 0 ) { printf("\nout of dct data\n"); return m;}
      n += m;
      ycbcr2macroblock( &ycbcr_macro, macro16x16 );
      rgbp = (RGB *) (image.ibuf) + (row * image.width + col);
      r = 0;
      for ( i = 0; i < 16; ++i ) {
        for ( j = 0; j < 16; ++j ) {
          *rgbp++ =  macro16x16[r++];
```

```
        }
        rgbp += ( image.width - 16 ); //next row within macroblock
      }
    } //for col
  }  //for row
  return n;
}
..............
(Functions presented in Listing 5-2 are omitted here.)
------------------------------------------------------------------------
```

Finally, the program **test_dct_ppm.cpp** of Listing 6-6 performs the tasks of DCT testing on an image file. It first reads RGB data from the testing PPM file "beach.ppm" and uses the function **encode_dct** () to convert the RGB data to 4:2:0 YCbCr macroblocks and then to 16-bit DCT coefficients, saving them in the file "beach.dct". Secondly, it uses the function **decode_dct**() to read the DCT data back from the file "beach.dct" and recover the RGB data. The recovered RGB data are saved in the PPM file "beach2.ppm". To generate an executable, we may link this file to the other object files discussed before using the following command:

```
$g++ -o test_dct_ppm test_dct_ppm.cpp ppm_ycc_dct.o \
            ../5/rgb_ycc.o encode.o decode.o dct_video.o
```

After executing the program, we can check the recovered data by issuing the command "display ../data/beach2.ppm". One can observe that the image of "beach2.ppm" is essentially identical to that of the original file, "beach.ppm". The images of these two files are shown at the end of this Chapter (Figure 6-6).

Program Listing 6-6 Testing Integer Implementation of DCT and IDCT Using a PPM Image

```
------------------------------------------------------------------------
/*
 * test_dct_ppm.cpp
 * Program to test integer implementations of DCT, IDCT, and
 * RGB-YCbCr conversions using macroblocks. PPM files are used
 * for testing. It reads "../data/beach.ppm" RGB data, converts
 * them to 4:2:0 YCbCr macroblocks, and then to 16-bit DCT
 * coefficients which will be saved in file "../data/beach.dct".
 * The program then reads back the DCT coefficients from
 * "../data/beach.dct", performs IDCT, converts them to YCbCr
 * macroblocks and the to RGB data. The  recovered RGB data are
 * saved in "../data/beach2.ppm".  PPM files can be viewed
 * using "display".
 * Compile:  g++ -o test_dct_ppm test_dct_ppm.cpp ppm_ycc_dct.o \
             ../5/rgb_ycc.o encode.o decode.o dct_video.o
 * Execute: ./test_dct_ppm
 */

#include <stdio.h>
#include <stdlib.h>
#include <string.h>
#include "../5/common.h"
#include "ppm_ycc_dct.h"

void encode_dct ( RGBImage *image, FILE *fpo );
int decode_dct ( RGBImage &image, FILE *fpi );
```

```
int main()
{
  FILE *fp;
  int c;
  int isize;        //image size

  fp = fopen ("../data/beach.ppm", "rb");//PPM file for testing
  RGBImage image;

  ppm_read_comments ( fp );                //read comments
  char temp[100];
  fscanf ( fp, "%2s", temp );
  temp[3] = 0;
  if ( strncmp ( temp, "P6", 2 ) )
    throw ppm_error();
  ppm_read_comments ( fp );
  fscanf ( fp, "%d", &image.width );
  ppm_read_comments ( fp );
  fscanf ( fp, "%d", &image.height );
  ppm_read_comments ( fp );
  int colorlevels;
  fscanf ( fp, "%d", &colorlevels );
  ppm_read_comments ( fp );
  while ((c = getc ( fp )) == '\n');//get rid of extra line returns
  ungetc ( c ,fp );

  if ( image.width % 16 != 0 || image.height % 16 != 0 ) {
    printf("\nProgram only works for image dimensions divisible
                by 16.\n
            Use 'convert' utility to change image dimension.!\n");
    return 1;
  }

  //convert RGB data to YCbCr 4:2:0 and then to DCT coeffs; save
  //  data in "beach.dct"
  isize = image.width * image.height;
  //allocate memory to hold RGB data
  image.ibuf = ( unsigned char *) malloc (3 * isize);
  fread ( image.ibuf,  3, isize, fp );
  fclose ( fp );

  fp = fopen ( "../data/beach.dct", "wb" );
  write_dct_header ( image.width, image.height, fp );
  encode_dct ( &image, fp );    //convert to 16-bit DCT coeffs,
                                // save data in "beach.dct"
  delete image.ibuf;            //remove the image buffer
  fclose ( fp );

  //read the DCT data back from "beach.dct" and convert to RGB
  fp = fopen ( "../data/beach.dct", "rb" );
  if ( read_dct_header ( image.width, image.height, fp ) == -1 ){
    printf("\nNot DCT File\n");
    return 1;
  }
  isize = image.width * image.height;
```

```
  image.ibuf = ( unsigned char *) malloc ( 3 * isize );
  decode_dct ( image, fp );//perform IDCT, convert data back to RGB
  fclose ( fp );

  //now save the decoded data in ppm again
  fp = fopen ("../data/beach2.ppm", "wb");       //output PPM file
  int ppmh[20];                                  //PPM header*
  make_ppm_header ( ppmh, image.width, image.height );
  for ( int i = 0; i < 15; ++i )                 //save PPM header
    putc ( ppmh[i], fp );
  save_ppmdata ( image, fp );                    //save RGB data
  printf("\nRecovered RGB data saved in ../data/beach2.ppm\n");
  fclose ( fp );
  delete image.ibuf;                             //deallocate memory

  return 0;
---------------------------------------------------------------------
```

We may use the command "ls -l ../data/beach*" to list the sizes of the *beach* files. If you do so, you may see something similar to the following, where the left column shows the file sizes:

```
73743  ../data/beach.ppm
73743  ../data/beach2.ppm
73740  ../data/beach.dct
36876  ../data/beach.ycc
```

We see that the file size of the DCT data is twice as large as that of the YCbCr data. This is because we have saved each DCT coefficient as a 16-bit number but each YCbCr sample value is only 8-bit. It seems that we have done something that have expanded rather than compressed the image data. Actually, the DCT is only an intermediate process. We do not really need to save any DCT coefficients. We do so here only for the purpose of testing and learning DCT. In the next chapter, we shall discuss what we shall do after the DCT step. At the moment, let us summarize what we have discussed, the encoding and decoding processes up to this point. The encoding stage consists of the following steps:

1. Converts RGB data to 4:2:0 YCbCr macroblocks. Each macroblock consists of four 8×8 Y sample blocks, one 8×8 Cb sample block, and one 8×8 Cr sample block. This step compresses the data by a factor of 2.
2. Applies DCT to each 8x8 sample block which gives an 8×8 array of 16-bit DCT coefficients. This step expands the data by a factor of 2.

On the other hand, the decoding stage consists of the following steps:

1. Applies IDCT to each 8×8 arrary of DCT coefficients to recover an 8×8 YCbCr 8-bit sample block. Reconstruct 4:2:0 YCbCr macroblocks from the sample blocks.
2. Converts YCbCr macroblocks to RGB data.

The encoding steps are shown in Figure 6-5.

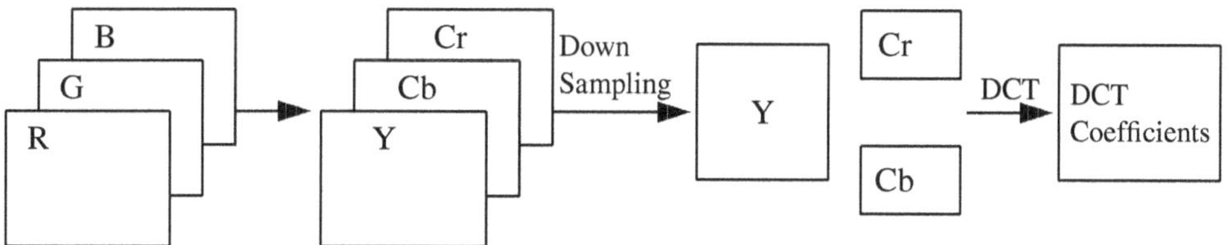

Figure 6-5. Encoding of RGB Data

Figure 6-6 Effect of down-sampling and DCT: The Original RGB Image (left) and The Restored Image (right)

Chapter 7

Quantization and Run-level Encoding

7.1 Introduction

In Chapter 6, we have discussed using DCT to transform image data to the frequency domain. We have seen that DCT alone does not achieve any data compression and does not lose any information. However, the transformation usually clusters the data that allow us to carry out compression in the next stage effectively. Typically, the 'low frequency' components of the DCT coefficients of a block of image position around the DC (0,0) coefficient. As shown in the data output of Section 6.6 of Chapter 6, the nonzero DCT coefficients are clustered around the top-left (DC) coefficient and the distribution is roughly symmetrical in the horizontal and vertical directions. This special characteristics inspire people to reorder the DCT coefficients so that more consecutive zeros are lined up together and thus are easier to encode.

After DCT, the next operation in our compression pipeline involves quantization which will generate even more zeros in a DCT block as small values are approximated by a zeros. After quantization, we shall reorder the data so that they can be encoded effectively using a technique called run-level encoding. The run-level values are then encoded using entropy encoding, which can be Huffman encoding or arithmetic encoding. In this book, we only discuss Huffman encoding, which is a lot faster than arithmetic encoding though the later may yield slightly lower compression ratio. Entropy encoding generates a bit stream, which is ready for transmission or storage. Figure 7-1 summarizes these encoding steps, which extend the steps shown in Figure 6-5.

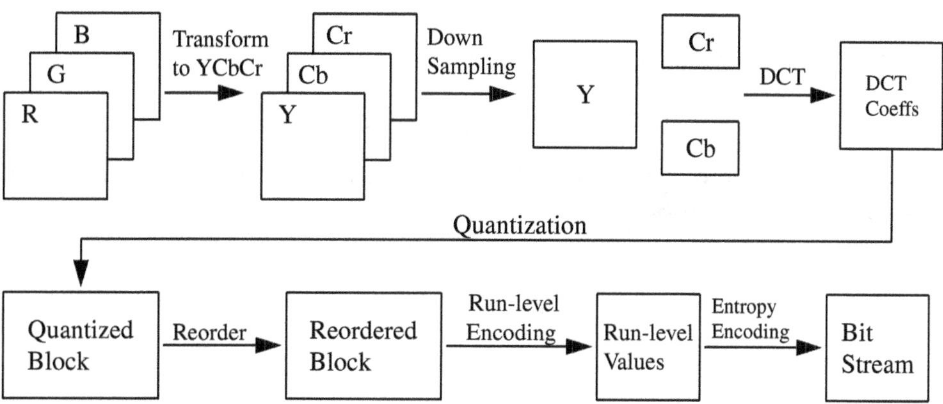

Figure 7-1. Encoding of RGB Image Block

Of all the stages shown in Figure 7-1, only the operations "Down Sampling" and "Quantization" are irreversible. Other stages are reversible; no information is lost in the operation. In particular, no rounding error will be introduced in the operations, "Reorder", "Run-level Encoding", and "Entropy Encoding"; the original data before each operation can be recovered exactly.

Compression occurs in stages "Down Sampling", "Run-level Encoding" and "Entropy Encoding". On the other hand, operations "DCT", "Quantization", and "Reorder" set up the data for these stages to compress them efficiently.

7.2 Quantization

We discussed in Chapter 3 that *quantization* is the procedure of constraining the value of a function at a sampling point to a predetermined finite set of discrete values. A *quantizer* maps a range of values X to a reduced range of values F. Therefore, a quantized signal can be represented by fewer bits than the original signal as the range of quantized values is smaller. To achieve high compression, we do not want to retain the full range of DCT coefficients as we did in Chapter 6 where we have used 16-bit (i.e. data type short) to save a DCT coefficient. In this Chapter, we discuss how to quantize DCT coefficients and represent a coefficient with significantly less bits.

Quantization can be done using a *scalar quantizer* or a *vector quantizer*. A *scaler quantizer* maps one sample of the input signal to one quantized output value. It is a special case of a *vector quantizer*, which maps a group of input samples (a 'vector') to an index of a codebook that contains vectors (groups) of quantized values. A vector quantizer in general yields better results but consumes a lot more computing power.

7.2.1 Scalar Quantization

An example of a simple *scalar quantizer* is an operation that rounds a real number to an integer. Obviously, the operation is a many-to-one mapping and is irreversible. Information is lost in the process; we cannot determine the exact value of the original real number from the rounded integer.

A more general example of scalar quantization is a uniform quantizer where an input value X is divided by a **quantization parameter** (or step size) q and rounded to the nearest integer F_q as shown in Equation (7.1) below:

$$F_q = round(\frac{X}{q}) \tag{7.1}$$

The quantized output level is given by

$$Y = F_q \times q \tag{7.2}$$

The output levels Y are spaced uniformly with step size q. The following example shows a uniform quantizer with various step sizes.

Example 7-1 A uniform quantizer with step sizes, 1, 2, 3, 5, and 8.

X	Y q = 1	Y q = 2	Y q = 3	Y q = 5	Y q = 8
-5	-5	-6	-6	-5	-8
-4	-4	-4	-3	-5	-8
-3	-3	-4	-3	-5	0
-2	-2	-2	-3	0	0
-1	-1	-2	0	0	0
0	0	0	0	0	0
1	1	2	0	0	0
2	2	2	3	0	0
3	3	4	3	5	0
4	4	4	3	5	8
5	5	6	6	5	8
6	6	6	6	5	8
7	7	8	6	5	8
8	8	8	9	10	8
9	9	10	9	10	8
10	10	10	9	10	8
11	11	12	12	10	8
12	12	12	12	10	16

Figure 7-2 shows two examples of scalar quantizer. The linear scalar quantizer shown on the left shows linear mapping between input and output values. The nonlinear quantizer on the right shows a dead zone where small input values are mapped to zero.

More precisely, we can define an N-point scalar quantizer Q as a mapping $Q : R \rightarrow C$ where R is the real line and

$$C \equiv \{y_1, y_2, ..., y_N\} \subset R \tag{7.3}$$

is the output set or codebook with size $|C| = N$. The output values, y_i, are referred to as output levels, output points, or reproduction values. Quite often, we choose the indexing of output values so that

$$y_1 < y_2 < ... < y_N \tag{7.4}$$

The resolution or code rate, r, of a scalar quantizer is defined as $r = log_2 N$, which measures the number of bits required to uniquely specify the quantized value.

Every quantizer can be viewed as making up of two successive operations (mappings), an encoder, E, (or forward quantizer FQ), and a decoder, D (or inverse quantizer IQ). The encoder E is a mapping

$$E : R \rightarrow I \tag{7.5}$$

where $I = \{1, 2, 3, ..., N\}$, and the decoder is the mapping

$$D : I \rightarrow C. \tag{7.6}$$

Therefore, if $Q(x) = y_i$, then $E(x) = i$ and $D(i) = y_i$. Consequently, $Q(x) = D(E(x))$. Note that the decoder can be implemented by a table-lookup process, where the table or codebook contains the output set, which can be stored with very high precision without affecting the transmission rate R.

The decoder is also referred to as inverse quantization and the encoder is sometimes referred to as forward quantization.

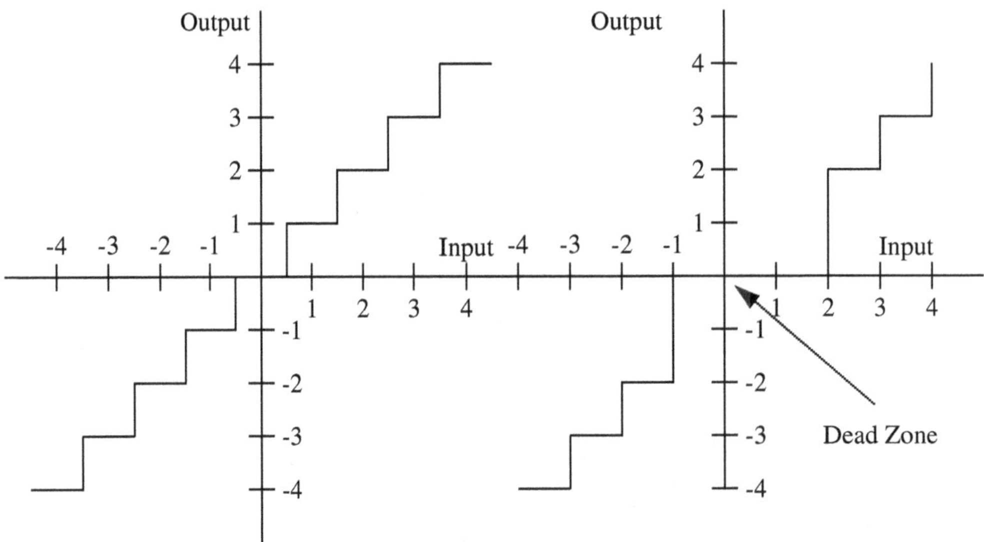

Figure 7-2. Linear and Non-linear Quantizers

7.2.2 Vector Quantization

Vector quantization (VQ) is a generalization of scalar quantization to the quantization of a vector, an ordered set of real numbers. Speech or image samples can be grouped together to form a vector. Thus vector quantization can be regarded as a form of pattern recognition where an input pattern is "approximated" by one of a predetermined set of patterns stored in a codebook.

We can define a vector quantizer Q of dimension k and size N as a mapping from a vector in k-dimensional Euclidean space, R^k, into a finite set C that contains N output or reconstructed vectors, called *code vectors* or *codewords*. That is,

$$Q:\ R^k \rightarrow C, \tag{7.7}$$

where

$$\begin{aligned} C &= \{y_1, y_2, ..., y_N\} \\ y_i &\in R^k \\ i &\in I \equiv \{1, 2, ..., N\} \end{aligned} \tag{7.8}$$

The set C is referred to as the *codebook* or the *code* with N distinct elements, each a vector in R^k. The *resolution* or *code rate* r of the vector quantizer is given by:

$$code\ rate\ r = \frac{log_2 N}{k} \tag{7.9}$$

In general, the code rate of a vector quantizer is the number of bits per vector component used to represent the input vector, indicating the accuracy or precision it can achieve with the quantizer. Note that for a given dimension k, the resolution is determined by the size N of the codebook but not by the number of bits used to specify the code vectors stored in the codebook. Even if we specify a code vector to a very high precision, we still can have a very low resolution by using a small codebook. Typically, a codebook is loaded as a lookup table in the main memory of a computer and the number of bits used in each table entry does not affect the quantizer's resolution or bit rate.

Associated with each of the N vectors in C is a partition of R^k into N regions or *cells*, R_i for $i \in I$:

$$R_i = \{\mathbf{x} \in R^k : Q(\mathbf{x}) = y_i\} \tag{7.10}$$

The ith cell R_i given by (7.10) is called the *inverse image* or *pre-image* of y_i under the mapping Q and can be denoted by:

$$R_i = Q^{-1}(y_i) \tag{7.11}$$

The application of VQ to image compression can be summarized as follows:

1. Partition an image into blocks of pixels.
2. Choose a vector from the codebook that best-approximates the current block.
3. Send the index pointing to the chosen vector to the decoder.
4. At the decoder, reconstruct an approximate copy of the original block using the chosen vector.

Figure 7-3 shows the concept of vector quantization.

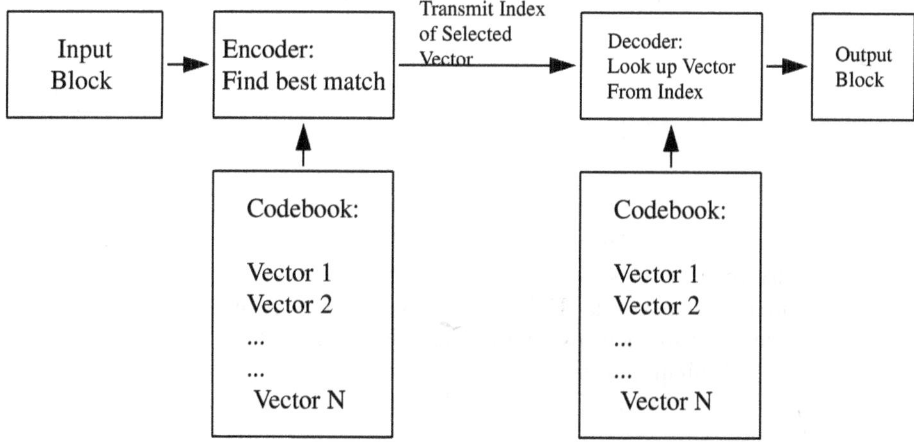

Figure 7-3. Vector Quantization

7.2.3 MPEG-4 Quantization

Video compression standard MPEG-4 allows two methods to quantize DCT coefficients. A parameter called quantizer_scale (quantization_parameter) is used to control how much information is discarded during the quantization process. The parameter can take values from 1 to 31 in the case of 8-bit textures and 1 to $2^{quant\_precision} - 1$ in the case of non 8-bit textures. Each frame may use a different value of quantizer_scale. The two methods are referred to as Method 2 (basic method) and Method 1 (more flexible but more complex). Method 2, which is the default method, specifies the quantization of the DC component, $F[0][0]$ using a fixed quantizer step:

$$Forward\ Quantization : F_q[0][0] = \frac{F[0][0]}{dc\_scalar}$$
$$Inverse\ Quantization : F'[0][0] = F_q[0][0] \times dc\_scalar \qquad (7.12)$$

where dc_scalar which has a value of 8 in the short header mode and depends on the quantizer_parameter is determined from the following table:

$quantizer\_parameter(Q_p)$	1 - 4	5 - 8	9 - 24	25 - 31
$dc\_scalar(luminance)$	8	$2Q_p$	$Q_p + 8$	$2Q_p - 16$
$dc\_scalar(chrominance)$	8	$\frac{2Q_p + 13}{2}$	$\frac{Q_p + 13}{2}$	$Q_p - 6$

Table 7-1: MPEG-4 Quantization Parameters.

All other coefficients are rescaled as follows.

$$\begin{aligned} |F| &= Q_p \times (2 \times |F_Q| + 1) && \text{if } Q_p \text{ is odd and } F_Q \neq 0 \\ |F| &= Q_p \times (2 \times |F_Q| + 1) - 1 && \text{if } Q_p \text{ is even and } F_Q \neq 0 \\ |F| &= 0 && \text{if } F_Q = 0 \end{aligned} \qquad (7.13)$$

where F_Q is the forward-quantized coefficient and F is the rescaled (inverse-quantized) coefficient.

In Method 1, which is also referred to as alternate quantizer, MPEG-4 uses a weighting factor to exploit properties of the human visual system (HVS). Since human eyes are less sensitive to some frequencies, we can quantize these frequencies with a coarser step-size, which results in a more compactly coded bit-stream and minimizes the image distortion. MPEG-4 recommends different weight matrices for the quantization of various sample blocks. The forward and inverse quantization can be described as follows.

Forward Quantization is described by the following equation (we shall explain the meaning of intra and inter blocks in a later chapter).

$$F_Q(u,v) = \frac{16F(u,v)}{2Q_p(W(u,v) - k \times Q_p)} \qquad (7.14)$$

where

$$k = \begin{cases} 0 & \text{for intra coded blocks} \\ sign(F_Q(u,v)) & \text{for inter coded blocks} \end{cases}$$

and

$$sign(x) = \begin{cases} -1 & \text{if } x < 0 \\ +1 & \text{otherwise} \end{cases}$$

Inverse Quantization is described by Eqaution (7.15) shown below.

$$F'(u,v) = \begin{cases} 0 & \text{if } F_Q(u,v) = 0 \\ \frac{(2F_Q(u,v) + k) \times W(u,v) \times Q_p}{16} & \text{if } F_Q(u,v) \neq 0 \end{cases} \quad (7.15)$$

Users can define the weighting factors $W(u,v)$ based on their particular applications. MPEG-4 suggests some default weighting factors, which are shown in Table 7-2, where the left table (Table 7-2a) shows the default weighting matrix for intra-coded macroblocks and the right one presents the default weighting matrix for inter-coded macroblocks. Again, we shall explain the difference between intra-coded and inter-coded blocks in a later chapter. The tables assume that a macroblock is of size 8×8. For example, if intra-coded blocks are used, $W(0,0) = 8$, and $W(7,7) = 45$. On the other hand, when inter-coded blocks are used, $W(0,0) = 16$ and $W(7,7) = 33$.

Table 7-2a Intra Block Weights $W(u,v)$

$u\backslash v$	0	1	2	3	4	5	6	7
0	8	17	18	19	21	23	25	27
1	17	18	19	21	23	25	27	28
2	20	21	22	23	24	26	28	30
3	21	22	23	24	26	28	30	32
4	22	23	24	26	28	30	32	35
5	23	24	26	28	30	32	35	38
6	25	26	28	30	32	35	38	41
7	27	28	30	32	35	38	41	45

Table 7-2b Inter Block Weights $W(u,v)$

$u\backslash v$	0	1	2	3	4	5	6	7
0	16	17	18	19	20	21	22	23
1	17	18	19	20	21	22	23	24
2	18	19	20	21	22	23	24	25
3	19	20	21	22	23	24	26	27
4	20	21	22	23	25	26	27	28
5	21	22	23	24	26	27	28	30
6	22	23	24	26	27	28	30	31
7	23	24	25	27	28	30	31	33

Listing 7-1 presents an implementation of a uniform quantizer. The implementation is simple and straightforward; the array *coef[]* holds an 8×8 sample block of DCT coefficients; *Qstep* is the quantization parameter discussed above; its default value is set to 12. The code shows both forward quantization (FQ) and inverse quantization (IQ).

Program Listing 7-1: Implementation of Uniform Quantizer

```
----------------------------------------------------------------------
void quantize_block ( short coef[8][8] )
{
  for ( int i = 0; i < 8; i++ )
    for ( int j = 0; j < 8; j++ )
      coef[i][j] = ( short ) round ( (double)coef[i][j] / Qstep );
}

//inverse quantize one block
void inverse_quantize_block ( short coef[8][8] )
{
  for ( int i = 0; i < 8; i++ )
    for ( int j = 0; j < 8; j++ )
      coef[i][j] = (short) (  coef[i][j] * Qstep );
}
----------------------------------------------------------------------
```

7.3 Reordering

After DCT transform and forward quantization, a sample block may have only a few nonzero coefficients and all others are zeros. It is desirable to group the zero coefficients together so that they can be represented effectively. The optimum reordering path (scan order) depends on the distribution of nonzero DCT coefficients. A commonly used scan order is a zigzag path starting from the DC coefficient at the top left corner of an 8×8 sample block as shown in Figure 7-4. After such a reordering, nonzero coefficients tend to cluster together at the beginning of the reordered array, followed by long sequences (runs) of zeros. Data consist of long runs of certain values can be efficiently encoded using a run-level coding technique that we shall discuss in the next section.

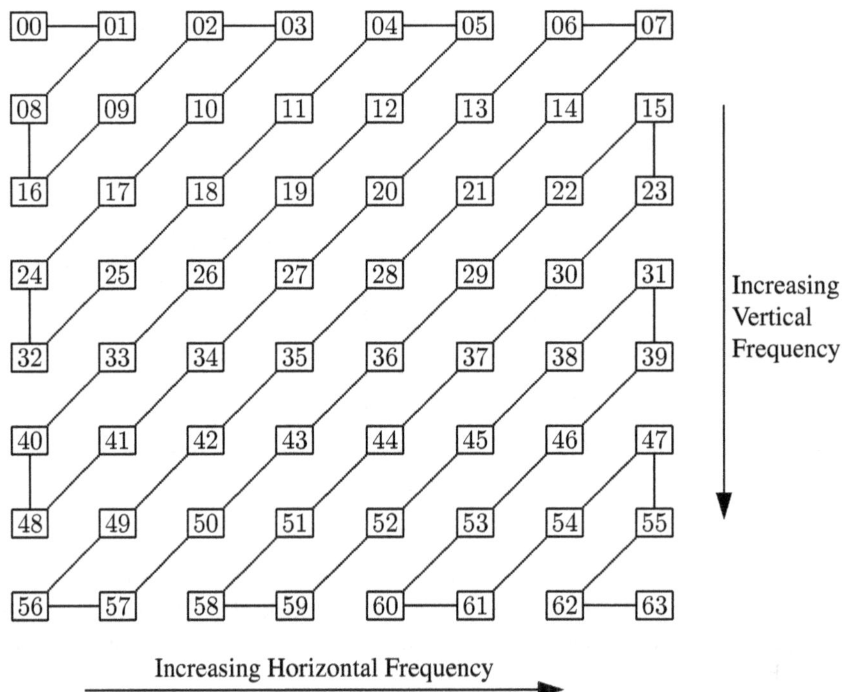

Figure 7-4. Zigzag scan order

Figure 7-4 shows that sample 0 is the first element to be read in a zigzag scan, followed by sample 1, then by sample 8, sample 16, sample 9, and so on. After a zigzag scan, the indices of the original DCT coefficients are reordered as below.

0	1	8	16	9	2	3	10
17	24	32	25	18	11	4	5
12	19	26	33	40	48	41	34
27	20	13	6	7	14	21	28
35	42	49	56	57	50	43	36
29	22	15	23	30	37	44	51
58	59	52	45	38	31	39	46
53	60	61	54	47	55	62	63

Researchers have explored and tried various scanning orders but the zigzag scan remains the most commonly used scan in video compression. However, for some applications such as a field block where the coefficient distribution is often skewed, an alternate scan is more effective. In an alternate scan, the left-hand coefficients are scanned before those on the right side as shown in Figure 7-5.

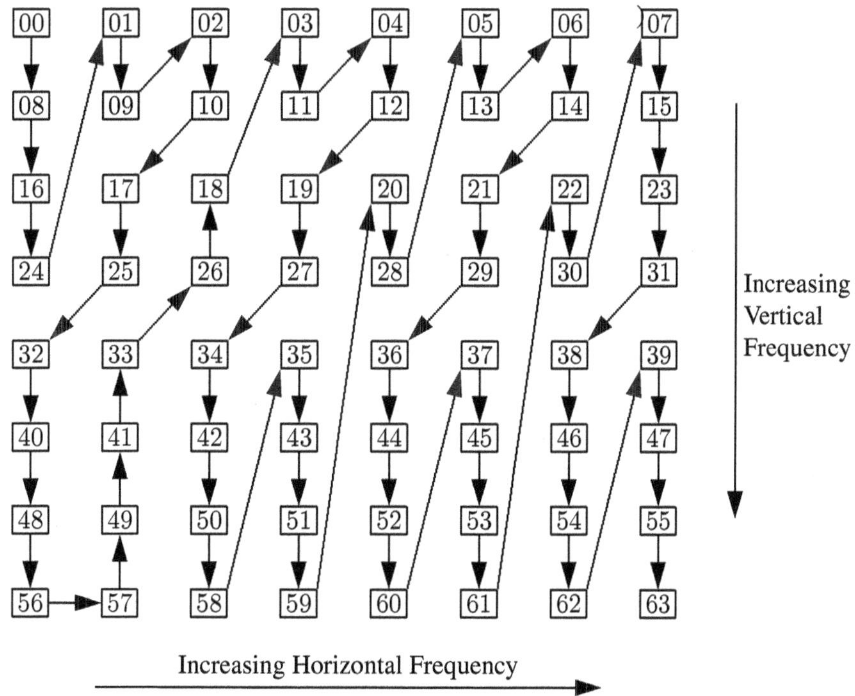

Figure 7-5. Alternate scan order

In our subsequent discussions, we shall only use the zigzag scan. Listing 7-2 shows the implementations of such a reordering and the reverse of it. The code assumes that 64 samples are arranged in an 8×8 sample block. The one dimensional index k is represented as a two-dimensional pair of integers (i, j) with $i = k/8, j = k\%8$. For example, 1 is represented by $(0, 1)$, 8 by $(1, 0)$, 23 by $(2, 7)$, and so on. The function **reorder()** uses zigzag scan to rearrange the 64 sample elements stored in the *Y*[][] array and save the reordered samples in the array *Yr*[][]. The function **reverse_reorder()** does the opposite; it restores the original order from array *Yr*[][] and saves the results in array *Y*[][].

Program Listing 7-2: Reordering

```
-------------------------------------------------------------------------
%\begin{verbbox}
\begin{verbatim}
int zigzag[] = {
    0,  1,  8, 16,  9,  2,  3, 10,
   17, 24, 32, 25, 18, 11,  4,  5,
   12, 19, 26, 33, 40, 48, 41, 34,
   27, 20, 13,  6,  7, 14, 21, 28,
   35, 42, 49, 56, 57, 50, 43, 36,
   29, 22, 15, 23, 30, 37, 44, 51,
   58, 59, 52, 45, 38, 31, 39, 46,
   53, 60, 61, 54, 47, 55, 62, 63
};
```

```
//input : Y,  output : Yr
void reorder ( short Y[8][8], short Yr[8][8] )
{
  int k, i1, j1;
  k = 0;
  for ( int i = 0; i < 8; i++ ){
    for ( int j = 0; j < 8; j++ ){
      i1 =  zigzag[k] / 8;
      j1 = zigzag[k] % 8;
      Yr[i][j] = Y[i1][j1];
      k++;
    }
  }
}

//input : Yr, output : Y
void reverse_reorder ( short Yr[8][8], short Y[8][8] )
{
  int k, i1, j1;
  k = 0;
  for ( int i = 0; i < 8; i++ ){
    for ( int j = 0; j < 8; j++ ){
      i1 = zigzag[k] / 8;
      j1 = zigzag[k] % 8;
      Y[i1][j1] = Yr[i][j];
      k++;
    }
  }
}
------------------------------------------------------------------------
```

7.4 Run-Level Encoding

After DCT, forward quantization and reordering, we may obtain long sequences of zeros followed by nonzero values. One of the effective methods to encode this kind of data is the three-dimensional (3D) run-level encoding. A 3D run-level codeword is represented by a tuple (*run, level, last*) where *run* is the number of zeros preceding a nonzero coefficient, *level* is the value of the nonzero coefficient, and *last* indicates whether the codeword is the final one with nonzero coefficient in the block. The following shows two examples of 3D run-level encoding.

Input Sequence: $1, 0, -2, 3, 0, 0, 0, 4, 5, 0, -1, 6, 0, 0, 0, ..., 0$

Output: $(0, 1, 0), (1, -2, 0), (0, 3, 0), (3, 4, 0), (0, 5, 0), (1, -1, 0), (0, 6, 1)$

Input Sequence: $0, 0, 2, 0, 0, 0, 0, 1, 0, 0, -2, 0, 7, 0, 0, 0, ..., 0$

Output: $(2, 2, 0), (4, 1, 0), (2, -2, 0), (1, 7, 1)$

We have to handle the special case when the whole block contains zeros separately; we code the whole block of zeros by (64, 0, 1):

$$\text{Input Sequence:} \quad 0, 0, 0, ..., 0$$
$$\text{Output:} \quad (64, 0, 1)$$

Implementation of run-level encoding can be done by defining a class *run3D* comprising public members *run, level*, and *last* as follows. A *run3D* object can hold one run-level codeword.

```
class Run3D {
public:
  unsigned char run;
  short level;
  char last;
};
```

Suppose a macroblock of 8 × 8 DCT coefficients have been quantized, zigzag-reordered, and saved in an array *Y*[]. Listing 7-3 presents a piece of code that can run-level-encode such a block of 64 coefficients. The function **run_block()** accepts the 8 × 8 block of coefficients saved in the array *Y*[] as input; the outputs are the run-level codewords returned in the run3D object array *runs*[]. Each run3D object holds the information of the tuple (*run, level, last*) that represents a codeword.

Program Listing 7-3: Run-level Encoding

```
--------------------------------------------------------------------------
/*
    Input: 64 quantized DCT coefficients in Y[][].
    Output: 3D run-level codewords in runs[].
*/
void run_block ( short Y[8][8], Run3D runs[] )
{
    unsigned char run_length = 0, k = 0;
    for ( int i = 0; i < 8; i++ ) {
      for ( int j = 0; j < 8; j++ ) {
        if ( Y[i][j] == 0  ) {
          run_length++;
          continue;
        }
        runs[k].run = run_length;
        runs[k].level = Y[i][j];
        runs[k].last = 0;
        run_length = 0;
        k++;
      }
    }
    if ( k > 0 )
      runs[k-1].last = 1;        //last nonzero element
    else {                       //whole block 0
      runs[0].run = 64;
      runs[0].level = 0;
      runs[0].last = 1;          //this needs to be 1 to terminate
    }
}
--------------------------------------------------------------------------
```

The corresponding code that recovers the block of 64 DCT coefficients from the run-level codewords is presented in Listing 7-4; the code first recovers the zeros and nonzero values from the run-level codewords saved in *runs*[] until it finds the *last* field of the codeword is 1; after detecting the *last* field to be 1, it sets the remaining values of *Y*[] to zero.

Program Listing 7-4: Run-level Decoding

```
/*
 *   Input: 3D run-level codewords of a macroblock in runs[].
 *   Output: 64 DCT coefficients in Y[][].
 */
void Run::run_decode ( Run3D runs[], short Y[8][8] )
{
     int i, j, r, k = 0, n = 0;

     while ( n < 64 ) {
       for ( r = 0;  r < runs[k].run; r++ ){
         i = n / 8;
         j = n % 8;
         Y[i][j] = 0;
         n++;
       }
       if ( n < 64 ){
         i = n / 8;
         j = n % 8;
         Y[i][j] = runs[k].level;
         n++;
       }
       if ( runs[k].last != 0 ) break;
       k++;
     }

     //run of 0s to end
     while ( n < 64 ) {
       i = n / 8;
       j = n % 8;
       Y[i][j] = 0;
       n++;
     }
}
```

Listing 7-5 presents the program **test_run.cpp**, which is a complete program that demonstrates the operations of quantization, reordering and run-level encoding and the reverse of the operations. It reads DCT coefficients from the file specified by argv[0] which has saved blocks of 8 × 8 DCT coefficients in short (16-bit) form as discussed in Chapter 6; the file of argv[0] can be obtained from the PPM image file "beach.ppm" after the operations of 4:2:0 YCbCr down sampling and DCT Transformation that we have discussed in Chapter 6. The functions **get64, print_blcock,** and **print_run** are member functions of the class **Run**; **get64** gets 64 sample values from the the specified input file and put them in the two-dimensional array *Y*[][], which will be returned to the calling function; **print_block** prints one 8 × 8 sample block; **print_run** prints the run-level codewords on one 64-sample block. We have grouped related functions into classes named **Quantizer**, **Reorder**, **Run**, and **Printer**.

Program Listing 7-5: Quantization, Reordering, and Run-level Encoding

```
--------------------------------------------------------------------------
/*
  test_run.cpp
  A demo program that illustrates the concepts of quantization, zigzag
  reordering and run-level encoding.  It reads DCT coefficients from the
  file specified by argv[0] which has saved 8x8 blocks of DCT
  coefficients in short ( 16-bit ) form.
*/
#include <stdio.h>
#include <string.h>
#include "run3D.h"
#include "run.h"
#include "reorder.h"
#include "quantizer.h"
#include "../util/printer.h"

using namespace std;

//function only used in this file
static int read_dct_header ( FILE *fp )
{
  char header[] =  { 'D', 'C', 'T', '4', ':', '2', ':', '0' };
  int len = strlen(header);
  char buf[len];

  fread ( buf, 1, len, fp );
  int width;
  int height;
  fread ( &width, 1, 2, fp );      //not used here
  fread ( &height, 1, 2, fp );      //not used here

  for ( int i = 0; i < len; ++i )
      if ( buf[i] != header[i] )
        return -1;       //wrong header

  return 1;
}

int main( int argc, char *argv[] )
{
    if (argc < 2) {
      printf("\nUsage: %s input_dct_filename", argv[0] );
      printf("\n  e.g. %s ../data/beach.dct\n", argv[0] );
      return 1;
    }

    //read the DCT data back from argv[1]
    FILE *fp = fopen ( argv[1], "rb" );
    if ( fp == NULL ) {
      printf("\nError opening file\n");
      return 1;
    }
```

```
    Run3D  runs[64];
    short  Y[8][8];
    short  Yr[8][8];
    Quantizer quantizer;
    Reorder reorder;
    Run run;
    Printer printer;

    if ( read_dct_header ( fp ) == -1 ){
        printf("\nNot dct File!\n");
        return 1;
    }

    while ( run.get64 ( Y, fp ) > 0 ) {        //read a block of 64 samples
        printf("\nA block of DCT coefficients:");
        printer.print_block ( Y );
        quantizer.quantize_block ( Y );

        printf("\nDCT block after quantization (Qstep=%d):",quantizer.Qstep);
        printer.print_block ( Y );
        reorder.reorder ( Y, Yr );

        printf("\nDCT block After zigzag reorder:");
        printer.print_block ( Yr );
        run.run_block ( Yr, runs );

        printf("\n3D run-level codewords of the reordered quantized
                                                      DCT coeficients:");
        printer.print_run ( runs );
        printf("\nHit any key to reverse the processes:");
        getchar();

        //reversing the process
        short new_Y[8][8];
        run.run_decode ( runs, new_Y );
        printf("\nDCT block after decode run:");
        printer.print_block ( new_Y );

        reorder.reverse_reorder ( new_Y, Y );
        printf("\nDCT block after reversing reorder:");
        printer.print_block ( Y );

        quantizer.inverse_quantize_block ( Y );
        printf("\nDCT block after inverse quantization:");
        printer.print_block ( Y );

        printf("\nDo you want another block? ( y/n) ");
        char c;
        scanf("%c", &c );
        if ( c == 'n' ) break;
    }
    fclose( fp );
    return 0;
}
----------------------------------------------------------------------
```

Listing 7-6 shows sample outputs of the program **test_run.cpp**. You can see from the data that reordering and run-level encoding are reversible while quantization is not.

Listing 7-6: Sample outputs of test_run.cpp

```
---------------------------------------------------------------------------
A block of DCT coefficients:
   629,     -5,     -1,     -1,      1,     -1,     -2,     -1,
    -8,     -5,     -1,      0,      0,     -1,     -2,     -2,
     2,     -3,     -1,     -1,     -4,     -4,     -3,     -2,
    -3,     -4,     -3,     -1,      1,     -2,     -4,     -3,
    -1,     -6,      0,     -1,     -1,      1,      0,      0,
    -4,     -5,     -3,      0,      2,     -1,     -1,      0,
    -1,     -2,     -2,     -1,     -1,     -1,     -1,     -2,
     1,     -1,      0,      0,      0,     -2,     -2,     -1,
DCT block after quantization ( Qstep = 12 ):
    52,      0,      0,      0,      0,      0,      0,      0,
    -1,      0,      0,      0,      0,      0,      0,      0,
     0,      0,      0,      0,      0,      0,      0,      0,
     0,      0,      0,      0,      0,      0,      0,      0,
     0,      0,      0,      0,      0,      0,      0,      0,
     0,      0,      0,      0,      0,      0,      0,      0,
     0,      0,      0,      0,      0,      0,      0,      0,
     0,      0,      0,      0,      0,      0,      0,      0,
DCT block After zigzag reorder:
    52,      0,     -1,      0,      0,      0,      0,      0,
     0,      0,      0,      0,      0,      0,      0,      0,
     0,      0,      0,      0,      0,      0,      0,      0,
     0,      0,      0,      0,      0,      0,      0,      0,
     0,      0,      0,      0,      0,      0,      0,      0,
     0,      0,      0,      0,      0,      0,      0,      0,
     0,      0,      0,      0,      0,      0,      0,      0,
     0,      0,      0,      0,      0,      0,      0,      0,
3D run-level codewords of the reordered quantized DCT coeficients:
( 0,  52, 0)    ( 1,  -1, 1)

Hit any key to reverse the processes:

DCT block after decode run:
    52,      0,     -1,      0,      0,      0,      0,      0,
     0,      0,      0,      0,      0,      0,      0,      0,
     0,      0,      0,      0,      0,      0,      0,      0,
     0,      0,      0,      0,      0,      0,      0,      0,
     0,      0,      0,      0,      0,      0,      0,      0,
     0,      0,      0,      0,      0,      0,      0,      0,
     0,      0,      0,      0,      0,      0,      0,      0,
     0,      0,      0,      0,      0,      0,      0,      0,
DCT block after reversing reorder:
    52,      0,      0,      0,      0,      0,      0,      0,
    -1,      0,      0,      0,      0,      0,      0,      0,
     0,      0,      0,      0,      0,      0,      0,      0,
     0,      0,      0,      0,      0,      0,      0,      0,
     0,      0,      0,      0,      0,      0,      0,      0,
     0,      0,      0,      0,      0,      0,      0,      0,
     0,      0,      0,      0,      0,      0,      0,      0,
```

```
     0,       0,       0,       0,       0,       0,       0,       0,
DCT block after inverse quantization:
   624,       0,       0,       0,       0,       0,       0,       0,
   -12,       0,       0,       0,       0,       0,       0,       0,
     0,       0,       0,       0,       0,       0,       0,       0,
     0,       0,       0,       0,       0,       0,       0,       0,
     0,       0,       0,       0,       0,       0,       0,       0,
     0,       0,       0,       0,       0,       0,       0,       0,
     0,       0,       0,       0,       0,       0,       0,       0,
     0,       0,       0,       0,       0,       0,       0,       0,
Do you want another block? ( y/n)
------------------------------------------------------------------------
```

Chapter 8

Huffman Encoding

8.1 Introduction

The 3D run-level tuples discussed in the last chapter can be encoded by an entropy encoder, which in general yields significant compression. Entropy encoding is a reversible or lossless process; exact data can be recovered in the decoding process from the encoded data. Arithmetic coding and Huffman coding are two popular methods of entropy encoding with the former giving slightly better results and consuming more computing power. This kind of encoding is also referred to as variable-length coding (VLC) because the codewords representing symbols are of varying lengths. We shall only discuss the Huffman encoding method here.

The commonly used generalized ASCII code uses 8 bits to represent a character and unicode uses 16 bits to do so; these are fixed-length codes, which are simple but inefficient in the representation. Huffman coding assigns a variable-length codeword to each symbol (or tuple here) based on the probability of the occurrence of the symbol. Frequently occurring symbols are represented with short codewords whilst less common symbols are represented with longer codewords; in this way we have a shorter average codeword length and thus save space to store the codewords, leading to data compression.

We say that a code has the **prefix property** and is a prefix code if no codeword is the prefix, or start of the codeword for another symbol. A code with codewords $\{1, 01, 00\}$ has the prefix property; a code consisting of $\{1, 0, 01, 00\}$ does not, because "0" is a prefix of both "01" and "00". A non-prefix code like { 1, 0, 01, 00 } cannot be instantaneously decoded because when we receive a bitstream such as "001", we do not know whether it consists of { '0', '0', '1' }, or { '0', '01' } or { '00', '1' }. On the other hand, a prefix code can be instantaneously decoded. That is, a message can be transmitted as a sequence of concatenated codewords, without any out-of-band markers to frame the words in the message. The receiver can decode the message unambiguously, by repeatedly finding and removing prefixes that form valid codewords, which are impossible if the message is formed by a non-prefix code as shown in the above example. Prefix codes are also known as prefix-free codes, prefix condition codes, comma-free codes, and instantaneous codes.

Not only that Huffman codes are prefix codes, they are also optimal in the sense that no other prefix code can yield a shorter average codeword length than a corresponding Huffman code. It is the foundation of numerous compression applications, including text compression, audio compression, image compression, and video compression. It is a building block of many contemporary multimedia applications.

Huffman code was developed by David A. Huffman while he was a Ph.D. student at MIT, and published in the 1952 paper "A Method for the Construction of Minimum-Redundancy Codes." Huffman codes are easiest to understand and implement if we use trees to represent them though the tree concept was not used when Huffman first developed the code. Briefly, Huffman tree is a **binary tree** (an ordered 2-ary tree) with a weight associated with each node. Let us first consider some simple examples to understand its principles.

Consider the following two codes.

Symbol	Code 1	Code 2
a	000	000
b	001	11
c	010	01
d	011	001
e	100	10

Code 1 is a fixed-length code with codeword length 3 and Code 2 is a variable-length code. Both of them have the prefix property (note that a fixed-length code always has the prefix property). They can be represented by binary trees like those shown in Figure 8-1. Decoding a bitstream is simply a process of traversing the binary tree; we start from the root of the tree and go left or right based on whether the current bit examined is 0 or 1 until we reach a leaf, which is associated with a symbol; we then start from the root again and examine the next bit and so on. For example, Code 2 decodes the string "000100111" uniquely to "aecb". The average codeword length of a code is equal to the average depths of of the leaves of the corresponding. It is obvious that Code 2 always has a shorter average codeword length when compared to Code 1, as the tree for Code 2 has a shorter average depth of its leaves.

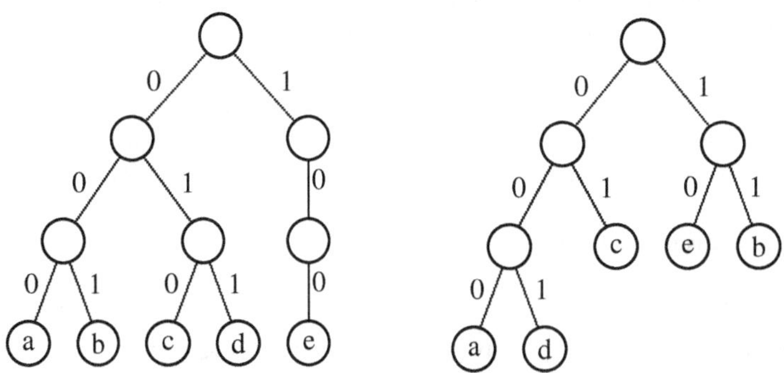

Figure 8-1. Binary Tree Representations of Code1 (left) and Code 2 (right)

8.2 Huffman Codes

Consider an example that the probabilities of the occurrence of symbols are known as shwon in the table below. In this case, we can calculate the average lengths $\overline{L}$ of the codewords of the two codes. Obviously, Code 1 is a fixed-length code and the average length is 3. For Code 2, we need to take into account the frequency of occurrence of each symbol:

$$\begin{aligned} \text{Code 1} : \overline{L} &= 3\ bits \\ \text{Code 2} : \overline{L} &= 0.35 \times 2 + 0.20 \times 2 + 0.20 \times 3 + 0.15 \times 3 + 0.10 \times 3 = 2.45\ (bits) \end{aligned} \tag{8.1}$$

Symbol	Frequency	Code 1	Code 2
a	0.35	000	00
b	0.20	001	10
c	0.20	010	011
d	0.15	011	010
e	0.10	100	110

Code 2 is a prefix code and has a significantly shorter average codeword length than that of Code 1. *But is Code 2 the best code for the given frequencies? Can we do better than Code 2, creating a code that has shorter $\overline{L}$ than Code 2?* This question can be answered by constructing a Huffman tree to obtain a Huffman code for the given symbols and frequencies. We start from a forest of trees; each tree in the forest has only one single node (which is a root as well as a leaf); each root consists of the symbol and the weight (probability) of it. In this example, we totally have five single-noded trees as shown in Figure 8-2:

a *b* c *d* e

0.35 0.20 0.20 0.15 0.10

Figure 8-2. A Forest of Single-noded Trees

Next, we merge the two trees whose roots have lowest weights and calculate the sum of the two weights. We assign the sum as the weight to the root of the merged tree. The resulted forest is shown in Figure 8-3, where we have merged two pairs of roots that have the lowest weights.

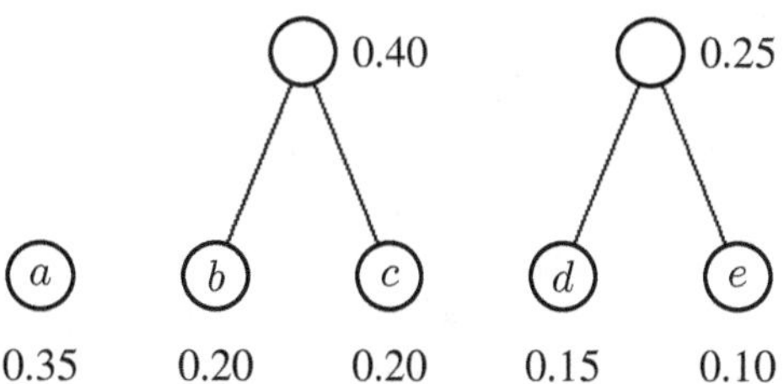

Figure 8-3. Merging Two Pairs of Roots with Lowest Weights

We repeat the above merging process until there is only one tree in the forest. Figure 8-4 and Figure 8-5 show two more iterations of the process. Note that for clarity of presentation, some node positions have been rearranged.

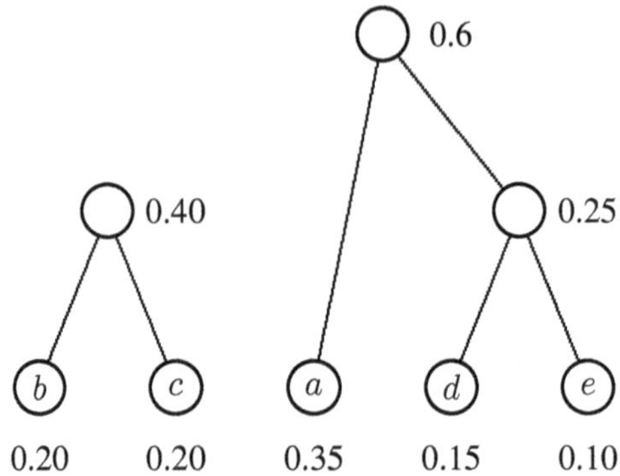

Figure 8-4. Merging Two More Roots with Lowest Weights

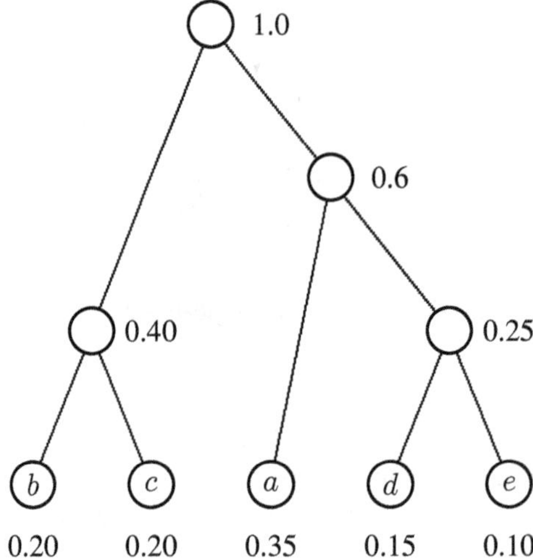

Figure 8-5. Merging All Trees Yields a Huffman Tree

As shown in Figure 8-5, the final single tree obtained is the Huffman tree that we need. To obtain the codeword for a symbol, we traverse the tree, starting from the root, until we arrive at a leaf, which contains the symbol; in the traversal, we generate a 0 on going left and a 1 on going right (it works just as well if we generate a 1 on going left and a 0 on right) as shown in Figure 8-6. The sequence of 1's and 0's parsed in the traversal from the root to the symbol is the codeword. The following table shows the Huffman code obtained from the Huffman tree of Figure 8-6.

Symbol	Codeword	Length
a	10	2
b	00	2
c	01	2
d	110	3
e	111	3

The average length of the Huffman code is

$$\overline{L} = 0.35 \times 2 + 0.20 \times 2 + 0.20 \times 2 + 0.15 \times 3 + 0.10 \times 3 = 2.25\ (bits) \tag{8.2}$$

which is shorter than that of Code 2 (2.45 bits) discussed above. Actually, one can prove that Huffman code is optimal. That is, a Huffman code always gives the shortest average code length of all prefix codes for a given set of probabilities of occurrences of symbols. (We'll skip the proof here.)

Note that the symbols are not limited to alphabets and letters. They can be any quantitative values or even abstract objects. Note also that a Huffman decoder does not need to know the probability distribution of the symbols in order to decode them. It only needs to know the Huffman tree to decode a bit-stream consisting of codewords encoded by a Huffman code. In the decoding process, we start from the root of the tree and traverse the tree according to the 0's and 1's we read from the bit-stream until we reach a leaf to recover the encoded symbol; we then start from the root again and read in further bits for traversal to obtain the next symbol and so on. For example, suppose the following is the output bit-stream resulted from encoding a sequence of symbols using the Huffman tree of Figure 8-6:

$$00101110110 \tag{8.3}$$

Upon decoding, we start from the tree root and first read in '0 0', reaching symbol 'b'; we then start from the root again and read in '1 0', reaching symbol 'a'; next, the bit sequence '1 1 1' gives symbol 'e'; next, '0 1' gives 'c' and finally '1 0' gives 'a'. Therefore, the encoded sequence of symbols of the bit-stream (8.3) is "b a e c a".

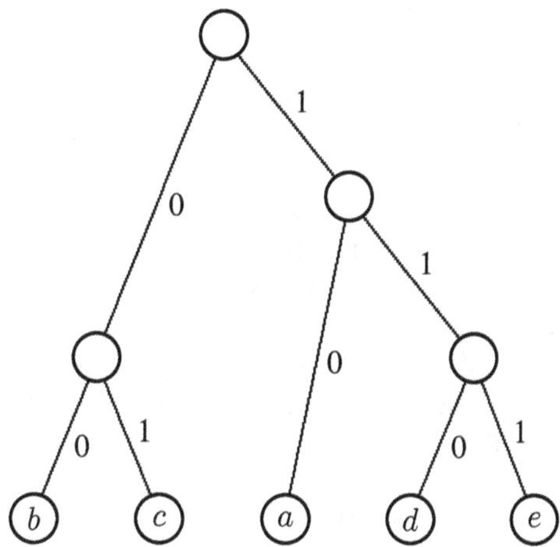

Figure 8-6. Traversing the Huffman Tree

8.3 Huffman Tree Properties

A Huffman tree can be conveniently constructed using a priority queue. A priority queue is a special queue that associates each element with a priority value. A general queue has the property of "First In First Out (FIFO)". That is, the first element that enters the queue is the first to be removed. In other words, the first entered-element is always at the front of the queue which is the next element to be deleted. This happens in a cashier station of a supermarket; the customer who arrives first at the cashier is the first one to be served. On the other hand, a priority queue does not follow the FIFO scenario; it is the element that has the highest priority in the queue that will be deleted first. This could happen when the president of a big company meets a number of visitors; she would first meet the most important visitor before meeting other less important people. Therefore, the element at the front of a priority queue always has the highest priority and is the first one to be deleted. In other words, when an element with a priority higher than the priorities of all the elements currently in the queue enters the queue, it will be moved to the front of the queue.

In our application, we can set the priority of a node (root of a tree) to be the reciprocal of its weight. That is, the lower the weight, the higher the priority. As an example, in Figure 8-2, node **e** has the highest priority, followed by node **d**, and node **a** has the lowest priority. With this association, a Huffman tree can be constructed by the following steps:

1. Start with a forest consisting of single-node trees; the root of a tree contains a symbol and its weight, which is the reciprocal of its priority value.
2. Insert the roots (nodes) of all trees of the forest into a priority queue.
3. Delete two nodes from the priority queue; the two deleted nodes always have the least weights (highest priorities).
4. Merge the deleted nodes to form a new root with combined weights; insert the new root back to the priority queue.
5. Repeat steps 3 - 4 until the priority queue is empty.

In the above steps, when the priority queue is empty, a single tree is formed and it is the required Huffman tree. In the process, we assume that a root always links to the rest of the nodes of the tree.

The priority queue implementation is straightforward and intuitive. However, it is not the most efficient method. and we shall not use it here. To make more efficient or customized implementations, it is helpful to learn some properties of a Huffman tree.

Firstly, we have learned that a Huffman tree is optimal. However, it is not unique. Given a set of frequencies, we can have more than one Huffman tree that yields an optimal average codeword length; different trees can be constructed by interchanging the assignment of 0 and 1 to the left and right traversal or by merging roots with equal weights in different orders.

Secondly, all internal nodes (non-leaves) of a Huffman tree always have two children. The binary tree that represents Code 1 in Figure 8-1 will never occur in a Huffman tree regardless of the occurrence frequencies of the symbols.

Thirdly, if the weights of the symbols are changing, the Huffman tree needs to be recomputed dynamically. This can be done by utilizing the *Sibling Property*, which defines a binary tree to be a Huffman tree if and only if:

1. all leaf nodes have non-negative weights,
2. all internal nodes have exactly two children,
3. the weight of each parent node is the sum of its childrenś weights, and
4. the nodes are numbered in increasing order by non-decreasing weight so that siblings are assigned consecutive numbers or rank, and most importantly, their parent node must be higher in the numbering.

The *Sibling Property* is usually used in *Dynamic Huffman Coding*, where we encode a stream of symbols on the fly and the symbol statistics changes as we read in more and more symbols.

Finally, we shall prove a lemma concerning binary trees to help us simplify the implementation of a Huffman tree when we use an array to implement it. Consider a binary tree where

n_0 = number of leaves (nodes of degree 0)

n_1 = number of nodes of degree 1 (nodes having one child)

n_2 = number of nodes of degree 2 (nodes having two children)

Lemma:

For a non-empty binary tree,

$$n_0 = n_2 + 1 \tag{8.4}$$

Proof:

The total number of nodes in the tree is

$$n = n_0 + n_1 + n_2 \tag{8.5}$$

Except the root, a node always has a branch leading to it. Thus the total number of branches is

$$n_B = n - 1 \tag{8.6}$$

But all branches stem from nodes of degree 1 or 2, so

$$n_B = n_1 + 2 \times n_2 \tag{8.7}$$

Combining (8.6) and (8.7), we have

$$n - 1 = n_1 + 2 \times n_2 \tag{8.8}$$

yielding

$$n_0 + n_1 + n_2 - 1 = n_1 + 2 \times n_2 \tag{8.9}$$

Simplifying (8.9), we obtain

$$n_0 = n_2 + 1$$

which is the result we want to prove.

From Huffman tree properties discussed above, we know that a Huffman tree does not have any node of degree 1 (i.e. $n_1 = 0$) and thus the number of internal nodes is equal to n_2. Also, the number of symbols is equal to the number of leaves (n_0) in the tree. Therefore, if we have n symbols, we know from the Lemma that the corresponding Huffman tree will have $n_2 = n_0 - 1 = n - 1$ internal nodes. To store a Huffman tree, we need an entry for each of the left and right child pointers and an entry for each symbol. The total number of entries N_T in the table that holds the Huffman Tree is equal to the number of pointers plus the number of symbols; this is given by

$$N_T = 2 \times (n - 1) + n = 3 \times n - 2 \tag{8.10}$$

For instance, consider a Huffman tree consisting of five symbols: a, b, c, d, e as shown in Figure 8-7.

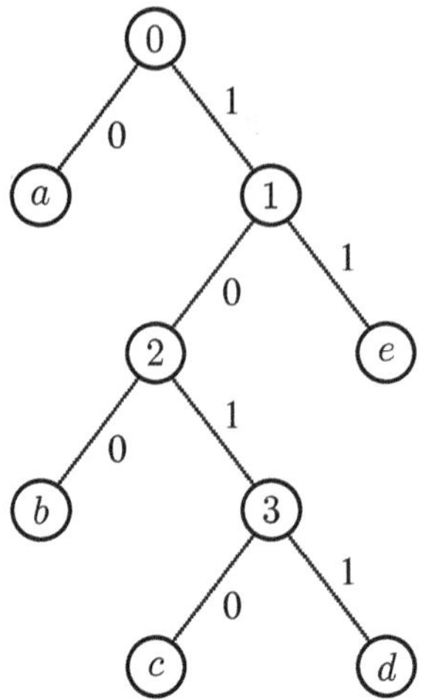

Figure 8-7. A Huffman Tree Consisting of Five Symbols

The following table shows the corresponding Huffman code of Figure 8-7.

Symbol	Codeword
a	0
b	100
c	1010
d	1011
e	11

In this example, the size of the table N_T that implements the Huffman tree is

$$N_T = 3 \times n - 2 = 3 \times 5 - 2 = 13 \tag{8.11}$$

The Huffman tree is represented by the following table (Table 8-1), where traversing left gives a 0, and traversing right gives a 1 and $N_T = 13$. Note that in the table, the root is pointing at the highest table location ($N_T - 1$) and when traversing the tree we move from the top of the table down to a location that contains a symbol. When we reach a location whose index is smaller than N_T, we know that we have reached a terminal node (leaf) containing a symbol.

Table 8-1

Table Index	Table Content	Comments
12	0	left child of node 0 (root)
11	10	right child of node 0
10	8	left child of node 1
9	4	right child of node 1
8	1	left child of node 2
7	6	right child of node 2
6	2	left child of node 3
5	3	right child of node 3
4	'e'	symbol at leaf
3	'd'	symbol at leaf
2	'c'	symbol at leaf
1	'b'	symbol at leaf
0	'a'	symbol at leaf

The following piece of C-like pseudo code shows how we traverse the table to obtain the symbols; in the code, htree[] is the table containing the Huffman tree:

```
loc = 3 * N - 3;              //start from root, N = # of symbols
do {
  loc0 = loc;                 //in is data pointer pointing to
                              //  encoded data
  if ( read_one_bit( in ) == 0 ) //a 0, go left
      loc = htree[loc0];
  else
      loc =  htree[loc0+1];   //a 1, go right

} while ( loc >= N );         //traverse until reach leaf
return htree[loc];            //return symbol
```

Table 8-1 can be simplified if we assert that the number of symbols n is smaller than a certain value and we associate each symbol with a value in the range 0 to $n-1$. For example, if we assert $n \leq 128$, which actually applies to many video compression applications, then

1. each pointer can be represented by a byte, with a left child denoted by the upper byte of a 16-bit word and right child by the lower byte,
2. table locations signify symbol values and do not need extra entries to hold the symbols, and
3. table size N_T is reduced to $n-1$.

The above Huffman tree example where the number of symbols is 5 can now be represented by a table with size of $5-1=4$ as shown below.

Table 8-2

Table Index (Symbol)	Left Child	Right Child	Comments
3 (8)	0 (a)	7	left, right children of node 0 (root)
2 (7)	6	4 (e)	left, right children of node 1
1 (6)	1 (b)	5	left, right children of node 2
0 (5)	2 (c)	3 (d)	left, right children of node 3

Table 8-2 only has 4 entries while Table 8-1 has 13 entries. The symbols are represented by the table indices with 0 representing 'a', 1 representing 'b' and so on. To resolve the case if a table entry holds a pointer or an actual symbol value, we've added the value N_T to all table indices before saving them as pointers. Therefore, in a table entry, if the pointer value is smaller than N_T, we know that it is a terminal node (symbol). The following piece of code shows how to decode such a table that represents a Huffman tree; a left mask and right mask are used to extract the correct pointer value.

```
                              //N = # of symbols
left_mask = 0xFF00;           //to extract upper byte(left child)
right_mask = 0x00FF;          //to extract lower byte(right child)
loc = ( N - 1 ) + N;          //start from root; add offset N to
                              // distinguish pointers from symbols
do {
  loc0 = loc - N;             //loc0 is real table location
  if ( read_one_bit( in ) == 0 ){  //a 0, go left
      loc = ( htree[loc0] & left_mask ) >> 8;
 } else{
      loc =  htree[loc0] & right_mask;
 }
} while ( loc >= N );         //traverse until reaches leaf
return loc;                   //symbol value = loc
```

8.4 Pre-calculated Huffman-based Tree Coding

The Huffman coding process has a disadvantage that the statistics of the occurrence of the symbols must be known ahead of the encoding process. Though we do not need to transmit the probability table to the decoder, we do need it before we can do any encoding. The probability table for a large video cannot be calculated until after the video data have been processed which may introduce unacceptable delay into the encoding process. Because of these, practical video coding standards define sets of codewords based on the probability distributions of generic video data. The following example is a pre-calculated Huffman table taken from MPEG-4 Visual (Simple Profile), which uses 3D run-level coding discussed before to encode quantized coefficients. A total of 102 specific combinations of (*run, level, last*) have variable-length codewords assigned to them and part of these are shown in Table 8-3. Each codeword can be up to 13 bits long and the last bit is the sign bit 's', which indicates if the decoded coefficient is positive (0) or negative (1). Any (*run, level, last*) combination that is not listed in the table is coded using an escape sequence; a special ESCAPE code of 0000011 is first transmitted followed by a 13-bit fixed-length codeword describing the values of *run, level,* and *last.* A valid codeword cannot contain more than eight consecutive zeros. Therefore, a sequence consisting of eight or more consecutive zeros, "00000000..." indicates an error in the encoded bitstream or possibly a start code, which might contain a long sequence of zeros. We shall use Table 8-3 in our entropy-encoding stage shown in Figure 7-1. The full implementation of the

Huffman encoding and decoding for our video codec is discussed in the next section.

Table 8-3

Run	Level	Last	Code
0	1	0	10s
1	1	0	110s
2	1	0	1110s
0	2	0	1111s
0	1	1	0111s
3	1	0	01101s
4	1	0	01100s
5	1	0	01011s
0	3	0	010101s
1	2	0	010100s
6	1	0	010011s
7	1	0	010010s
8	1	0	010001s
9	1	0	010000s
1	1	1	001111s
2	1	1	001110s
3	1	1	001101s
4	1	1	001100s
0	4	0	0010111s
10	1	0	0010110s
11	1	0	0010101s
12	1	0	0010100s
5	1	1	0010011s
6	1	1	0010010s
7	1	1	0010001s
8	1	1	0010000s
ESCAPE			0000011s
..	..	..	..

8.5 Huffman Coding Implementation

Because Huffman coding involve reading and writing one bit at a time, we need to first develop some functions that can process an arbitrary number of bits of a file. We provide the program "fbitios.cpp" along with its header file "fbitios.h" that has this capability. The files can be downloaded from this book's web site at *http://www.forejune.com/vcompress*. We do not intend to discuss the details of this program as it does not directly relate to video compression. All we need to know is how to use it, which is straightforward. The following are the prototypes of the functions that have been grouped to a class that does the job that processes files on a bit-basis.

```
class  BitFileIO{
public:
  BitFileIO ( char *argv_in,  char *argv_out );    //constructors
  BitFileIO :: BitFileIO( char *argv_out, int in_out );
  int  inputBit();                           //input one bit from file
  void outputBit( int bit );                 //output one bit to file
  long inputBits( int n );                   //input n bits from file
  void outputBits(unsigned long data, int n);//send n bits to file
  void closeOutput();                        //close_output
  void closeInput();                         //close input
};
```

The constructor **BitFileIO** (char **argv_out*, int *in_out*) opens the file specified by *argv_out* for input or output depending on the value of *in_out*. If *in_out* is 1, the file is opened for input, otherwise it is for output. The main purpose of the Huffman code here is to encode the run-level codewords of the DCT coefficients after forward quantization and reordering. Recall that we have defined a class to represent a 3D run-level codeword:

```
class Run3D {
public:
  unsigned char run;
  short level;
  char  last;
};
```

Each Run3D object represents a run-level codeword, and the Huffman code is used to encode these codewords. We define a class called *RunHuff* that will help encode and decode run-level codewords with a Huffman code. This class "has-a" Run3D class. As you'll see, we'll insert *RunHuff* objects into a **set**, which involves the ordering of nodes. **Sets** and **bags** are data structures that are useful in problems in which multiple collections naturally occur. A **set** is an unordered collection of elements in which each element is unique like the figure below, which shows a set of 3D run-level codewords.

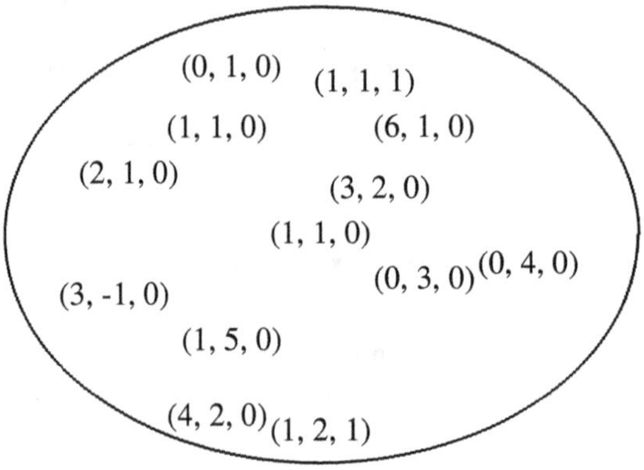

(0, 1, 0) (1, 1, 1)
(1, 1, 0) (6, 1, 0)
(2, 1, 0) (3, 2, 0)
(1, 1, 0)
(0, 3, 0) (0, 4, 0)
(3, -1, 0)
(1, 5, 0)
(4, 2, 0) (1, 2, 1)

On the other hand, a **bag** can have duplicate elements. Actually, the concept of a **set** underlies much of mathematics and is as well an integral part of many computing algorithms. The fundamental operations of a set include adding and removing elements, testing for inclusion of an element, and forming unions, intersections and differences of other sets.

Theoretically, a set is a collection of unordered elements; there is no key associated with each element and thus we cannot order the elements in a set. However, the people who wrote the STL C++ library have modified (or wrongly interpreted) the definition of a set and allow an element associate with a key. Therefore, the elements in an STL C++ set can be ordered. The modified set behaves more like a **map**. **Maps** and **multimaps** are data structures that are useful in problems in which multiple collections naturally occur.

A **map**, sometimes also referred to as a dictionary or a table is an associative container where records (data) are specified by key values. It is an indexed collection; the key can be used to generate an index to access the corresponding record. A map can be considered as a collection of associations of key and value pairs. The key is used to find the value as shown below:

$$key_1 \rightarrow value_1$$

$$key_2 \rightarrow value_2$$

$$key_3 \rightarrow value_3$$

....

$$key_n \rightarrow value_n$$

For example, we can use the telephone number as the key to lookup the information of a person. The keys in a map must be ordered and unique. A multimap is similar to a map except that a multimap permits multiple entries to be accessed using the same key value. (i.e. The keys in a multimap do not need to be unique.)

To utilize an STL C++ set (which behaves like a map) properly, we have to define the comparison operator "<" so that *RunHuff* objects (nodes) can be ordered. In this case, we order the objects using the values of (run, level, last) of the *Run3D* objects. We first compare the runs of the two objects, whichever is smaller determines the smaller *RunHuff* object. If the runs are equal, we compare levels and so on. The data member index will point to the table location where the run-level codeword will be saved. Note that in the STL C++ set data abstraction, the equality testing operator (operator ==) is not used to test objects for equality. Instead, two objects X and Y are considered to be equal when "$X < Y$" and "$Y < X$" are both **false**. Each element in a set is unique. If one tries to insert an element which is already in the set, the "insert" operation will be ignored. The class *RunHuff* is defined below.

Program Listing 8-1: *RunHuff* Class

```
-----------------------------------------------------------------------
class RunHuff {
public:
  run3D r;
  unsigned int codeword;
  char hlen;                //length of the Huffman codeword
  short index;              //table index where codeword saved
  RunHuff() {}              //constructors
  RunHuff ( run3D a, unsigned c, char len, short idx )
  {
    r = a, codeword = c, hlen = len; index = idx;
  }
  //'<' operator is to order run-level tuples so that
  //  they can be saved in a binary tree ( set )
```

```
  friend bool operator < ( RunHuff left, RunHuff right ) {
    if ( left.r.run < right.r.run )
      return true;
    if ( left.r.run >  right.r.run )
      return false;
    //runs equal
    if ( left.r.level < right.r.level )
      return true;
    if ( left.r.level > right.r.level )
      return false;
    //both runs and levels equal
    if ( left.r.last > right.r.last )
      return true;
    return false; //so, left object is not smaller than the right
  }
};
------------------------------------------------------------------------
```

We assume that a pre-calculated Huffman Table like the one shown in Table 8-3 is provided. Listing 8-2 presents the class *Hcodec* that makes use of a pre-calculated Huffman Table to build the encoder and the decoder. We declare a variable *htable* to be a map to collect *RunHuff* objects, each of which contains a 3D run-level tuple and the corresponding Huffman codeword (Table 8-2).

Program Listing 8-2: *Hcodec* class for Huffman Coding-Decoding

```
------------------------------------------------------------------------
class Hcodec
{
private:
  const static int NSymbols = 256;    //maximum symbols allowed
  const static short ESC = 127;       //Escape run
  const static short ESC_HUF_CODE = 0x60;  //Escape code
  const static short EOS = 126;       //End of Stream 'symbol' ( run )
  const static short EOS_HUF_CODE = 0x0a;  //End of Stream 'symbol'
  bool tableNotBuilt;
  set<RunHuff> htable;

public:
  //default constructor
  Hcodec();
  //use a set ( htable ) to collect all pre-calculated run-level
  //  and Huffman codewords
  void build_htable ();
  void escape_encode ( BitFileIO *outputs, Run3D &r );
  void huff_encode ( Run3D runs[], BitFileIO *outputs );
  //Encode End of Stream symbol
  void huff_encode_EOS ( BitFileIO *outputs );
  short huff_decode( BitFileIO *inputs, Dtables &d,  Run3D runs[] );
};
------------------------------------------------------------------------
```

The function **build_htable()** of the class *Hcodec* has all codewords and run-level tuples hard-coded in the code and saved in variables *hcode, runs, levels,* and *last* respectively. The function collects all these pre-calculated run-level tuples and Huffman codewords and saves them in the set *htable*. We can conveniently do this using the C++ Standard Template Library (STL) **set**. We use the member function **insert()** of the **set** class to insert all *RunHuff* objects into the set as shown below. (As a matter of fact, the STL **set** class is implemented using a balanced binary tree structure, which gives efficient search and insert operations. This is why we need to define a comparison operator in *htable* in order to use the STL **set** since a binary tree is fully ordered.) In the function, the special run value 127 is used to represent the ESC (escape) symbol. Listing 8-3 shows the code of this function:

Program Listing 8-3: Function build_htable() of Class *Hcodec*

```
//htable is a set of RunHuff objects
void Hcodec::build_htable() {
    //N = number of pre-calculated codewords with positive levels
    //  In practice, N should be larger than 100
    short i, j, k, N = 11;
    //lengths of Huffman codewords (not including sign-bit)
    char hlen[] = { 2, 3, 4, 4, 4, 5, 5, 5, 6, 6,  7 };
    //Huffman codewords, 0x60 for ESC, 0x3a for EOS;
    //  a codeword should NEVER be a prefix of another
    unsigned short hcode[] = {0x01,0x3,0x7,0xf,0xe, 0x16, 0x6, 0x1a,
                                    0x2a, EOS_HUF_CODE, ESC_HUF_CODE};
    //data of 3D run-level tuples ( codewords )
    unsigned char runs[] = {0, 1, 2, 0, 0, 3, 4, 5, 0, EOS, ESC};
    //Note: don't set Escape level to 0, otherwise leads to duplicate key
    short levels[] = {1, 1, 1, 2, 1, 1, 1, 1, 3, 1, 1};
    char  lasts[] = {0, 0, 0, 0, 1, 0, 0, 0, 0, 0, 0 };
    Run3D r;              //a 3D run-level codeword ( tuple )
    RunHuff rf[128];      //table containing RunHuff objects
    //inserting RunHuff objects into rf[]
    k = 0; j = 0;
    for ( i = 0; i < N; i++ ) {
      r.run = runs[i];
      r.level = levels[i];
      r.last = lasts[i];
      //construct a RunHuff object, positive level, so sign=0
      rf[k++] =  RunHuff ( r, hcode[i] << 1,  hlen[i], j++ );
      //do the same thing for negative level, sign = 1
      r.level = (short) -r.level;
      rf[k++] = RunHuff ( r, (short)((hcode[i]<<1) | 1), hlen[i], j++ );
    }
    k = 2 * N;            //insert all 2N RunHuff objects into htable
    for ( i = 0; i < k; ++i )
      htable.insert ( rf[i] );
    tableNotBuilt = false;
}
```

After we have collected all the pre-calculated run-level Huffman codewords in the **set** *htable*, the encoding of 3D run-levels tuples becomes simple. To encode a run-level codeword, all we need to do is to lookup the **set** *htable*; if the run-level codeword is in the set, we output the Huffman codeword along with the sign-bit; if it is not in the set, we "escape" and output the run-level codeword "directly".

Suppose the array *runs*[] contains all the run-level codewords of a macroblock; the following piece of code shows how to encode them using the pre-calculated Huffman codewords saved in *htable*. In the code, we define an iterator *itr* to traverse *htable*. If it finds the run-level tuple in *htable*, it outputs the Huffman codeword and the sign-bit, otherwise it escape-encodes the tuple by first outputting the

ESCAPE code followed by a fixed-length codeword for the tuple. (In C++, an iterator is an object that can access members of an array or a container class. It has the ability to traverse the elements in a certain range using certain operators such as increment (++) and dereference (*). Very often, it is used in a manner similar to pointers.). The following function of Listing 8-4, **huff_encode()** does the job:

Program Listing 8-4: Function huff_encode() of Class *Hcodec*

```
-----------------------------------------------------------------------
void Hcodec::huff_encode ( Run3D runs[], BitFileIO *outputs )
{
  short i, j, k;
  set<RunHuff>::iterator itr;          //iterator to traverse htable

  if ( tableNotBuilt )
      build_htable();
  i = 0;  k = 0;
  while ( i < 64 ) {                  //a macroblock has at most 64 samples
    RunHuff rf ( runs[k], 0, 0, 0 ); //construct a RunHuff object;
                                      //  only runs[k] is relevant
    if ( (itr = htable.find ( rf )) != htable.end() )    //found
      outputs->outputBits ( itr->codeword, itr->hlen + 1);
    else                                                  //not found
      escape_encode( outputs, rf.r );//need to 'escape encode' 3D tuple
    if ( runs[k].last ) break;        //end of run-level codewords
    i += ( runs[k].run + 1 );      //for handling the special case of whole
                                   //  block of run being 0
    k++;
  }
}
-----------------------------------------------------------------------
```

To encode a run-level tuple using the ESC symbol, we first check if the level is negative. If it is negative, we output a '1' bit otherwise we output a '0' bit. We then send the special code for the ESC symbol followed by the binary numbers representing the values of run, level and last. The following piece of code shows how to do this precisely.

```
void Hcodec::escape_encode ( BitFileIO *outputs, Run3D &r ) {
  if ( r.level < 0 ) {                 //value of level negative
    outputs->outputBit ( 1 );           //output sign-bit first
    r.level = -r.level;                //change level to positive
  } else
    outputs->outputBit ( 0 );           //value of level negative
  outputs->outputBits(ESC_HUF_CODE, 7); //ESCAPE code
  if ( r.run == 64 ) r.run = 63;       //r.level differentiates
                                       // whether last element nonzero
  outputs->outputBits ( r.run, 6 );     //6 bits for run value
  outputs->outputBits ( r.level, 8 );   //8 bits for level value
  outputs->outputBit ( r.last );        //1 bit for last value
}
```

The functions **huff_encode**() and **escape_encode**() encode the 3D run-level tuples of a macroblock. Also, at the end of the encoding process, we need to encode a special symbol 'End of Stream' (EOS) to indicate that there are no more encoding data. When the decoder sees the symbol EOS, it knows that the decoding process is done.

In the encoding process, the Huffman tree is not needed. However, to decode the encoded bit-stream, we have to use the Huffman tree to recover the 'symbols' (run-level tuples). We can easily construct the Huffman tree in the form of a table from the **set** *htable*. Note that here we build the Huffman tree from pre-calculated codewords, not from symbol weights as people normally do. Therefore, the process is a lot simpler as Huffman codewords have been provided. The following function **build_huff_tree**() builds the Huffman tree from *htable* and saves it in the table (array) *huf_tree*[] of data type short. An entry of *huf_tree*[] holds a node's pointer to a child or an index ('symbol') if the node is a leaf; the index points to an entry of another table,*run_table*[], which contains the actual run-level tuple (see Table 8-2). For convenience of programming, we put *huf_tree*[] and *run_table*[] in a public class (i.e. a struct) called *Dtables*. (The 'D' stands for 'Decoding'.) Listing 8-5 shows the class *Dtables* and the function build_huff_tree().

Program Listing 8-5: Constructing Huffman Tree

```
-------------------------------------------------------------------------------
class Dtables {
public:
  short huf_tree[1024];       //table containing Huffman Tree
  Run3D run_table[512];       //table containing run-level codewords
};

void Hcodec::build_huff_tree ( Dtables &d )
{
  set<RunHuff>::iterator itr;       //iterator to traverse set htable

  short i, j, n0, free_slot, loc, loc0, root, ntotal;
  unsigned int mask, hcode;

  n0 = NSymbols;                    //number of symbols (# of leaves in tree)
  ntotal = 2 * n0 - 1;              //Huffman tree has  n0-1  internal nodes
  root = 3 * n0 - 3;                //location of root with offset n0 added
  free_slot = root - 2;             //next free table entry for filing in
                                    //  with a pointer or an index
  for ( i = 0; i < ntotal; ++i )    //initialize the table
    d.huf_tree[i] = -1;             //all entries empty
  for ( itr = htable.begin(); itr != htable.end(); ++itr ) {
     if ( itr->r.level < 0 ) continue; //only save positive levels
     //save run-level codeword;divide by 2 as only postive levels saved
     d.run_table[itr->index/2]=itr->r;
     loc = root;                    //always start from root
     mask = 0x01;                   //for examining bits of Huffman codeword
     hcode = itr->codeword >> 1;    //the rightmost bit is sign-bit
     for ( i = 0; i < itr->hlen; ++i ){ //traverse the Huffman codeword
         loc0 = loc - n0;              //everything shifted by offset n0

       if ( i == ( itr->hlen - 1 ) ){  //last bit, should point to leaf
         if ( (mask & hcode) == 0 )    //a 0, save it at 'left' leaf
           d.huf_tree[loc0] = itr->index/2;
         else                          //a 1, save it at 'right' leaf
           d.huf_tree[loc0-1] = itr->index/2;
         continue;                  //get out of for i for loop,next codeword
       }
       if ( (mask & hcode) == 0 ){     //a 0 ( go left )
         if (d.huf_tree[loc0] == -1){  //slot empty
```

```
          d.huf_tree[loc0]=free_slot; //point to left new child
          free_slot -= 2;             //next free table entry
        }                             //else : already has left child
        loc = d.huf_tree[loc0];       //follow the left child
      } else {                        //a 1 ( go right )
        if (d.huf_tree[loc0-1]== -1){ //slot empty
          d.huf_tree[loc0-1]=free_slot;//point to right new child
          free_slot -= 2;
        }                             //else: already has right child
        loc = d.huf_tree[loc0-1];     //follow the right child
      }
      mask <<= 1;                     //consider next bit
    } //for i
  } //for itr
}
------------------------------------------------------------------------
```

After we have built the Huffman tree, decoding becomes simple. We read in a bitstream and traverse the tree starting from the root. If the bit read is a 0, we traverse left, otherwise we traverse right until we reach a leaf where we recover a symbol. If the symbol is an ESCAPE code, we need to further read in a fixed-number of bits to determine the 'symbol' (the run-level tuple). Then we read in another bit and start the tree-traversal from the root again. The details are shown in the function **huff_decode**() listed below.

Program Listing 8-6: Huffman Decoder

```
------------------------------------------------------------------------
short Hcodec::huff_decode( BitFileIO *inputs, Dtables &d,  Run3D runs[] )
{
  short n0, loc, loc0, root, k;
  char c, sign;
  bool done = false;
  Run3D r;

  n0 = NSymbols;                      //number of symbols
  root = 3 * n0 - 3;                  //points to root of tree
  k = 0;
  while ( !done ) {
    loc = root;                       //starts from root
    sign = inputs->inputBit();        //sign-bit
    do {
      loc0 = loc - n0;
      c = inputs->inputBit();         //read one bit
      if (c < 0) {done = true; break;} //no more data, done
      if ( c == 0 )                   //a 0, go left
        loc = d.huf_tree[loc0];
      else                            //a 1, go right
        loc = d.huf_tree[loc0-1];
    } while ( loc >= n0 );            //traverse until reaches leaf
    r = d.run_table[loc];
    if ( r.run == ESC ) {  //ESCAPE code, read actual run-level tuple
        r.run   = inputs->inputBits ( 6 );     //read 6 bits for run
        r.level  = inputs->inputBits ( 8 );  //read 8 bits for level
        r.last = inputs->inputBit();         //read 1 bit for last
        if ( sign )          //if sign is 1, level should be negative
```

```
          r.level = -r.level;
      } else {                                    //not ESCAPE code
         if ( sign )                              //1 => negative
          r.level = -r.level;
     }
     if ( (r.run == 63) && (r.level == 0) ) r.run = 64;  //whole block 0
     runs[k++] = r;                              //save tuple in table runs[]
     if ( r.last )                               //end of macroblock
       break;
   } //while
   if ( done ) return -1;                        //if (done) => no more data
   else return 1;
}
-------------------------------------------------------------------------
```

Putting all these together, we provide two driver programs,

```
test_huf_encode.cpp, and
test_huf_decode.cpp
```

for you to do the testing of the concepts discussed above. (The programs can be downloaded from the web site of this book, *http://www.forejune.com/vcompress/.*) A Makefile is provided for you to create the executables **test_huf_encode** and **test_huf_decode**. You may use the command,

```
$test_huf_encode ../data/beach.dct ../data/beach.huf
```

to encode the DCT coefficients of the file "beach.dct" and save the Huffman codeword bitstream in "beach.huf". The command

```
$test_huf_decode ../data/beach.huf t.dec
```

decodes the Huffman codeword bitstream saved in "beach.huf" and saves the decoded DCT coefficients in the file "t.dec". The original data file "beach.dct" and recovered data file "t.dec" are not the same as quantization and rounding errors have occurred in the process.

Chapter 9

Image Prediction and Motion Compensation

9.1 Introduction

In previous chapters, we combined various well-developed techniques, which are shown in Figure 7-1 to compress image data. You may be amazed to see that the techniques can achieve high compression ratios with high-quality reproduced decompressed images. Actually, the best is yet to come. So far, we have only considered static images and have used .ppm files in our examples; the techniques employed in Figure 7-1 have only exploited the correlations between pixels (or spatial redundancy). These techniques are very similar to those used by the JPEG standard to compress static images. Actually, they can be applied to encode a sequence of images, compressing each image individually. This method of compressing each frame independently is known as motion JPEG or M-JPEG. Obviously, M-JPEG has not made use of the correlations between frames (temporal redundancy) to achieve higher compression. M-JPEG is usually used in very high quality video captures and the scenes are normally captured in the raw data format which are then edited and compressed into another format. Encoding each frame individually is also referred to as *intra-frame* coding, where at a certain instance, data processing is applied only to the data of the current frame but not to any other frame in the video sequence. This contrasts with *inter-frame* coding, where processing is applied simultaneously to the data of the current frame and the adjacent frames. If you watch a movie played by a DVD player and at some point change it to play at a slow-motion mode, you would notice that most consecutive frames within a sequence are very similar to the frames both before and after the frame of interest. By exploiting the inherent temporal, or time-based redundancies between frames, considerably more compression efficiency can be obtained.

Intra-frames are often referred to as I-frames and inter-frames are called P-frames. P here refers to 'prediction'. This is because people use motion estimation and a technique known as block-based motion compensated prediction to exploit the temporal correlations between frames in order to reduce the redundancies. Indeed, in Chapter 2 we have discussed that the information conveyed by a set of data closely relates to its predictability. A perfectly predictable message conveys no information. Actually, besides temporal prediction, we can also use spatial prediction to reduce data redundancies.

9.2 Temporal Model

A temporal model exploits inter-frame correlations to reduce redundancies. Very often, a predicted frame is calculated or formed by certain procedures and is subtracted from the current frame, producing a residual or difference frame. The more accurate the prediction, the less information the residual data contain and the higher compression we can achieve. The residual data are encoded in the usual way as presented in Figure 7-1. Besides decoding the encoded residual data, the decoder has to recreate the predicted frame and adds it to the decoded residual to reconstruct the current frame (usually this is a lossy process; the reconstructed frame is not identical to the original one). The predicted frame is often created from one or more past or future frames which are referred to as 'reference frames'. Predictions in general can be improved by compensating for motion between the current frame and reference frames. We will discuss motion compensation in detail in the next section.

For instance, MPEG predicts images from previous frames (P frames) or bidirectionally from previous and future frames (B frames). After predicting frames using motion compensation, the coder calculates the residual which is then compressed using the methods shown in Figure 7-1.

9.3 Block Based Motion Estimation and Motion Compensation

A simple and commonly used method for temporal prediction is to use the previous frame as the predictor for the current frame. However, very often for many frames of a video scene, the main difference between one frame and another is the result of either the camera moving or an object in the frame moving. This means much of the information that represents one frame will be the same as the information used in the next frame. A direct subtraction of the previous frame (predictor) from the current frame could produce substantial nonzero residual values. For instance, consider an example where the images are shown in Figure 9-1 and Figure 9-2 (for simplicity, we assume that a white pixel has a zero value and a black pixel has a nonzero value). The objects in the two figures are identical except that one is displaced with respect to the other. Direct calculation of the difference between the two frames yields substantial residual values as shown in Figure 9-3. Actually, this example is quite extreme as the difference has more nonzero values than Frame 1 and Frame 2, resulting in a less efficient compression. However, if we make compensation for the motion by translating the object in Frame 1 to the position of the object in Frame 2 before carrying out the subtraction, then the residual will consist of all zeros, which result in a very efficient compression.

The residual can be compressed and decompressed as usual (Figure 7-1). *But how do we recover the current frame (Frame 2)?* To reconstruct the current frame, the decoder needs to know the the image data of the previous frame (Frame 1) and the displacement of the object, which is known as **motion vector**. The process of obtaining the motion vector is known as **motion estimation**, and using the motion vector to remedy the effects of motion is known as **motion compensation**.

Once we have reconstructed Frame 2, we can use it as the predictor for Frame 3 and the reconstructed Frame 3 is used as the predictor for Frame 4 and so on. Therefore, we only need to send one complete frame to be used as the predictor along with the residual and motion vectors at the very beginning. After that, the predictor (reference frame) is reconstructed from other information.

Of course in reality, the objects in two different frames are rarely identical. Moreover, many objects in a scene are deformable and it is very difficult to identify all the objects in a large number of frames. Then in practice, how do we do motion compensation?

Figure 9-1. Frame 1

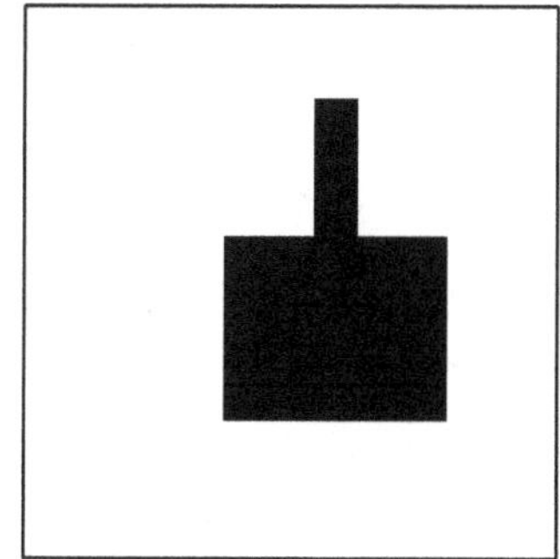

Figure 9-2. Frame 2

Figure 9-3. Residual = Frame 1 - Frame 2

Figure 9-4. Motion Compensated Residual

The most commonly used technique in motion compensation is the block-based motion estimation. In this method, a current frame is divided into rectangular sections or 'blocks'. We handle each block independently and search in the reference frame a block that matches this block best. The following procedures explain more precisely how the search is carried out for each block of size $M \times N$:

1. Search a region in the reference frame that best matches the $M \times N$ sample block. This is done by comparing the $M \times N$ block of the current frame with some or all of the possible $M \times N$ regions of the reference frame. The best matched region can be determined using an objective quality measure such as the minimum absolute difference (MAD) or sum of absolute difference (SAD) discussed below. That is, we want to find an $M \times N$ block in

the reference frame so that the sum of absolute difference (SAD) between it and the given sample block is minimized. This is the motion estimation procedure.

2. Set the selected block in the reference frame to become the predictor for the $M \times N$ sample block of the current frame and subtract it from the current block to form a residual $M \times N$ block. Also, calculate the motion vector (displacement) between the two blocks. This is the motion compensation procedure.

3. Encode the residual block using methods discussed in previous chapters (Figure 7-1). We may also encode the motion vector using a pre-calculated Huffman code. Send the encoded values to the decoder.

The decoder first decodes the encoded motion vector and residual block. It uses the motion vector to identify the predictor region in the reference frame and adds the predictor to the residual to reconstruct a version of the original block.

From the above discussions, we see that encoding one frame usually involves more than one motion vector. This is the reason that we encode a motion vector with a Huffman code. Figure 9-5a presents the video compression that extends Figure 7-1 to include temporal prediction, motion estimation and motion compensation; the steps of RGB-YCbCr transformation and down sampling are omitted in the diagram. The corresponding diagram for decoding the encoded stream is shown in Figure 9-5b.

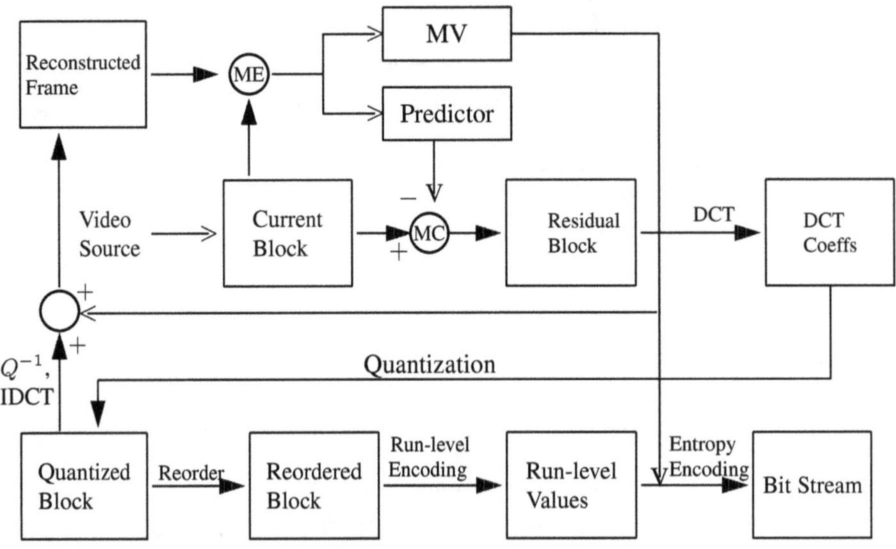

Figure 9-5a. Video Compression with ME and MC

In Figure 9-5, the terms MV, ME, MC, and Q^{-1} represent motion vector, motion estimation, motion compensation, and inverse quantization respectively. Block-based motion compensation (MC) is commonly used in video compression. This is because it is simple, and straightforward to implement. The algorithm could be efficient, depending on the choice of block size and search details. The method also fits well with commonly used rectangular video frames and the block-based Discrete Cosine Transform (DCT). On the other hand, there are some drawbacks in using block-based MC. Objects in a scene are often non-rectangular and their boundaries rarely match well with rectangular edges. Very often, an object may move by a fraction of the distance between pixels from one frame to another; the motion may not be simple translations but more complex motions like shrinking, rotation, and vibration. Also, objects like animals and liquid could be deformable and some objects such as clouds, smoke and fire may not even have any regular shape.

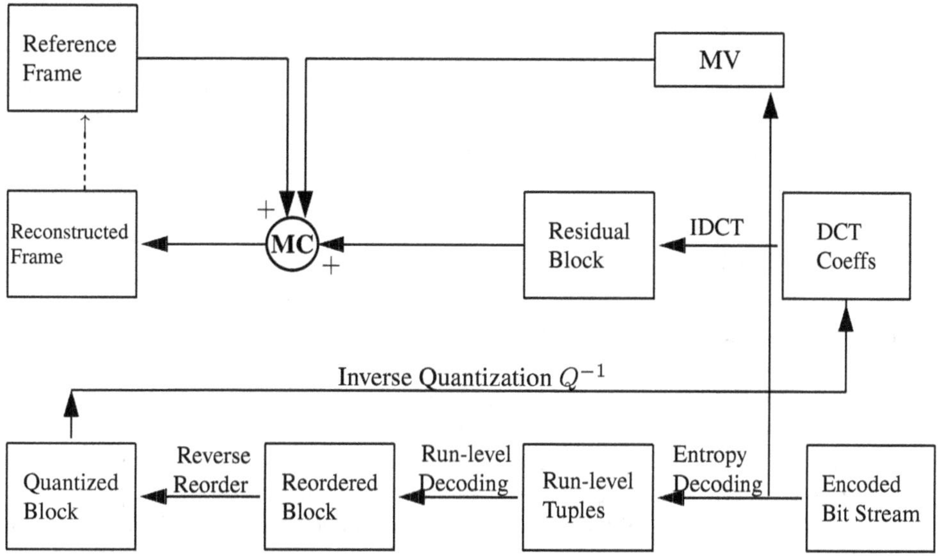

Figure 9-5b. Decoding of Compressed Stream with ME and MC

9.4 Matching Criteria

Before we perform any search, we need some criteria to determine which is the best match. Some of these criteria are simple to evaluate, while others are more involved. Different kinds of algorithms may use different criteria for comparison of blocks. The commonly used criteria are the "Sum of Differences" (SAD), the "Mean Absolute Difference" (MAD), and the "Mean Squared Difference" (MSD). If the compensation block size is $N \times N$ samples, and I_{ij} and I'_{ij} are the current and reference sample values respectively at location (i, j), the formulas for these criteria are presented in equations (9.1a), (9.1b), and (9.1c) below:

$$SAD = \sum_{i=0}^{N-1} \sum_{j=0}^{N-1} |I_{ij} - I'_{ij}| \tag{9.1a}$$

$$MAD = \frac{1}{N^2} \sum_{i=0}^{N-1} \sum_{j=0}^{N-1} |I_{ij} - I'_{ij}| \tag{9.1b}$$

$$MSD = \frac{1}{N^2} \sum_{i=0}^{N-1} \sum_{j=0}^{N-1} (I_{ij} - I'_{ij})^2 \tag{9.1c}$$

The functions SAD, MAD, and MSD presented in (9.1) are also referred to as distortion functions. Because of its simplicity, SAD is probably the most commonly used measure to determine the best match. In subsequent discussions, we shall also use "minimizing SAD" as our criterion to find the best match.

In practice, instead of searching in the RBG space, we search in the YCbCr space. The residuals are actually the differences of the YCbCr components between two frames. Also, we need to send the motion vectors to the decoder. Very often, small vectors occur more frequently, and a pre-calculated Huffman coder 'bias' towards smaller values. Therefore, we usually encode smaller vectors with less number of bits than larger vectors. Consequently, it may be useful to 'bias' the choice of a vector towards the location of the current block which is assumed to be at (0, 0). We can accomplish this by subtracting a constant from the SAD at location (0, 0).

9.5 Choice of Block Size

The next question arises on motion compensation is what block size should we use in the search. Intuitively, a smaller block size would give smaller SADs, yielding 'better' residual results (more zeros and small values). However, a smaller block size requires more search operations and motion vectors encoding. Encoded motion vectors increase the overhead bits required for decoding and the increase in bits may outweigh the benefits of improved residual compression. For instance, consider the extreme case that we were to use a block consisting of only a single pixel (i.e. block size = 1). Then in the searching process, a pixel with the same intensity value would result in a perfect match and produce a motion vector. However, we would not gain any compression in this situation because instead of encoding a set of pixel values, we would encode the same number of two dimensional motion vectors, which could be less correlated and make the compression worse.

On the other hand, a large block size requires much less search and motion vectors. However, a large block may contain small moving objects, giving rise to a poor predictor block and thus poor residual results. The larger the block, the less likely we will find a predictor block that matches reasonably well with the current block.

One effective way to compromise between choosing a large block size and a small block size is to adapt the block size to the image characteristics. For example, we choose a large block size in flat, and homogeneous areas of a frame and choose a small block size in regions of rapid or complex motion. In practice, video compression standards, including MPEG-1, MPEG-2, MPEG-4, H.261, H.263 and H.264 use a macroblock as the basic block for motion compensation. H.264 also uses adaptive motion compensation block sizes which are organized in a tree structure. In Chapter 5, we discussed that a macroblock is a 16×16 region of a frame. It shows in Figure 5-1 that a 4:2:0 formatted macroblock consists of a 16×16 luminance (Y) sample block, an 8×8 blue chrominance (Cb) sample block and an 8×8 red chrominance (Cr) sample block. Motion estimation is done by searching a 16×16 sample region in a reference frame that best matches the current macroblock consisting of Y, Cb, and Cr samples. The Minimum Absolute Difference (MAD) criterion or the Sum of Absolute Differences (SAD) is usually used to determine the best-match. Motion compensation is done by subtracting the chosen best matching region in the reference frame from the current macroblock to generate a residual macroblock, which is encoded in the usual manner (Figure 7-1 of Chapter 7) and sent to the decoder along with an encoded motion vector that describes the position of the selected region relative to the current macroblock. Within the encoder, we have to decode encoded residual macroblock and make use of the motion vector to add it to the matching region to form a reconstructed macroblock frame which is stored as a reference for future motion compensation operations (see Figure 9-5). You may wonder why we obtain the reference frame by reconstructing the macroblock rather than using one from the video source. This is because the encoder and decoder need to use an identical reference frame for motion compensation otherwise errors will accumulate over time. Sometimes, if there is a rapid scene change, causing a significant difference between adjacent frames, it is better not to use motion compensation in the encoding.

To carry out the compression effectively, one can allow the encoding to switch between *intra* mode that encodes without motion compensation and *inter* mode that uses motion compensation for each macroblock. Also, objects may move by a fraction of the distance between two pixels rather than an integral value. In this case, we may be able to find better predictions by first interpolating the reference frame to sub-pixel positions before searching a best-match of these positions.

9.6 Motion Estimation Algorithms

Often motion estimation (ME) is the most computationally intensive part of a video encoder. Reduction of the required computational complexity is one of the most challenging issues for motion compensation. It is the state of the art in video encoding and is particularly critical in real-time video compression. On the other hand, nonreal-time applications can do the compression offline and can afford to spend more time on optimizing the compression. The decoder does not need to do any motion compensation and in general runs a lot faster than the encoder. Moreover, in many applications such as the distribution of a video clip, compression has to be done only once but decompression will be done many times. Therefore, these applications may afford to pay the cost of computation even if they are very high during the compression process.

As mentioned in the previous section, a common way to do motion estimation is to find a region in the reference frame that best matches the current macroblock and compute the motion vector between the two regions. *How do we find the best-matched region?* A model that is commonly used in searching is the *block-translation* model, where an image is divided into non-overlapping rectangular blocks. Each block in the predicted image is formed by translating a similar source region from the reference frame. This model does not consider any rotation or scaling of the block. The brute-force exhaustive search, which is also known as full search is one of such models.

9.6.1 Full Search

In a full search (or exhaustive search), we test every block within a defined range against the block it is defined to match (target block). In terms of minimizing SAD, exhaustive search always finds the optimal motion vector because the method compares all possible displacements within the search range. The following C-like pseudo code shows this algorithm:

```
for ( int i = 0; i < 256; ++i ) {
  x[i] = pixel in current macroblock
  y[i] = pixel in a 16x16 block in reference frame
  for each k = 16x16 block in reference frame {
    D[k] = sum of distortion( x[i], y[i][k] )
  }
}

return k-th 16x16 block in reference frame that minimizes D
```

If the search window size is 2S + 1, and its center (0, 0) is at the position of the current macroblock, the search window is typically a rectangular region with lower-left and upper-right corners defined by the coordinates $(-S, -S)$, and $(+S, +S)$. Full search evaluates SAD at each point of the window, for a total of $(2S + 1)^2$ points. A simple full search strategy is to start from the upper-left corner at $(-S, +S)$ and proceed in raster scan order, from left to right and top to bottom until SADs at all positions have been evaluated. However, in a typical video sequence, movements of objects between frames are small and small SAD positions are concentrated around (0, 0). It is not likely that we find a minimum SAD near the corners of the search window. Therefore, we can simplify a full search by starting the search at the center (0, 0) and proceeding to evaluate points in a spiral pattern as shown in Figure 9-6. Of course, if we evaluate the SAD at every position as usual, we do not gain an advantage. However, we can make a short cut by adopting an early termination strategy, in which the evaluation of a SAD terminates once its value is larger than the previous SAD minimum (note that we just terminate the SAD evaluation at the position but we do **not** terminate the search until all positions in the window have been covered). By using this early termination strategy, it is increasing likely that the search will terminate early as the search pattern expands outward, and thus saving a significant amount of time in calculating SADs.

There are various strategies to decide on the search range. The search range usually depends on how fast objects move in the image sequence, and how well we want to track the fastest objects. If our reference frames are adjacent frames, it is not possible to track an object that moves more than an image width or height between successive frames. It might be reasonable to track an object that moves about half an image width between successive frames but in terms of TV, this corresponds to an object that appears in a frame and might disappear in the subsequent frame in one tenth of a second, which is faster than what we need. If we aimed at tracking an object that traverses a frame in about half a second, and the video dimension is about 512×512 and is played at a rate of 40 frames per second (fps). we would need to accommodate a movement of about 12 pixels per frame. If we wish to make predictions from two successive frames instead of one, we would need to double the search range to about 24 pixels.

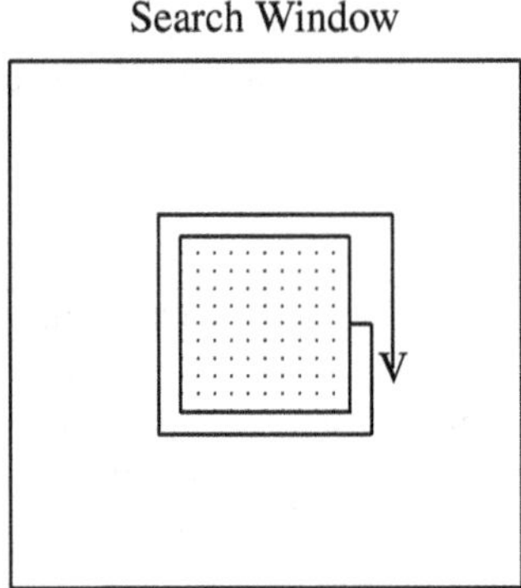

Figure 9-6. Full Search with Spiral Scan

Also, in real-world scene, there are usually more and faster movements in the horizontal direction than in the vertical direction. People found that it was best to search the width about twice as much as the height.

Full search is rather easy to implement. However, the best match as determined by a criterion like minimum SAD may not represent the real match of the object that appears in two frames. Good matches tend to minimize the residual errors, resulting in good compression, but if the matches do not represent true motion, the motion vectors of subsequent matching blocks may not correlate well, and encoding these vectors become inefficient.

9.6.2 Fast Searches

Though full search gives optimal results for a given criterion, it is computationally intensive. There are suboptimal search algorithms, usually referred to as fast search algorithms that trade the quality of the image prediction with the efficiency of searching. These algorithms evaluate the search criterion at a subset of the locations of the search window.

Three Step Search (TSS)

The Three Step Search (TSS),introduced by Koga et al in 1981 is a popular and robust search algorithm that gives near-optimal results. The N-Step Search (NSS) is a modified version of the TSS that calculates the SADs at a specified subset of locations within the search window. It searches for the best motion vectors in a coarse to fine search pattern. Figure 9-7 illustrates the search positions of this algorithm. Suppose the origin (0, 0) is at the center of the figure. We start by choosing the origin as our center of searching and pick a step size b, which is 4 in Figure 9-7. In the first stage, in addition to the origin, we choose eight locations of blocks at a "distance" of b from the center for comparison; in Figure 9-7 these first 9 search locations are labeled '1'. We pick the location that gives the smallest SAD as our new center of search, which is marked by a concentric circle in Figure 9-7. In the second stage search, the step size is halved and a further 8 locations around the new center are chosen with the new step size which is 2 in this example. The search locations for this stage is labeled '2' in Figure 9-7. Once again, we pick the best-matched location to be the new search center and repeat the procedure until the step size cannot be subdivided further.

In an N-step search, the step size in general is $2^{(N-1)}$ and there are N searching levels. The number of searches is only $8N + 1$ as compared to $(2^{N+1} - 1)^2$ in a corresponding full search. However, NSS uses a uniformly allocated checking point pattern in the first step, which could be inefficient for small motion estimation.

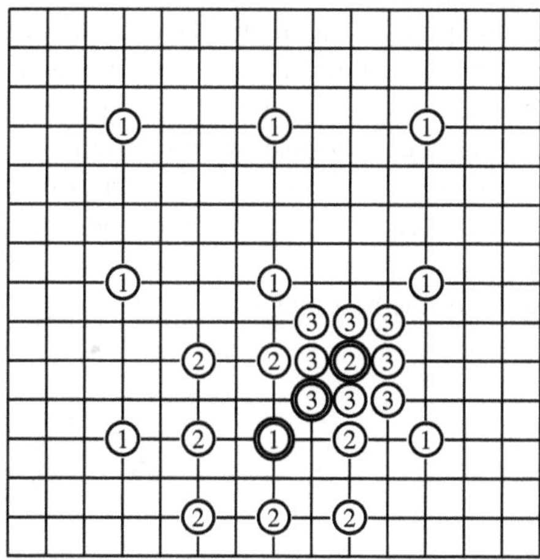

Figure 9-7. Three Step Search (TSS)

Hierarchical Search

Hierarchical search employs the coarse-to-fine approach to reduce computations at the coarse levels. At a coarse level, a 'large' block may contain many pixel positions but only a small number of searching locations; the sample value at a location may be the average (filtered value) of many adjacent pixel values. The algorithm first searches a large block to obtain a first approximation of the motion, which can be successively refined by searching smaller regions using smaller blocks, each block being appropriately filtered. The method has a better chance of getting the "real" motion vector because we first establish the general trend of motion using large filtered blocks and accomplish more accurate measurement using small blocks. It has been shown that motion vectors obtained by hierarchical search has significantly lower entropy, implying that they require less number of bits to encode.

For example, the mean pyramid method constructs different pyramidal images by subsampling, and estimates motion vectors starting from higher levels (coarse levels) and proceeding to lower ones. We can reduce the noise at higher levels by constructing the image pyramids using low pass filters, and use a simple averaging to construct the multiple-level pyramidal images. For instance, suppose $g_L(x, y)$ is the gray level value at the position (x, y) of the L-th level and $g_0(x, y)$ represents the original image at level 0. We obtain the pixel value at a level by averaging the four pixel values in a nonoverlapping window of the next lower level as shown in Equation (9.2):

$$g_L(x, y) = \lfloor \frac{1}{4} \sum_{i=0}^{1} \sum_{j=0}^{1} g_{L-1}(2x + i, 2y + j) \rfloor \tag{9.2}$$

where $\lfloor x \rfloor$ denotes the floor function of x, which truncates x to the nearest integer. If there are totally three levels in the pyramid, one pixel at level 2 corresponds to a 2×2 block and a 4×4 block at level 1 and level 0 respectively. Therefore, a block of size 16×16 at level 0 produces a block of size $16/2^L \times 16/2^L$ at level $L > 0$. After constructing the mean pyramid, we can search the images starting at level 2 using the minimum SAD (Sum of Absolute Differences) criterion; we select the motion vector with the smallest SAD as the coarse motion vector at that level. We send the motion vector detected at the higher level to the next lower level (level 1), which uses the received motion vector to guide the refinement step at that level. We repeat the motion estimation process once more down to level 0. Since SAD's are computed at the highest level based on relatively small blocks, the same values are likely to appear at several points. To solve this problem, we can use more than one candidate at the highest level (level 2 for our special case). A number of motion vectors at level 2 are propagated to the lower one. Full search in a small window around the candidates is used at level one to find the minimum difference location as the search center at layer 0. Figure 9-8 shows the search locations of the algorithm. At level 2 of the figure, three best matched points are selected as centers for search windows in the next level, which are shown at level 1 of the figure. Level 0 shows the search window where we search for the best match.

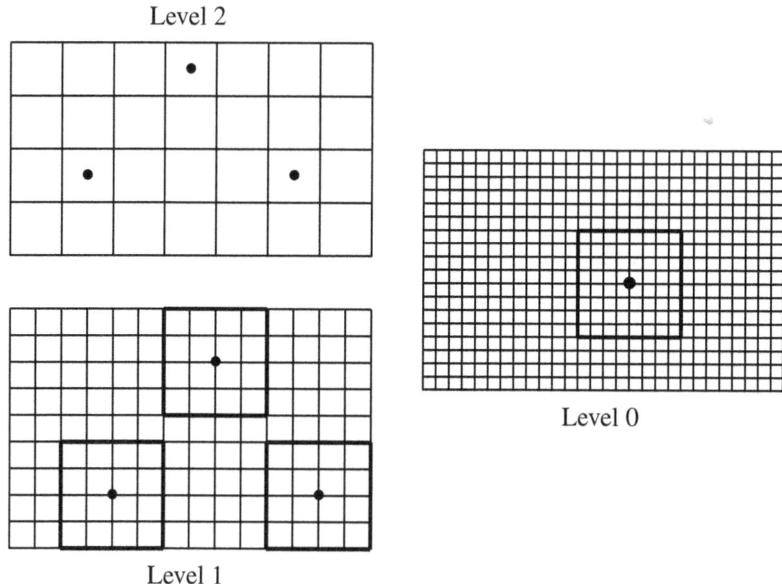

Figure 9-8. Search Locations for Hierarchical Search

Nearest Neighbours Search

One problem of the TSS, Hierarchical Search and many other suboptimal searches is that the searches may quickly get trapped in local minima, as the distortion function does not necessarily increase monotonically when we move away from the global minimum distortion candidate. This could result in a significant loss in estimation accuracy, and hence compression performance as compared to Full Search. This problem can be alleviated by incorporating prediction into a fast-search algorithm. We can predict the the current motion vector (MV) from previously coded motion vectors that represent spatially or temporally neighbouring macroblocks. Localizing the search origin in this way reduces the possibility of getting trapped in local minima, as the predicted motion vector is usually closer than the vector (0, 0) to the global minimum candidate. If the predicted MV is accurate, we can quickly find the "optimal" MV by searching a relatively small neigbourhood.

Nearest Neighbours Search (NNS) makes use of the above-mentioned motion vector prediction method and highly localized search pattern to give estimation accuracy approaching that of Full Search in many applications but with much lower computational complexity. The algorithm offers a more reliable MV prediction that detects potential non-motion changes in the video sequence. In the algorithm, we predict an MV based on previously coded MVs and transmit the difference (MVD) between the current MV and the predicted MV. NNS exploits this property by giving preference to MVs that are close to the predicted MV, and thus minimize the MVD. Figure 9-9 shows an example of search positions of NNS, which first evaluates the SAD at the search origin (labeled '0') and then calculates the SAD at the locations of the predicted MV as well as the SADs of the surrounding points in a diamond shape (labeled '1'). If the SAD at '0' or the center of the diamond is lowest, the search terminates, otherwise the location that gives the smallest SAD is chosen (double-circled '1' in Figure 9-9), and becomes the center of a new diamond-shaped search pattern (labeled '2') and the search process continues. In the example, the next search center is double-circled '2' and the final selected location is double-circled '3'.

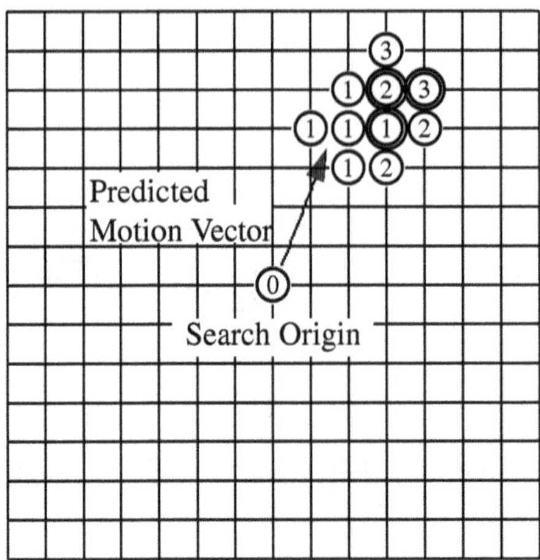

Figure 9-9. Nearest Neighbours Search (NNS)

Others

Many other fast search algorithms have been proposed. More popular ones include Binary Search (BS), Two Dimensional Logarithmic Search (TDL), Four Step Search (FSS), Orthogonal Search Algorithm (OSA), One at a Time Algorithm (OTA), Cross Search Algorithm (CSA), and Spiral Search (SS). In each case, we can evaluate its performance by comparing it with Full Search. We can compare the time an algorithm used and the compression ratio achieved against that of Full Search. Sometimes an algorithm may be good for certain applications but not for others. For example, algorithms such as Hierarchical Search are more easily to be implemented with customized hardware than others.

9.7 Frame Types

There are two types of video frames concerning motion compensation. An **intraframe** or **I-frame** is a frame that is encoded using only the information from within that frame. On the other hand, **inter-** or non-intra frames are encoded using information from within that frame as well as information from other frames. Inter-frames can be further classified as P-frames and B-frames.

9.7.1 Intraframes (I-frames)

Intra frames are coded without motion estimation and compensation. That means it is encoded spatially with no information from any other frame. In other words, no temporal processing is performed outside of the current picture or frame. Coding an I-frame is similar to coding an image in JPEG. Compressing a video using I-frames only is similar to the techniques in motion JPEG. The compression ratio obtained is in general significantly lower than that of compressing with inter-frame coding.

Spatial prediction can be used in intra-frame coding. In spatial prediction, we make use of previously-transmitted samples to predict an image sample in the same image or frame. Figure 9-10 shows a pixel d that is to be encoded. If the pixels in the frame are processed in the order from left to right and top to bottom, then the neighbouring pixel values at a, b, and c have been processed and are available in both the encoder and decoder. The encoder predicts a value $P(d)$ for the current pixel d based on some combinations of previously coded pixel values, $I(a), I(b)$, and $I(c)$. It then subtracts the actual pixel value $I(d)$ of d from $P(d)$ and encodes the residual (the difference resulted from the subtraction). The decoder uses the same prediction formula and adds the decoded residual to construct the pixel value.

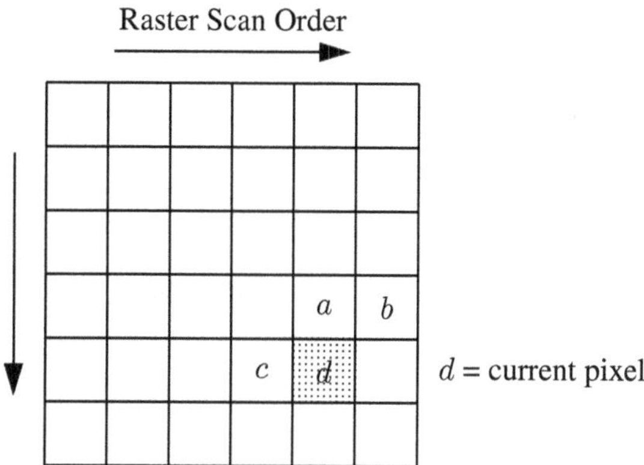

Figure 9-10. Spatial Prediction

The following is an example of spatial prediction for Figure 9-10. In the example, pixel c has a larger weight than b and a because it is the most recently scanned pixel. We also assume that the encoding of the residuals is a lossless process, which means that the pixel values can be recovered exactly from the decoded residuals.

Example 9-1 Spatial Prediction for Figure 9-10.

Encoder prediction: $P(d) = \frac{2I(c) + I(b) + I(a)}{4}$

Residual: $R(d) = I(d) - P(d)$ is encoded and transmitted.

Decoder decodes $R(d)$, and

obtain $P(d)$ using same prediction formula: $P(d) = \frac{2I(c) + I(b) + I(a)}{4}$

Reconstruct sample value at d: $I(d) = R(d) + P(d)$

If the residual encoding involes lossy operations such as quantizations, the decoded sample values, $I'(a), I'(b)$, and $I'(c)$ may not be identical to the original sample values, $I(a), I(b)$, and $I(c)$ of pixels a, b, and c. In this case, the decoder does not know the values of $I(a), I(b)$, and $I(c)$ and if we still use $I(a), I(b)$, and $I(c)$ to calculate $P(d)$ in the encoder as it does in the example, the process could lead to a cumulative error between the encoder and decoder. Therefore, in this situation, the encoder should first reconstruct the sample values $I'(a), I'(b)$, and $I'(c)$ from the previous residuals before calculating the current prediction $P(d)$. The encoder uses the reconstructed sample values to form the prediction in the above example:

$$\begin{aligned} P(d) &= \frac{2I'(c) + I'(b) + I'(a)}{4} \\ R(d) &= I(d) - P(d) \\ R'(d) &= Decode(Encode(R(d))) \\ I'(d) &= P(d) + R'(d) \end{aligned} \tag{9.3}$$

In this way, just like what we discussed in Section 9.5, where we obtain the reference frame by reconstructing the macroblock rather than using one from the video source, the encoder and decoder use the same sample values in calculating $P(d)$, and the cumulative error can be avoided. The prediction equation of (9.3) is a special case of the more general linear prediction:

$$P(d) = C_a I'(a) + C_b I'(b) + C_c I'(c) \tag{9.4}$$

where C_x is a constant for pixel x. In the example of (9.3), the constants for pixels a, b, and c are 0.25, 0.25, and 0.5 respectively. For things to work properly, the sum of the constants in the linear prediction of (9.4) must be equal to 1. If the predicted values I' have been scaled in the process, the original sample value $I(d)$ of the current pixel d must be scaled accordingly before subtracting $P(d)$ from it to form the residual $R(d)$.

In practice, we may perform intra-prediction after DCT transformation at a block-based level with block size 8×8. Very often, the low-frequency DCT coefficients of neighbouring blocks are correlated. Therefore, we can predict the DC coefficient (i.e. F_{00} of Chapter 6) and AC coefficients of the first row and column ($F_{0i}, F_{i0},\ 0 < i < 8$) from neigbouring coded blocks. Table 9-1 shows the DCT coefficients for each of the four luma 8×8 block of a macroblock. The data are obtained from the same PPM file, "beach.ppm" that we have used for testing in previous chapters. The DC coefficients (629, 637, 653, and 662) are clearly similar but it is less obvious whether there is correlation between the first row and first column of the AC coefficients in the blocks.

Table 9-1 Four 8×8 luma blocks of a DCT Macroblock

629	-5	-1	-1	1	-1	-2	-1	637	-5	0	1	2	0	0	-1
-8	-5	-1	0	0	-1	-2	-2	-4	2	-1	-2	-1	1	0	0
2	-3	-1	-1	-4	-4	-3	-2	4	-1	1	-2	1	2	1	1
-3	-4	-3	-1	1	-2	-4	-3	2	0	-3	-1	0	1	0	0
-1	-6	0	-1	-1	1	0	0	2	-1	-1	0	-1	1	-1	3
-4	-5	-3	0	2	-1	-1	0	2	-2	-1	-1	-1	0	-1	0
-1	-2	-2	-1	-1	-1	-1	-2	0	0	1	2	1	-1	0	-2
1	-1	0	0	0	-2	-2	-1	-1	-1	1	1	0	0	0	-1
653	1	0	0	-1	1	-1	0	662	-6	1	-1	0	-2	0	0
-9	1	1	-2	-1	0	-1	2	-7	1	1	-2	0	1	0	1
0	1	0	0	0	0	0	-1	1	1	1	1	-1	0	-1	-1
-2	0	-2	1	1	-1	2	0	0	-1	-1	1	-1	-2	0	0
0	-1	-1	0	-1	0	0	0	2	1	1	0	-1	-1	1	0
1	-1	1	-1	0	0	-1	1	0	0	-1	-1	-1	0	0	1
0	-1	1	0	0	0	0	0	-1	-1	-2	-1	0	2	-2	0
0	0	1	2	2	0	1	-2	1	0	-1	0	1	1	-2	0

Suppose F^X_{ij} represent the coefficient of block X at location (i, j). Figure 9-11 presents an example of prediction for the current block D from neigbouring blocks. We predict F^D_{00}, the DC coefficient of the current block from the DC coefficients of the previously coded neighbouring 8×8 blocks, A, B, and C. The question is which block should we choose to form the prediction. *Should we choose A, B or C, or a combination of them?* A simple solution is to use either B or C as they are adjacent to the current block D. This is shown in Figure 9-11. In determining whether we should choose B or C, we can examine the *gradients* of the DC values between the blocks. We choose the block that gives the smaller gradient. That is, the choice of prediction is determined by:

$$\begin{aligned} &\text{if } \; |F^A_{00} - F^C_{00}| < |F^A_{00} - F^B_{00}| \\ &\qquad \text{Predict from Block B;} \\ &\text{otherwise} \\ &\qquad \text{Predict from Block C;} \end{aligned} \tag{9.5}$$

The prediction value P^D_{00} of block D is set to the DC coefficient of the chosen block and is subtracted from the actual DC value of the current block. For example, if block C is chosen,

$$\begin{aligned} P^D_{00} &= F^C_{00} \\ R^D_{00} &= F^D_{00} - P^D_{00} \end{aligned} \tag{9.6}$$

The residual R^D_{00} is then coded and transmitted.

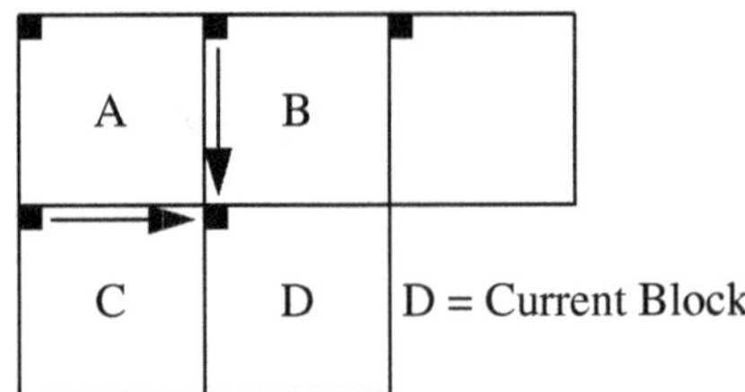

Figure 9-11. Prediction of DC of 8 × 8 DCT Block

We predict the AC coefficients in a similar way as shown in Figure 9-12, with the first row or column predicted in the direction determined by gradients of DC coefficients of (9.5). For example, if the prediction direction is from Block B, we predict the first row of AC coefficients of Block D from the first row of Block B. If the prediction direction is from Block C, we predict the first column of Block D from the first column of Block C.

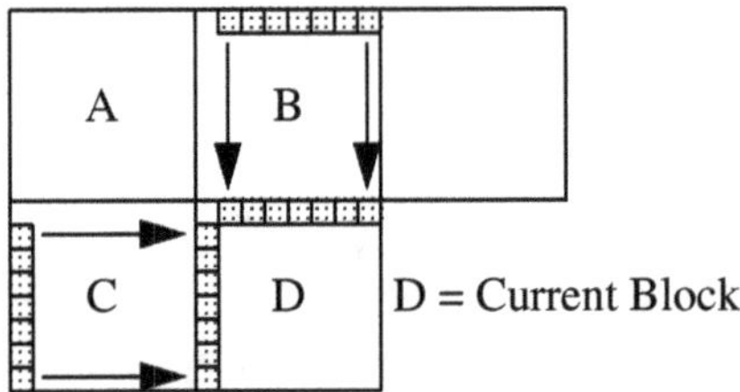

Figure 9-12. Prediction of AC of 8 × 8 DCT Block

9.7.2 Inter-frames

In addition to the techniques used in intra-frame coding, Inter-frame (or nonintra-frame) coding utilizes motion estimation and compensation to improve the compression of videos; it exploits the temporal correlations to make good predictions to reduce data redundancies. There are two types of inter-frames, **predicted frames (P-frames)** and **bidirectional frames (B-frames)**. The difference between P-frames and B-frames is that they use different kinds of reference frames to make predictions. These two kinds of frames and I-frames usually join in a GOP (Group of Pictures), which is often required to synchronize the encoder and decoder, when the encoded data are transmitted over a network and errors may occur. We can use an I-frame as a reliable reference for synchronization as it does not require information from other frames to be decoded. I-frames are also important for random access of compressed video files. Because of these, I-frames are also known as key frames or access points.

P-frames

Starting with an I-frame, we can forward-predict a future frame, which is commonly referred to as a P-frame. We can also use a P-frame to predict other P-frames in the future. Therefore, a P-frame is always predicted from a past frame, a frame that has been coded earlier.

As an example, consider a GOP that has 6 frames. The ordering of the frames will be:

$$I, P, P, P, P, P, I, P, P, P, P, P, \ldots$$

We predict each P-frame in the sequence from the frame immediately preceding it, whether it is an I-frame or a P-frame. The I-frame can be used for synchronization.

B-frames

B-frames are bidirectionally predicted frames. They can be predicted or interpolated from earlier and/or later frames. That is, we not only search a past frame to find the best match but also a future frame to find the optimal result. It is easy to understand making predictions using information of a previously coded frame. *But how do we make predictions from a future frame, something that has not happened?* The trick is that the terms "past" and "future" are artificial; we call the frames occurred before the current frame the past frames and frames occur after the current one, the future frames. To make predictions from a future frame, we must look ahead and buffer it, encoding and decoding it for it to be used as a reference frame. This is called backward prediction. Therefore, if video compression and decompression is to be done in "real time", there must be a time delay between the compression and decompression process if B-frames are used. Figure 9-13 shows various prediction modes for inter-frames.

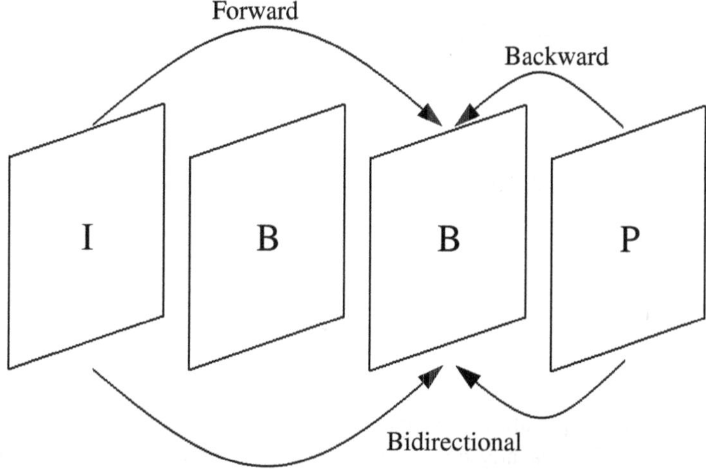

Figure 9-13. Prediction Modes of Inter-frames

9.8 Typical GOP Structure

Figure 9-14 shows a typical group of picture (GOP) structure, "IBBPBBP...". We can categorize the I-frames and P-frames as *anchor frames*, because they may be used as reference frames in the coding of other frames. On the other hand, B-frames are not anchor frames as they are never used as a reference. Note that the structure starts with an I-frame; it is essential to start coding with an I-frame as there is no previous information that can be used for reference in motion estimation.

Figure 9-15 shows a prediction scheme of the GOP structure. We use the I-frame to predict the first P-frame, and use these two frames (I and P) to predict the first and second B-frame. Then we use the first P-frame to predict the second P-frame. The first and second P-frames are joined to predict the third and fourth B-frames.

As you can see from the prediction scheme, we need the fourth frame (P-frame) to predict the second and the third (B-frames). So we need to transmit the P-frame to the decoder before the B-frames and consequently we have to delay the transmission in order to keep the P-frame or to buffer the frames.

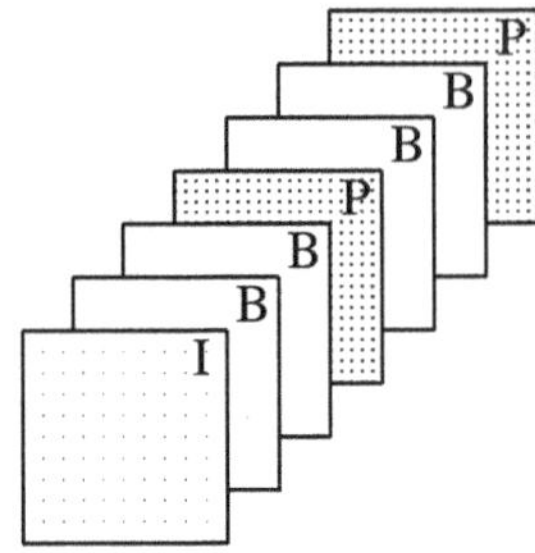

Figure 9-14. A Typical Group of Pictures (GOP)

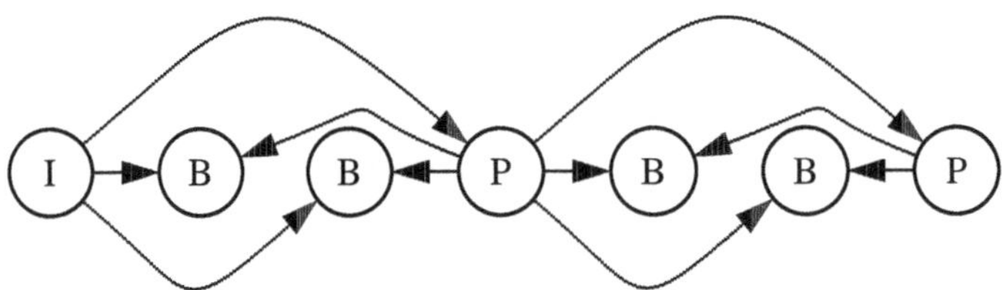

Figure 9-15. A Prediction Scheme for GOP of Figure 9-14

9.9 Rate Control

In many video compression applications, compressed data are sent over a network as bitstreams. The traffic in a large network is usually bursty. It may be idle for some of the time but may have congestion at some other time. This may make available bandwidth to clients change from time to time. Also, if the encoding parameters of a video codec are kept constant, the number of coded bits may change for each macroblock, depending on the video content; this will lead to variations of the output bit rate of the encoder. Typically, high-motion scenes or scenes with fine details generate more bits and low motion or coarse-detail scenes produce fewer bits. These can cause problems in delivering video data and it is necessary for the video encoder to adjust the bit rate to match the available bit rate of the transmission channel.

One simple way to control bit rate is to buffer the encoded data before transmission, which can 'smooth' the impact of fluctuations in the available bandwidth. Figure 9-16 shows a block diagram explaining this mechanism. The variable bit rate output is buffered by a queue, which is first-in first-out (FIFO). The data in the queue are deleted at a constant rate to match the available bandwidth of the delivering channel. Another queue at the receiving end of the channel is used to buffer data to the decoder which deletes the data from the queue at variable bit rate; this is because for the same number of input bits, the decoder may produce a different number of output bits depending on the context of the data. If the decoder needs to produce data at a constant frame rate, it has to consume input bits at a variable rate to counter the variations in the amount of data produced for a given number of bits. Of course, if the fluctuations in the channel capacity or the data context is too large, queues with limited size may not be able to maintain a constant bit rate, but at least the queues can 'smooth' the fluctuations.

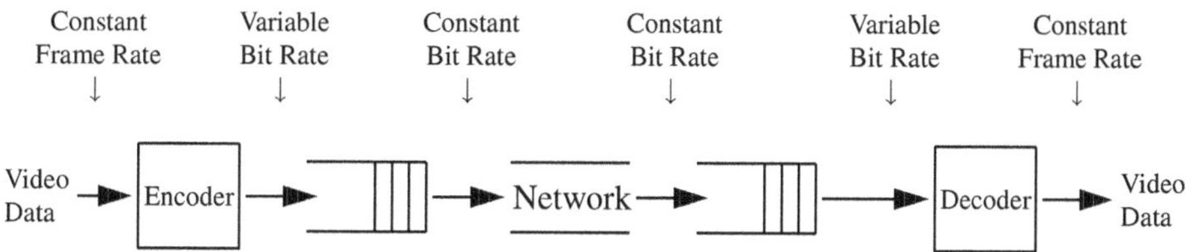

Figure 9-16. Controlling Bit Rate Using Queues

Another way to control the bit rate of the bitstream generated by a video encoder is to vary the encoding parameters from time to time in order to maintain a target bit rate. One important parameter that can change the encoding bit rate is the quantization parameter (Q_p). The encoder can control the bit rate by analyzing the rate at which the encoder is producing data and comparing it with the desired target bit rate. If the encoder is producing too much data, it simply raises Q_p. If too little data is being produced, it lowers Q_p. Note that the larger the Q_p, the better the compression but the lower the quality. There are many different algorithms for varying Q_p depending on the criteria of performance. Some of these algorithms also use the option of dropping frames of video as well as adjusting Q_p. The trade-off of the quality of each frame with the jerkiness in the video caused by frame dropping determines the extent to which we adjust Q_p and the number of frames we want to drop. Alos, the bit rate profiles and characteristics of these algorithms will differ, and often the choice of algorithm is dependent on the network and target application.

9.10 Implementations

We shall discuss the implementation of motion estimation and motion compensation in the next few chapters. We do not intend to cover many of the search algorithms and the prediction methods. We shall only discuss two simple cases, the encoding of the residual between two frames without any motion estimation, and the use of Three Step Search (TSS) to improve upon the encoding.

Chapter 10

Video Programming

10.1 Introduction

In order to experiment with the encoding and decoding of video data, we need to have a way to play the video on a PC. We need some well-developed tools to help us achieve this goal. Ideally, the tools we are going to use are free and platform independent, and hopefully are simple to use. Surprisingly, such tools are available, thanks to the open-source community that provides many high-quality free useful software applications. The main tool that we shall use to play video is the Simple DirectMedia Layer (SDL) (*http://www.libsdl.org*). We also need some tools to process some video files that you can find in Internet and download them to carry out the tests and experiments. There exists a lot of video formats but we do not intend to address all of them; exploring video formats is **not** a goal of this book. Rather, we shall only discuss in detail the relatively simple AVI (Audio Video Interleaved) format and we use it as an intermediate format that we can read and save video data. There exists free utilities that allow us to change AVI files to other video formats and vice versa. To simplify things, we shall also make use of an open-source AVI (Audio Video Interleaved) library that can help us process AVI files.

In this chapter, we shall first use the SDL library to develop a simple video player (without audio part). Our goal of course is to decode the compressed data and render them on the screen. *Can we integrate the decoder and player seamlessly? Could we separate the decoder and the player functionalities so that changing the decoder would not affect the rendering and vice versa?* It turns out that this can be easily handled by the using the paradigm of the producer-consumer problem, which is a well-studied synchronization problem in Computer Science. In this case, the decoder is the producer which provides data and the player is the consumer that consumes the data. To accomplish these, they have to be run using different threads. SDL provides simple thread functions that allow us to implement all these with relative ease. We shall discuss the principles and implementations of the player and related issues in the following sections.

10.2 Simple DirectMedia Layer (SDL)

Simple DirectMedia Layer (SDL) is a cross-platform multimedia library designed to provide low level access to audio, keyboard, mouse, joystick, 3D hardware via OpenGL, and 2D video framebuffer. It is used by MPEG playback software, emulators, and many popular games. It supports Linux, MS Windows and many other platforms. It is ideal to be used in embedded Linux as it is small and does not require X-window to do graphics. Embedded systems frequently have highly constrained resources and can afford neither the program storage space nor the memory footprint of desktop graphics software like X Window, KDE and GNOME. Because of these, SDL has been particularly popular in embedded Linux. It has been applied to a number of Embedded Linux implementations such as Microwindows, Paragui, and Superwaba.

SDL was designed and written by a group of experienced and highly professional game programmers and is supported by a huge collection of good programmers. In summary, it is a lean, portable, well-defined and reliable API (Application Programming Interface) , which is simple to learn and use. It is reported in an article
(*http://gameprogrammer.com/sdl.html*) that the author spent several months writing test programs both as a way to learn SDL and to try to find bugs in SDL. In all that time he only found a couple of minor documentation bugs and what he would call a miss-feature for which there was an easy work around. He tried ridiculous things with SDL, such as writing a program that used 10,000 timers, and wasn't able to break it. Every time he found what he thought was a bug it turned out to be either the result of minor errors in the documentation or the result of his misunderstanding of the documentation. The one time he thought he had found a serious bug in SDL it turned out that it had already been fixed.

SDL can be used in games, emulators, and multimedia applications including the following:

- video: it can set a video at any depth (8 bits per pixel or greater) with optional conversion; write directly to a linear graphics framebuffer; create surfaces with colorkey or alpha blending attributes,
- events: provides event change detection like keyboard input, mouse input; each event can be enabled or disabled with SDL_EventState(),
- audio: set audio playback of 8-bit and 16-bit audio, mono or stereo; audio runs independently in a separate thread, filled via a user callback mechanism; provides complete CD audio control API,
- threads: provides simple thread creation API and simple binary semaphores for synchronization, and
- timers: gets the number of milliseconds elapsed and waits a specified number of milliseconds.

The most important application of SDL, though, is game programming.

The SDL library consists of several sub-APIs, providing cross-platform support for video, audio, input handling, multithreading, OpenGL rendering contexts and other amenities.

10.3 SDL API

The complete SDL API can be found at *http://www.libsdl.org/cgi/docwiki.cgi/SDL_20API.* We discuss here only some of the basic SDL functions that relate to playing videos.

10.3.1 Initializing the Library

We use SDL_Init() to dynamically load and initialize the library. This function takes a set of flags corresponding to the portions you want to activate:

SDL_INIT_AUDIO

SDL_INIT_VIDEO

SDL_INIT_CDROM

SDL_INIT_TIMER

SDL_INIT_EVERYTHING

We use SDL_Quit() to clean up the library when we are done with it. The following are the synopsis and explanations of the the usage of the functions SDL_init(), SDL_Quit(), and SDL_QuitSubSystem(), where "Uint32" refers to data type 32-bit unsigned integer.

Synopsis #include "SDL.h"

int **SDL_Init**(Uint32 flags);

Description Initializes SDL. This should be called before all other SDL functions.

The flags parameter specifies what part(s) of SDL to initialize. (Flags should be bitwise-ORed together, e.g. "SDL_INIT_AUDIO | SDL_INIT_VIDEO".)

SDL_INIT_TIMER	Initializes the timer subsystem.
SDL_INIT_AUDIO	Initializes the audio subsystem.
SDL_INIT_VIDEO	Initializes the video subsystem.
SDL_INIT_CDROM	Initializes the cdrom subsystem.
SDL_INIT_JOYSTICK	Initializes the joystick subsystem.
SDL_INIT_EVERYTHING	Initialize all of the above.
SDL_INIT_NOPARACHUTE	Prevents SDL from catching fatal signals.
SDL_INIT_EVENTTHREAD	Run the event manager in a separate thread.

Returns -1 on error, 0 on success. When error occurred, you can obtain more information about it by calling SDL_GetError().

Synopsis #include "SDL.h"

void **SDL_Quit**(void);

Description Shuts down all SDL subsystems and frees the resources allocated to them.

You can set SDL_Quit as your atexit call for simplicity, like:

atexit(SDL_Quit);

However, it is not advisable to use atexit for large programs or dynamically loaded code.

Returns none

Synopsis #include "SDL.h"

void **SDL_QuitSubSystem** (Uint32 flags);

Description Shuts down a particular component of SDL, leaving others untouched.

Returns none

The following example shows the initialization of SDL audio and video:

```
#include <stdlib.h>
#include "SDL.h"

main(int argc, char *argv[])
{
    if ( SDL_Init(SDL_INIT_AUDIO|SDL_INIT_VIDEO) < 0 ) {
        fprintf(stderr, "Unable to init SDL: %s\n", SDL_GetError());
        exit(1);
    }
    //atexit(SDL_Quit);
    SDL_Quit();
    ...
}
```

10.3.2 Video API

Every personal computer has a video card to process graphical data. There are numerous brands of video cards which differ in structures and functions. To hide the low-level programming details of the video hardware, people introduce the concept of **framebuffer** device, which is an abstraction for the graphic hardware. It represents the frame buffer of some video hardware, and allows application software to access the graphic hardware through a well-defined interface, so that the software doesn't need to know anything about the low-level interface stuff. We may regard framebuffer as an area of memory that describes the image on the computer screen, with each screen pixel corresponding to a memory location.

SDL uses structures called **surfaces** to handle graphical data. A surface can be regarded as a memory block that stores a rectangular region of pixels. Like a framebuffer, a surface has widths, heights, and specific pixel formats. The rectangular region of data of a surface is often referred to as **bitmaps** or **pixmaps**.

SDL surfaces can be copied onto each other efficiently with one-to-one pixel mapping, which is referred to as **block image transfer** or **blit**. Blit operations are important in graphics programming as they allow a portion or complete image to be transferred from a memory buffer working in the background to the display screen effectively. Since the framebuffer can be also regarded as a surface, one can display the entire image on the screen with a single blitting operation. In practice, graphics applications such as video games rely mainly on blits to show the graphics rather than writing to individual pixels one by one. As an example, a video game's artwork is created by artists and saved in files. The game program assembles the images on screen from those predrawn graphics.

Choosing and setting video modes

Before writing to the frame buffer, we need to tell the video card what features we need. We can choose our desired bit-depth and resolution, and set it using the SDL_SetVideoMode() function, which returns an SDL_Surface where all graphics data, including the screen, are stored. You can choose a video mode based on the following information: *Full screen* or *windowed, Screen size, Window properties* (has-border, resize, ..), *Bits per Pixel*, and *Surface type* (software surface, hardware surface).

The following two examples ask for a 640 × 480 screen software surface with a pixel format that is the same as the current display setting:

```
---------------------------------------------------------------------
//Example:
```

```
int options = (
    SDL_ANYFORMAT   |
    SDL_FULLSCREEN |
    SDL_SWSURFACE
);

SDL_Surface *screen = NULL;

screen = SDL_SetVideoMode(640, 480, 0, options);
if (NULL == screen)
{
    printf("Can't set video mode");
    exit(1);
}

//Example:

//setvideo.cpp
//compile by: g++ -o setvideo setvideo.cpp -I/usr/include \
//            -L/usr/local/lib -lSDL
#include <SDL/SDL.h>
#include <stdio.h>
#include <stdlib.h>

int main()
{
  SDL_Surface *screen;

  //initialize video system
  if ( SDL_Init( SDL_INIT_VIDEO ) < 0 ) {
  fprintf(stderr, "Unable to init SDL: %s\n", SDL_GetError());
    exit(1);
  }
  //ensure SDL_Quit is called when the program exits
  atexit(SDL_Quit);

  //set video mode of 640 x 480 with 16-bit pixels
  screen = SDL_SetVideoMode(640, 480, 16, SDL_SWSURFACE);
  if ( screen == NULL ) {
    fprintf(stderr,"Unable to set video:%s\n",SDL_GetError());
    exit(1);
  }

  SDL_Delay ( 2000 ); //delay 2 seconds before exit
  printf("Setting video mode successful!\n");
  return 0;
}
------------------------------------------------------------------------
```

Drawing pixels on the screen

Drawing to the screen is done by writing directly to the graphics framebuffer, and calling the screen update function. Nothing we draw on a software surface is visible until it has been copied from memory to the display buffer on the video card. SDL provides two ways to do that: **SDL_Flip**()

and **SDL_UpdateRect**(). **SDL_Flip**() copies the entire software surface to the screen. If the screen is set to 640×480 at 4 bytes per pixel, **SDL_Flip**() will copy 1.2 megabytes per frame and the frame rate will be limited by how fast our computer can copy images to the screen.

SDL_UpdateRects() is designed to let us use a "dirty pixels" scheme. It lets us specify a list of rectangular areas that have been changed and only copies those areas to the screen. This technique is ideal for a game with a complex background but only a small number of moving or changing items. Tracking dirty pixels can give us a dramatic improvement in performance. **SDL_UpdateRect**() updates one rectangular area.

Synopsis #include "SDL.h"

int **SDL_Flip**(SDL_Surface *screen);

Description Swaps the background and foreground buffers for systems that support double-buffering. For systems not supporting double-buffering, it is the same as SDL_UpdateRect(screen, 0, 0, 0, 0).

Returns none

Synopsis #include "SDL.h"

void **SDL_UpdateRect**(SDL_Surface *screen, Sint32 x, Sint32 y,
Sint32 w, Sint32 h);

Description Makes sure the given area is updated on the given screen. The rectangle must be confined within the screen boundaries (no clipping is done). If 'x', 'y', 'w' and 'h' are all 0, SDL_UpdateRect will update the entire screen.

Returns none

Program Listing 10-1 presents an example that draws a pixel on a screen with arbitrary format. In the program, Uint8, Uint16, and Uint32 represent data types 8-bit, 16-bit and 32-bit unsigned integer (unsigned char, unsigned short, and unsigned int) respectively.

Program Listing 10-1: Drawing a Pixel on Screen

```
------------------------------------------------------------------------
//Example: Drawing a pixel on screen
void DrawPixel(SDL_Surface *screen, Uint8 R, Uint8 G, Uint8 B){
  Uint32 color = SDL_MapRGB(screen->format, R, G, B);

  if ( SDL_MUSTLOCK(screen) )
    if ( SDL_LockSurface(screen) < 0 )
      return;
  switch (screen->format->BytesPerPixel) {
  case 1: { /* Assuming 8-bpp */
    Uint8 *bufp;
    bufp = (Uint8 *)screen->pixels + y*screen->pitch + x;
```

```
    *bufp = color;
  } break;
  case 2: { /* Probably 15-bpp or 16-bpp */
    Uint16 *bufp;
    bufp = (Uint16 *)screen->pixels + y*screen->pitch/2 + x;
    *bufp = color;
  } break;
  case 3: { /* Slow 24-bpp mode, usually not used */
    Uint8 *bufp;
    bufp = (Uint8 *)screen->pixels + y*screen->pitch + x;
    *(bufp+screen->format->Rshift/8) = R;
    *(bufp+screen->format->Gshift/8) = G;
    *(bufp+screen->format->Bshift/8) = B;
  } break;
  case 4: { /* Probably 32-bpp */
    Uint32 *bufp;
    bufp = (Uint32 *)screen->pixels + y*screen->pitch/4 + x;
    *bufp = color;
  } break;
  }
  if ( SDL_MUSTLOCK(screen) )
    SDL_UnlockSurface(screen);
  SDL_UpdateRect(screen, x, y, 1, 1);
}
-----------------------------------------------------------------------
```

Loading and displaying images

SDL provides one single image loading function, **SDL_LoadBMP**() for users to load a Windows BMP image onto an SDL surface. The function returns a pointer to an SDL_Surface structure containing the image, or a NULL pointer for failure of loading the image. The user can then display the loaded image by using **SDL_BlitSurface**() to blit it into the graphics framebuffer. SDL_BlitSurface() automatically clips the blit rectangle, which should be passed to SDL_UpdateRect() to update the portion of the screen, which has changed. Bitmaps use dynamically allocated memory; if no longer needed they should be freed by using the function **SDL_FreeSurface**(). Conversely, the function **SDL_SaveBMP**() allows us to save an SDL surface as a BMP file.

If we need to process images in other popular formats such as **.png, .jpg** or **.gif**, we need to install the **SDL_image**- library. After we have installed it, our program needs to include SDL/SDL_image.h and link with "-lSDL_image". Documentation of this library can be found at *http://jcatki.no-ip.org/SDL_image/SDL*. The library supports BMP, PNM (PPM/PGM/PBM), XPM, LBM, PCX, GIF, JPEG, PNG, TGA, and TIFF formats. We can use the function **IMG_Load**() to load an image onto an SDL surface. It is best to call this function outside of event loops, and keep the loaded images around until you are really done with them. This is because the loading process could be time-consuming. When we have finished using the image, we should use **SDL_FreeSurface**() to free the allocated resources. The usage of **IMG_Load()** is shown below.

Synopsis #include "SDL_image.h"

SDL_Surface *IMG_Load (const char *ifile*);

Description Loads *ifile* for use as an image onto a new SDL_Surface.

Returns A pointer to the new SDL_Surface where the image is loaded.

If we are loading an image to be displayed many times, we can improve blitting speed by converting it to the format of the screen. The function **SDL_DisplayFormat**() does this conversion.

Listing 10-2 presents a complete program that loads an image using **IMG_Load**(). You also need to include the following headers in your program:

```
#include <SDL/SDL.h>
#include <SDL/SDL_image.h>
#include <stdlib.h>
```

Program Listing 10-2: Loading Image using IMG_Load()

```
--------------------------------------------------------------------------
//Example: Loading an Image using IMG_Load()
/*
loadimage.cpp
compile by: g++ -o loadimage loadimage.cpp -I/usr/include \
            -L/usr/local/lib -lSDL -lSDL_image
*/
bool load_image(SDL_Surface *screen, char *image_name,int x,int y){
  SDL_Surface *image;
  SDL_Rect source, offset; //offset is the destination

  image = IMG_Load(  image_name );
  if ( image == NULL ) {
    printf ( "Unable to load image\n" );
    return false;
  }
  source.x = 0;     source.y = 0;
  source.w = image->w; source.h=image->h;//display the whole image
  offset.x = x;     offset.y = y; //position to display the image
  offset.w = image->w;    //width and height here actually NOT used
  offset.h = image->h;

  //Draws image data to the screen:(image,source) is the source,
  //  (screen, offset) is the destination
  SDL_BlitSurface ( image, &source, screen, &offset );
  //free the resources allocated to image
  SDL_FreeSurface ( image );
  return true;
}

int main(){
  SDL_Surface *screen;
  //initialize video system
  if ( SDL_Init( SDL_INIT_VIDEO ) < 0 ) {
        fprintf(stderr, "Unable to init SDL: %s\n", SDL_GetError());
        exit(1); }
  //ensure SDL_Quit is called when the program exits
  atexit(SDL_Quit);
  //set video mode of 640 x 480 with 16-bit pixels
  screen = SDL_SetVideoMode(640, 480, 16, SDL_SWSURFACE);
  if ( screen == NULL ) {
        fprintf(stderr, "Unable to set video: %s\n",SDL_GetError());
```

```
        exit(1);
    }
    //put image near center of screen
    if ( !load_image ( screen, "test-image.gif", 320, 240 ) )
          exit ( 1 );
    //update the entire screen
    SDL_UpdateRect ( screen, 0, 0, 0, 0 );
    SDL_Delay ( 4000 );    //delay 4 seconds before exit
    return 0;
```

10.4 SDL Events

Programs that operate in a GUI environment are event-driven. An event is an action that takes place within a program when something happens. Part of writing a GUI application is to create event listeners. An event listener is an object or a loop that triggers certain action when a specific event occurs. In the SDL programming environment, an event is produced whenever we move or click the mouse, press a key, or resize the SDL video window. Event handling allows our application to receive input from the user. SDL stores unprocessed events in an internal event queue which allows SDL to collect as many events as possible each time it updates an event. Using functions like **SDL_PollEvent, SDL_PeepEvents** and **SDL_WaitEvent** we can observe and handle waiting input events. There are four main categories of events: keyboard, mouse, window, and system-dependent events. Window events handle gaining and losing focus, as well as exit requests. System-dependent events process raw messages from the windowing system that SDL otherwise would ignore. Information of an event is stored in the structure type SDL_Event. The event queue itself is composed of a series of **SDL_Event** unions, one for each waiting event. **SDL_Event** unions are read from the queue with the **SDL_PollEvent** function and it is then up to the application to process the information stored with them. Its definition is shown below.

Synopsis SDL_Event : General event structure, which is a union of all possible event types for receiving events from SDL.

Definition
```
typedef union{                              Uint8 type;
   SDL_ActiveEvent active;                  SDL_KeyboardEvent key;
   SDL_MouseMotionEvent motion;             SDL_MouseButtonEvent button;
   SDL_JoyAxisEvent jaxis;                  SDL_JoyBallEvent jball;
   SDL_JoyHatEvent jhat;                    SDL_JoyButtonEvent jbutton;
   SDL_ResizeEvent resize;                  SDL_ExposeEvent expose;
   SDL_QuitEvent quit;                      SDL_UserEvent user;
   SDL_SysWMEvent syswm;                    } SDL_Event;
```

Description For reading and placing events on the event queue.

The SDL event subsystem is intertwined with the video subsystem. We basically cannot separate the use of them. Therefore, they are both initialized with **SDL_INIT_VIDEO** parameter to **SDL_Init**().

10.4.1 Event Processing

To process an event, we need to read the **SDL_Event** unions from the event queue using the **SDL_PollEvent**() or **SDL_WaitEvent**() function. We can also add events onto the event queue using **SDL_PushEvent**(), which returns 0 on success or -1 on failure. We can wait for events to occur using the SDL_WaitEvent() function, which waits indefinitely and returns only if an event or an error has occurred as explained below. On the other hand, we can peek at events in the event queue without removing them by passing the **SDL_PEEKEVENT** action to **SDL_PeepEvents**().

Synopsis #include "SDL.h"

int **SDL_WaitEvent**(SDL_Event **event*);

Description Waits indefinitely for the next available event.

Returns 0 if there was an error while waiting for events, 1 otherwise.

Information of the event detected will be stored in the structure

pointed by event and the event is removed from the event queue.

The following example, **waitevent.cpp** of Program Listing 10-3 shows how to use **SDL_Wait_Event**() to wait for various events.

Program Listing 10-3: Waiting for an event

```
------------------------------------------------------------------------
//waitevent.cpp: Waiting for an event to occur.
bool wait_for_events () {
  SDL_Event event;
  int status;  char *key;
  bool quit = false;
  printf("waiting for events, press 'q' or 'ESC' to quit\n");
  while ( !quit ) {
    //wait indefinitely for an event to occur
    status = SDL_WaitEvent(&event);
                        //event will be removed from event queue
    if ( !status ) {     //Error has occurred while waiting
       printf("SDL_WaitEvent error: %s\n", SDL_GetError());
       return false;
    }
    switch (event.type) {             //check the event type
      case SDL_KEYDOWN:               //if a key has been pressed
        key = SDL_GetKeyName(event.key.keysym.sym);
        printf("The %s key was pressed!\n", key );
        if (event.key.keysym.sym == SDLK_ESCAPE)//quit if 'ESC'
          quit = true;
        else if ( key[0] == 'q'  )    //quit if 'q'  pressed
          quit = true;
        break;
      case SDL_MOUSEMOTION:           //mouse moved
        printf("Mouse motion x:%d, y:%d\n",
               event.motion.x, event.motion.y );   break;
      case SDL_MOUSEBUTTONUP:         //mouse button pressed
```

```
        printf("Mouse pressed x:%d, y:%d\n",
                event.button.x, event.button.y );  break;
      case SDL_QUIT:                        //'x' of Window clicked
         exit ( 1 );
    }
  } //while
  return true;
}
int main() {
  SDL_Surface *screen;
  if ( SDL_Init( SDL_INIT_VIDEO ) < 0 ) {
    fprintf(stderr, "Unable to init SDL: %s\n", SDL_GetError());
    exit(1);
  }
  //ensure SDL_Quit is called when the program exits
  atexit(SDL_Quit);
  //set video mode of 640 x 480 with 16-bit pixels
  screen = SDL_SetVideoMode(640, 480, 16, SDL_SWSURFACE);
  if ( screen == NULL ) {
    fprintf(stderr, "Unable to set video: %s\n", SDL_GetError());
    exit(1);
  }
  wait_for_events();        return 0;
}
```

We can also poll for events using the **SDL_PollEvent**() function. In addition to handling events directly, each type of event has a function, which allows us to check the application event state. If we use this exclusively, we should ignore all events with the **SDL_EventState**() function, and call **SDL_PumpEvents**() periodically to update the application event state. The following piece of code shows how to poll events and pump events:

```
    //Example: Polling Event State
    { SDL_EventState(SDL_MOUSEMOTION, SDL_IGNORE);}

    void CheckMouseHover(void)
    { int mouse_x, mouse_y;
      SDL_PumpEvents();
      SDL_GetMouseState(&mouse_x, &mouse_y);
      if ( (mouse_x < 32) && (mouse_y < 32) )
       printf("Mouse in upper left hand corner!\n");
    }

    //Example: Pumping events.
    { SDL_EventState(SDL_MOUSEMOTION, SDL_IGNORE); }

    void CheckMouseHover(void) {
      int mouse_x, mouse_y;
      SDL_PumpEvents();
      SDL_GetMouseState(&mouse_x, &mouse_y);
      if ( (mouse_x < 32) && (mouse_y < 32) )
        printf("Mouse in upper left hand corner!\n");
    }
```

10.5 SDL Threads

The effective use of threads is very important in modern programming. It allows a program to execute multiple parts of itself simultaneously in the same address space. In many cases, we basically cannot accomplish the tasks without using threads. For instance, consider a game program that needs to accept inputs from the mouse and keyboard, and at the same time has to play music at the background and generate some special sounds at various stages; it will be extremely difficult if not impossible to achieve these effects in our program without using threads. Of course, we use threads only when we have to. We are not replacing simple nonthreaded programs with fancy, complex, threaded ones. Threads are just one more way we can use to make our programming tasks easier. The main benefits of using threads in programming include the following:

- gaining performance from multiprocessor hardware,
- easier programming for jobs with multi-tasks,
- increasing job throughput by overlapping I/O tasks with computational tasks,
- more effective use of system resources by sharing resources between threads,
- using only one binary to run on both uniprocessors and multiprocessors,
- creating well-structured programs, and
- maintaining a single source for multiple platforms.

Multithreaded applications are ubiquitous in modern computing systems. For example, a Web server makes use of threads to dramatically improve performance and interactivity. Typically, a Web server receives requests from remote clients for Web pages, images, multimedia data and other information; the Web server has one main thread listening to the requests and creates a seperate thread to service each request. Upon receiving a request, the main thread spawns a new thread that interprets the request, retrieves the specified Web pages and transmits the data to the client (typically a Web browser). After spawning a new thread, the main thread (the parent) can continue to listen for new requests. If the Web server runs on a multiprocessor system, it can receive and fulfill several requests at the same time by creating different threads, and thus improves both the throughput and response time of the system. Another commonly cited example that makes use of threads to enhance user productivity and improve interactivity is a word processor, which uses one thread to accept commands from a user and another thread to carry out the commands at the background. For example, many modern word processors detect mispelled words as they are typed and periodically save a copy of the document to disk to prevent loss of data. Each feature is implemented with a separate thread; consequently, the word processor can respond to keyboard interrupts even if one or more of its threads are blocked because of other I/O activities (e.g. saving a copy of the document to disk).

10.5.1 What Are Threads

A thread is also referred to as a **light weight process** (**LWP**). A process is a program in execution. It is a unit of work in a modern time-sharing system. You can create several processes from the same program. A process not only includes the program code, which is sometimes referred to as the text section, but also the current activities and consumed resources including the program counter, processor registers, the process stack (which contains temporary data such as function parameters, return address, and local variable), and the data section, which contains global variables. A process may also have a heap, which is the memory dynamically allocated to it during run time.

A **thread** is a basic unit of CPU utilization, comprising a **thread ID**, a **program counter**, a **register set**, and a **stack**. It shares with its other threads of the same process its code section, data section, and other operating-system resources, such as open files, signals, and global variables. The various states of a thread can be represented by Figure 10-1, where quantum refers to the time the computer allocated to run a thread before switching to running another thread.

10.5.2 Pthreads

IEEE defines a POSIX standard API, referred to as **Pthreads** (IEEE 1003.1c), for thread creation and synchronization. Many contemporary systems, including Linux, Solaris, and Mac OS X implement Pthreads. To use Pthreads in your program, you must include **pthread.h** and link with **-l pthread**. The following exmaple, **pthreads_demo.cpp** of Listing 10-4 shows how to use Pthreads.

Program Listing 10-4: Pthread Example

```
-----------------------------------------------------------------------
/*
  pthreads_demo.cpp
  A very simple example demonstrating the usage of pthreads.
  Compile: g++ -o pthreads_demo pthreads_demo.cpp -lpthread
  Execute: ./pthreads_demo
*/
#include <pthread.h>
#include <stdio.h>
using namespace std;

//The thread
void *runner ( void *data )
{
  char *tname = ( char * )data;

  printf("I am %s\n", tname );

  pthread_exit ( 0 );
}

int main ()
{
  pthread_t id1, id2;              //thread identifiers
  pthread_attr_t attr1, attr2;     //set of thread attributes
  char *tnames[2] = { "Thread 1", "Thread 2" }; //names of threads

  //get the default attributes
  pthread_attr_init ( &attr1 );
  pthread_attr_init ( &attr2 );

  //create the threads
  pthread_create ( &id1, &attr1, runner, tnames[0] );
  pthread_create ( &id2, &attr2, runner, tnames[1] );

  //wait for the threads to exit
  pthread_join ( id1, NULL );
  pthread_join ( id2, NULL );

  return 0;
}
-----------------------------------------------------------------------
```

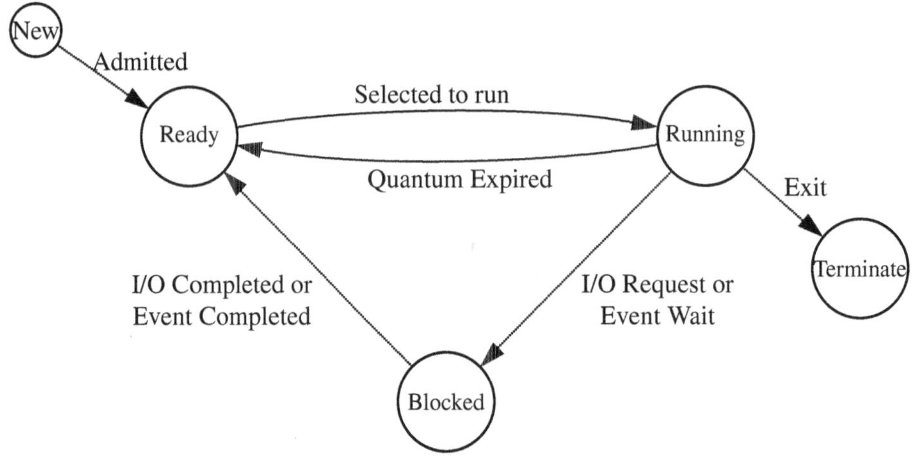

Figure 10-1. States of a Thread

In the example of **pthreads_demo.cpp** shown in Program Listing 10-4, we use **pthread_tid** to declare the identifiers for the threads we are going to create. Each thread has a set of attributes containing information about the thread such as stack size and scheduling information. We use **pthread_attr_t** to declare the attributes of the threads and set the attributes in the function called by **pthread_attr_init**(). As we did not explicitly set any attributes, the default attributes will be used. The function **pthread_create**() is used to create a separate thread. In addition to passing the thread identifier and the attributes to the thread, we also pass the name of the function, *runner*, where the new thread will begin execution. The last argument passed to **pthread_create**() in the example is a string parameter containing the name of the thread. At this point, the program has three threads: the initial parent thread in **main**() and two child threads in **runner**(). After creating the child threads, the **main**() thread will wait for the **runner**() threads to complete by calling the **pthread_join**() function.

Pthreads specification has a rich set of functions, allowing users to develop very sophisticated multithreaded programs. In the applications discussed here, we do not need to use many of the Pthread functions. So instead we will use SDL threads, which are much simpler and only consist of a few functions. Moreover, SDL is platform independent. Besides POSIX threads, different crucial thread programming schemes exist in the market. MS Windows has its own threading interface which is very different from POSIX threads. Though Sun's Solaris supports Pthreads, it also has its own thread API. Other UNIX systems may also have their own thread APIs. SDL solves this inconsistency with its own set of portable threading functions.

10.5.3 SDL Thread Programming

The mechanisms of using SDL Threads are basically the same as that of Pthreads. The thread functions are similar except that the names are different. We start new threads with the **SDL_CreateThread**() function, which returns a thread handle of type **SDL_Thread** for subsequent thread operations. The above Pthreads example can be rewritten using SDL threads as shown in Listing 10-5. The code is similar to and a little simpler than the Pthreads code of Listing 10-4. The **SDL_WaitThread**() function works in the same way as the Pthreads **pthread_join**(), which waits a thread to complete. We need to do a **-lpthread** link in compilation because some of the SDL thread implementations are based on the Pthreads libraries.

As mentioned above, the SDL's threading API is a simplified set of threading functions. Its implementation is somewhat incomplete. For example, SDL does not allow a program to change a thread's scheduling priority or other low-level attributes. Actually, these features are highly system-dependent and supporting them would be difficult to make SDL platform independent. For many video applications, the SDL's threading API is sufficient. The following shows the detailed usage of some of the basic threading functions of SDL.

Synopsis #include "SDL.h"

#include "SDL_thread.h"

SDL_Thread ***SDL_CreateThread**(int (**fn*)(void *), void **data*);

Description Creates a new thread of execution that shares all of its parent's global memory, signal handlers, file descriptors, etc, and runs the function fn(), which utilizes the void pointer data passing to it. The thread quits when fn() returns.

Returns A pointer to the thread of type SDL_Thread.

Synopsis #include "SDL.h"

#include "SDL_thread.h"

void **SDL_KillThread** (SDL_Thread **thread*);

Description racelessly terminates the thread associated with the thread. You should avoid using it to terminate a thread. If possible, use some other form of IPC to signal the thread to quit.

Returns None

Synopsis #include "SDL.h"

#include "SDL_thread.h"

void **SDL_WaitThread**(SDL_Thread **thread*, int **status*);

Description Waits for a thread to finish (timeouts are not supported).

Returns The return code for the thread function is placed in the area pointed to by status, if status is not NULL.

Program Listing 10-5: Example of SDL Thread Programming

```
-----------------------------------------------------------------------
/*
  sdlthreads_demo.cpp
  A very simple example demonstrating the usage of sdl threads.
  Compile:g++ -o sdlthread_demo sdlthread_demo.cpp -lSDL -lpthread
  Execute:  ./sdlthread_demo
*/
#include <SDL/SDL.h>
#include <SDL/SDL_thread.h>
#include <stdio.h>
```

```
using namespace std;

//The thread
int runner ( void *data )
{
  char *tname = ( char * )data;
  printf("I am %s\n", tname );
  return 0;
}

int main ()
{
  SDL_Thread *id1, *id2;                    //thread identifiers
  char *tnames[2] = { "Thread 1", "Thread 2" }; //names of threads

  //create the threads
  id1 = SDL_CreateThread ( runner, tnames[0] );
  id2 = SDL_CreateThread ( runner, tnames[1] );

  //wait for the threads to exit
  SDL_WaitThread ( id1, NULL );
  SDL_WaitThread ( id2, NULL );

  return 0;
}
-----------------------------------------------------------------------
```

The following table lists all the SDL Thread functions:

Table 10-1 SDL Threading Functions

Functions	Descriptions
SDL_CreateThread()	Creates a new thread that shares its parent's properties.
SDL_ThreadID()	Gets the 32-bit thread identifier for the current thread.
SDL_GetThreadID()	Gets the SDL thread ID of a SDL_Thread
SDL_WaitThread()	Waits for a thread to finish.
SDL_KillThread()	Gracelessly terminates the thread.
SDL_CreateMutex()	Creates a mutex.
SDL_DestroyMutex()	Destroys a mutex.
SDL_mutexP()	Locks a mutex.
SDL_mutexV()	Unlocks a mutex.
SDL_CreateSemaphore()	Creates a new semaphore and assigns an initial value to it.
SDL_DestroySemaphore()	Destroys a semaphore that was created by SDL_CreateSemaphore.
SDL_SemWait()	Locks a semaphore; suspends the thread if semaphore value is zero.
SDL_SemTryWait()	Attempts to lock a semaphore but does not suspend thread.
SDL_SemWaitTimeout()	Locks a semaphore; waits up to a specified maximum time.
SDL_SemPost()	Unlocks a semaphore.
SDL_SemValue()	Returns the current value of a semaphore.
SDL_CreateCond()	Creates a condition variable.
SDL_DestroyCond()	Destroys a condition variable.
SDL_CondSignal()	Resumes a thread waiting on a condition variable.
SDL_CondBroadcast()	Resumes all threads waiting on a condition variable.
SDL_CondWait()	Waits on a condition variable.
SDL_CondWaitTimeout()	Waits on a condition variable, with timeout Time.

10.6 A Simple PPM Viewer

We have discussed the reading and writing of PPM files in Chapter 4. Here we want to develop a program that displays the image of a PPM file on the screen so that we can visually compare images before and after compression directly. It is surprisingly simple to use SDL to render an image. The program **ppmviewer.cpp** presented in Listing 10-6 accomplishes the task. The program is a slight modification of the PPM demo program, **ppmdemo.cpp** of Listing 4-1 discussed in Chapter 4. A few lines of codes related to SDL are added to display a PPM image. An SDL surface is created using the SDL function **SDL_SetVideoMode**(), and we use the variable *screen* to point to the newly created surface. After loading the image data into the memory buffer *ibuf*, we simply point the framebuffer to the data buffer, which is done by the statement "screen→pixels = ibuf;". There is a catch here. While PPM saves image data in the order red, green, and blue, SDL processes data in the opposite order, blue, green and red. To make things consistent, we provide the function **ppm2sdl**() that converts the PPM format to SDL format. After making the conversion, the function **SDL_UpdateRect**() is used to send the data to the screen efficiently. **SDL_Delay**() is called to delay the program exit by four seconds. In other words, the image will be displayed for four seconds on the screen.

Program Listing 10-6: Viewing PPM Images Using SDL

```
/* ppmviewer.cpp
 * Demostrate rendering a PPM file.
 * Slight modification of ppmdemo.cpp; SDL is used to display image.
 *
 * Compile: g++ -o ppmviewer ppmviewer.cpp -L/usr/local/lib -lSDL
 * Execute: ./ppmviewer
 */

#include <stdio.h>
#include <stdlib.h>
#include <SDL/SDL.h>

//A public class is the same as a 'struct'
class CImage {
public:
  unsigned char red;
  unsigned char green;
  unsigned char blue;
};

void ppm_read_comments ( FILE *fp )
{
  int c;
  while ( (c = getc ( fp ) )  == '#' ) {
    while (  getc( fp )  != '\n' )
;
  }
  ungetc ( c, fp );
}

class ppm_error
{
  public:
    ppm_error() {
      printf("\nIncorrect PPM format!\n");
      exit ( 1 );
    }
};


//change from (R, G, B) to (B, G, R)
void  ppm2sdl  ( CImage *ibuf, int width, int height )
{
  unsigned char temp;

  for ( int i = 0; i < height; ++i ) {
    int row_offset = i * width;
    for ( int j = 0; j < width; ++j ){
      int offset =  row_offset + j;
      temp = ibuf[offset].red;
      ibuf[offset].red = ibuf[offset].blue;
      ibuf[offset].blue = temp;
    }
  }
}
```

```
int main()
{
  int ppmh[20], c;              //PPM header
  int width, height;         //image width and height
  SDL_Surface *screen;
  char filename[] = "../data/beach.ppm"; //hard-coded filename

  FILE *input = fopen (filename, "rb");  //PPM file for testing read
  if ( !input ) {
    printf("\nError opening input file!\n");
    return 1;
  }

  //read PPM input file
  ppm_read_comments ( input );  //read comments
  char temp[100];
  fscanf ( input, "%2s", temp );
  temp[3] = 0;
  if ( strncmp ( temp, "P6", 2 ) )
    throw ppm_error();
  ppm_read_comments ( input );
  fscanf ( input, "%d", &width );
  ppm_read_comments ( input );
  fscanf ( input, "%d", &height );
  ppm_read_comments ( input );
  int colorlevels;
  fscanf ( input, "%d", &colorlevels );
  printf("\n%s PPM file: ", temp );
  printf(" \n\twidth=%d\theight=%d\tcolorlevles=%d\n", width,
             height,colorlevels+1 );
  ppm_read_comments ( input );
  while (( c = getc ( input )) == '\n');//get rid of extra returns
  ungetc ( c ,input );

  // May use CImage ibuf[width][height] if we do not use SDL_QUIT;
  CImage *ibuf = (CImage *) malloc ( width * height * 3 );
  fread ( ibuf,  3, width * height, input );   //read image data
  fclose ( input );

  //initialize video system
  if ( SDL_Init( SDL_INIT_VIDEO ) < 0 ) {
    fprintf(stderr, "Unable to init SDL: %s\n", SDL_GetError());
    exit(1);
  }
  //ensure SDL_Quit is called when the program exits
  atexit(SDL_Quit);//if not use this, we need to
                 //  do house cleaning manually when program ends

  //set video mode of width x height with 24-bit pixels
  screen = SDL_SetVideoMode( width, height, 24, SDL_SWSURFACE);
  if ( screen == NULL ) {
      fprintf(stderr, "Unable to set %dx%d video: %s\n", width,
                height, SDL_GetError());
      exit(1);
```

```
  }

  //convert PPM format (R, G, B)  to SDL format (B, G, R)
  ppm2sdl ( ibuf,  width, height );

  screen->pixels = ibuf;  //point framebuffer to data buffer
  //  ibuf needs to be dynamically allocated if SDL_QUIT is used
  SDL_UpdateRect ( screen, 0, 0, 0, 0 );    //blit data to screen

  SDL_Delay ( 4000 );      //delay 4 seconds before exit
  printf("Displaying PPM image %s successful!\n", filename );

  //do NOT free(ibuf) if use SDL_QUIT which does the house cleaning
  return 0;
}
-------------------------------------------------------------------
```

10.7 The Producer-Consumer Problem

The program **ppmviewer.cpp** presented in the previous section is a single-threaded program. We can modify it to a "video player" by adding a loop in **main**() to display a sequence of images: it reads in the image data from a file and saves it in the buffer *ibuf*, points the framebuffer to the data buffer, blits the data to the screen, waits for a fixed period of time, and repeats the process by reading in another set of image data. Such a "video player" is very inflexible. The whole program is dedicated to a single task, reading and displaying images. It cannot do other things like playing music or accepting inputs. If we add a decoder in the loop, it becomes difficult to synchronize the displaying speed and the decoding speed. We can overcome these shortcomings by changing the program to a multi-threaded program, and using the producer-consumer concept to handle the synchronization between decoding and rendering.

The producer-consumer problem is a common paradigm for thread synchronization. A **producer** thread produces information which is consumed by a **consumer** thread. This is in analog with whats happening in a fast-food restaurant. The chef produces food items and put them on a shelf; the customers consume the food items from the shelf. If the chef makes food too fast and the shelf is full, she must wait. On the other hand, if the customers consume food too fast and the shelf is empty, the customers must wait.

To allow producer and consumer threads to run concurrently (simultaneously), we must make available a buffer that can hold a number of item and **shared** by the two threads; the producer fills the buffer with items while the consumer empties it. A producer can produce an item while the consumer is consuming another item. Trouble arises when the producer wants to put a new item in the buffer, which is already full. The solution is for the producer to go to sleep, to be awakened when the consumer has removed one or more items. Similarly, if the consumer wants to remove an item from the buffer and finds it empty, it goes to sleep until the producer puts something in the buffer and wakes the consumer up. The **unbounded-buffer** producer-consumer problem places no practical limit on the size of the buffer. The consumer may have to wait for new items, but the producer can always produce new items without waiting. The **bounded-buffer** producer-consumer problem puts a limit on the buffer size; the consumer must wait when it is empty, and the producer must wait when the buffer is full.

The approach sounds simple enough, but if not properly handled, the two threads may **race** to access the buffer and the final outcome depends on who runs first. There is a simple technique to resolve the *race conditions*. E.W. Dijkstra introduced the concept of **semaphore** to handle synchronization problems in 1965. A semaphore is an integer variable associated with two operations, *down* and *up*, a generalization of *sleep* and *wakeup*, respectively. The *down* operation checks if the semaphore value is greater than 0. If yes, it decrements it and continues; if the semaphore value is 0, the thread is put on sleep. Checking the value, changing it, and possibly going to sleep are all done in a single, indivisible, **atomic action**. This it to guarantee that once a semaphore operation has started, no other thread can access the semaphore until the operation has completed or blocked. SDL provides semaphore operations, **SDL_SemPost()**, and **SDL_SemWait()** corresponding to the *up* and *down* operations we just mentioned.

The program **proconsumer.cpp** presented in Listing 10-7 is a simple example of using SDL threads as well as an example of solving the producer-consumer problem using semaphores. The program uses three semaphores, *nfilled*, *nempty*, and *mutex* to do synchronization, with *nfilled* used for counting the number of slots that are filled, *nempty* for counting the number of empty slots, and *mutex* to ensure the producer and consumer do not access the buffer at the same time. *nfilled* initially has a value of 0; *nempty* has an initial value equal to the number of slots in the buffer, and *mutex* has an initial value of 1. In general, the variable *mutex* refers to **mutual exclusion**, which is initialized to 1 and used by two or more threads to ensure only one of them can access a certain piece of code referred to as a critical section. This kind of special semaphore is called a **binary semaphore**; if each thread does a *wait* (down) operation just before entering the critical section and a *post* (up) operation just after leaving it, mutual exclusion is guaranteed.

In the program, the buffer we use is a circular queue. The producer inserts an item at the tail of the queue and the consumer removes an item at the head of it. We advance the tail and head pointers after an insert and a remove operation respectively. The pointers wrap around when they reach the "end" of the queue. This concept is illustrated in Figure 10-2.

Program Listing 10-7: Solving Producer-Consumer Problem Using Semaphores

```
--------------------------------------------------------------------------
/*
  proconssumer.cpp
  An example of using SDL threads and semaphores.
  The producer-consumer problem using semaphores.
  Compile:  g++ -o proconsumer proconsumer.cpp -lSDL -lpthread
  Execute:  ./proconsumer
*/
#include <SDL/SDL.h>
#include <SDL/SDL_thread.h>
#include <stdio.h>
#include <stdlib.h>
using namespace std;

#define N     5              //number of slots in buffer
SDL_sem *mutex;              //controls access to critical region
SDL_sem *nempty;             //counts number of empty slots
SDL_sem *nfilled;            //counts number of filled slots
int buffer[N];

int produce_item()
{
  int n = rand() % 1000;
  return n;
}
void insert_item ( int item )
{
  static int tail = 0;
```

```
  buffer[tail] = item;
  printf("insert %d at %d", item, tail );
  tail = ( tail + 1 ) % N;
}

int producer ( void *data )   //a producer thread
{
  int item;
  char *tname = ( char *) data;     //thread name
  while ( true ) {
    SDL_Delay ( rand() % 1000 );    //random delay
    printf("\n%s : ", tname );
    item = produce_item();          //produce an item
    SDL_SemWait ( nempty );         //decrement empty count
    SDL_SemWait ( mutex );          //entering critical section
    insert_item ( item );
    SDL_SemPost ( mutex );          //leave Critical Section
    SDL_SemPost ( nfilled );        //increment nfilled
  }
  return 0;
}

int remove_item ()
{
  static int head = 0;
  int item;
  item = buffer[head];
  printf("remove %d at %d", item, head );
  head = ( head + 1 ) % N;
  return item;
}

int consumer ( void *data ) //a consumer thread
{
  int item;
  char *tname = ( char * ) data;    //thread name

  while ( true ) {
    SDL_Delay ( rand() % 1000 );    //random delay
    SDL_SemWait ( nfilled );        //decrement filled count
    SDL_SemWait ( mutex );          //entering critical section
    printf("\n%s : ", tname );
    item = remove_item ();          //take item from buffer
    SDL_SemPost ( mutex );          //leave Critical Section
    SDL_SemPost ( nempty );         //increment empty slot count
    //can do something with item here
  }
}

int main () {
  SDL_Thread *id1, *id2, *id3;          //thread identifiers
  char *tnames[3] = { "Producer", "Consumer" }; //names of threads

  mutex = SDL_CreateSemaphore ( 1 );  //initialize mutex to 1
```

```
  nempty = SDL_CreateSemaphore ( N ); //initially all slots empty
  nfilled  = SDL_CreateSemaphore ( 0 );  //no slot filled
  id1 = SDL_CreateThread ( producer, tnames[0] );
  id2 = SDL_CreateThread ( consumer, tnames[1] );
  //wait for the threads to exit
  SDL_WaitThread ( id1, NULL );
  SDL_WaitThread ( id2, NULL );
  return 0;
}
```

The program can be compiled with the command,

```
$g++ -o proconsumer proconsumer.cpp -lSDL -lpthread
```

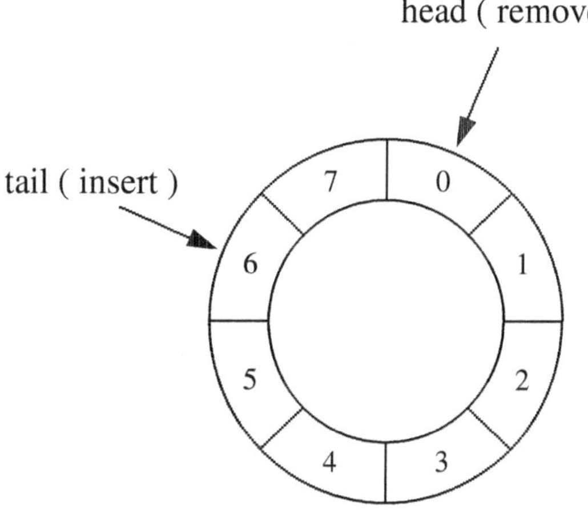

Figure 10-2. Circular Queue with Eight Slots

The following are sample outputs of the program when we execute **proconsumer**:

Table 10-2 Sample Outputs of **proconsumer**

```
Producer : insert 777 at 0
Consumer : remove 777 at 0
Producer : insert 335 at 1
Consumer : remove 335 at 1
Producer : insert 649 at 2
Producer : insert 362 at 3
Producer : insert 690 at 4
Consumer : remove 649 at 2
Producer : insert 926 at 0
Producer : insert 426 at 1
Producer : insert 736 at 2
Consumer : remove 362 at 3
Producer : insert 567 at 3
%Consumer : remove 690 at 4
%Producer : insert 530 at 4
%Consumer : remove 926 at 0
%Consumer : remove 426 at 1
%Consumer : remove 736 at 2
%Producer : insert 929 at 0
%Consumer : remove 567 at 3
%Consumer : remove 530 at 4
```

10.8 Using Condition Variables

We have seen that semaphores are elegant tools, which can be conveniently used to solve many synchronization problems. However, for many other problems, it is cumbersome to use semaphores and their solutions expressed in semaphores could be complex. Therefore, many computing systems provide an additional construct called *condition variable* for concurrent programming. A *condition variable* is a queue of threads (or processes) waiting for some sort of notifications. This construct has been supported by POSIX, SDL, and Win-32 events in C/C++ programming environments. As a matter of fact, the Java utility library and the mobile phone Android platform also provide support of this construct.

A condition variable queue can only be accessed with two methods associated with its queue. These methods are typically called **wait** and **signal**. The **signal** method is also referred to as **notify** in Java. This tool provides programmers a convenient way to implement guarded commands. Threads waiting for a guard to become true to enter the queue. Threads that change the guard from false to true could wake up the waiting threads in the queue.

The following figure of code segments shows the general approach presented in guarded commands and an outline of implementation using SDL functions. The code shows that the execution of statements is protected by a guard, which is shown on the left side of the figure. The notation means that the operations enclosed by the square brackets are executed only when the expression ecnclosed by parenthisis and following **when**, known as the *guard*, is true; the statements enclosed by the square brackets, known as the *command sequence*, are effectively executed simultaneously.

In the implementation, to evaluate a guard safely, a thread must mutually exclude all other threads evaluating it. This is accomplished by declaring a condition variable, (*condVar* in the example), which always associate with a lock (*mutex* in the example). The thread first locks the lock *mutex* to achieve mutual exclusion. If the guard is true, the thread can execute the command sequence, still locking *mutex*. It unlocks *mutex* only when all statements of the command sequence have been executed.

An interesting situation arises when the guard is false, which makes the thread execute the **wait**() method of the condition variable *condVar*; the operation puts the thread in the queue of the condition variable and the thread is suspended. It seems that the thread would wait forever in the queue as the guard is locked by *mutex* and no other thread can access it. But what we want is that the thread waits until the guard becomes true. Here is what the condition variable comes into play. Right before the thread enters the queue and gets suspended, it **unlocks** *mutex* temporarily so that another thread can change the value of the guard. The thread that changes the guard from false to true is also responsible for waking up the waiting thread.

Guarded Command

```
When ( guard ) [
    statement 1
    .....


    statement n
]
```

SDL Implementation

```
SDL_bool condition = SDL_FALSE;
SDL_mutex *mutex;
SDL_cond *condVar;
.....
SDL_LockMutex ( mutex );
while ( !condition )
   SDL_CondWait ( condVar, mutex );
statement 1;
.....
statement n;
SDL_UnlockMutex ( mutex ); ‘
```

So the **wait**() method of a condition variable works in the following way.

1. It causes the current thread to wait until it is signaled or interrupted.
2. The lock associated with the condition variable is atomically released and the current thread is suspended until one of four events happens:
   (a) Some other thread executes the **signal**() method of this condition variable and the current thread happens to be selected from the queue as the thread to be awakened.
   (b) Some other thread executes the **signalAll**() method of this condition variable, which wakes up all waiting threads in the queue.
   (c) The current thread is interrupted by some other thread, and interruption of thread suspension is supported.
   (d) An event of *spurious wakeup* occurs.

   In any of the four cases when the current thread wakes up, before the method returns, the thread must re-acquire the lock associated with the condition variable. This guarantees that the thread works in the same way when the guard is true at the beginning.

The following code segment shows the situation that the guard is modified by a thread.

Guarded Command

```
//code modifying guard
    .....
```

SDL Implementation

```
SDL_LockMutex(mutex);
.....
condition = SDL_TRUE;
.....
SDL_CondSignal ( condVar );
SDL_UnlockMutex ( mutex );
```

In SDL, the **wait** method is called **SDL_CondWait** and the **signal** method is called **SDL_CondSignal**. The variable *mutex*, short for *mutual exclusion*, acts like a lock for accessing critical resources.

10.9 A Multi-threaded Raw Video Player

In this section, we put together what we have learned to develop a simple multi-threaded video player. Our concern here is to illustrate the concept of playing video data in an effective way. To simplify things, we hard-code the dimensions of a frame and assume that there's no compression in the data. We shall see that we can easily generalize the player to accommodate encoded data and data attributes.

A single-thread raw video player is easy to implement: it just sits in a main loop to read in the video data and blits them to the screen, waits for a while and repeats the data reading and blitting. In practice, a player has to handle various tasks besides blitting data on the screen. It may have to decode the data or to process the audio; a single-threaded player tangles all the tasks together and one needs to worry about the coordination between various tasks. On the other hand, a multi-threaded program can handle these tasks much better, as playing data (sending data to screen) can be cleanly separated from other tasks. The following section describes how to develop a multi-threaded program named **tplayer.cpp** to play raw video data. The program and the sample raw data can be downloaded from this book's web site at *http://www.forejune.com/vcompress*.

In its simplest form, besides **main**(), our multi-threaded player needs two threads, one for sending data to the screen and one for 'decoding' data (at this moment, 'decoding' is simply reading from the file); suppose we name these threads **player**() and **decoder**() respectively. This becomes a classical producer-consumer problem. Here, **decoder**() is the producer which produces resources (video data) and **player**() is the consumer which consumes resources (video data).

As discussed above, in the producer-consumer problem, to allow producer and consumer threads to run concurrently, we must have available a buffer for holding items that can be filled by the producer and emptied by the consumer. A producer can produce zero or more items while the consumer is consuming an item; the number of items that can be produced or consumed depends on the production rate as well as the consumption rate and other factors that may influence the production and consumption operations. The producer and consumer must be synchronized, so that the consumer does not try to consume an item that has not yet been produced and the producer suspends production when the buffer is full as there will not be any space to hold the produced item. Therefore, the producer (**decoder**()) must wait when the buffer is full and the consumer (**player**()) must wait when the buffer is empty.

Typically, when the buffer is empty, the consumer goes to sleep and when the producer has finished producing an item and put it in the buffer, it is responsible to wake up the consumer. On the other hand, when the buffer is full, the producer goes to sleep and the consumer is responsible to wake up the producer after it has consumed an item. These can be implemented using the SDL semaphores and condition variables discussed above.

In our implementation, we create a buffer that can hold four frames of video data:

```
const int NSlots = 4;
char *buf[NSlots];
for ( int i = 0; i < NSlots; ++i ) {
    buf[i] = ( char * ) malloc ( frameSize );
    assert ( buf[i] );
}
```

The buffer *buf* acts as a circular queue. As usual, we maintain two pointers, *head* and *tail* like those in Figure 10-2 to manage the queue. Data are entered into the queue at the 'rear' where *tail* points at and are deleted (consumed) at the front where *head* points at. Each time, an item is produced, *tail* is advanced by 1 and when an item is consumed, *head* is advanced. When *head* equals *tail*, indicating that the buffer is empty, the **player**() thread must wait:

```
while ( !quit ) {
   SDL_LockMutex (mutex); //CondWait releases mutex before sleep
   while ( head == tail && !quit )    //shared Buffer empty
     SDL_CondWait (condVar, mutex);
   if ( head == tail ){               //no more data
     SDL_CondSignal ( condVar );
     SDL_UnlockMutex ( mutex );
     return 0;
   }
   SDL_UnlockMutex ( mutex );
   ....
}
```

When *tail* is 4 ahead of *head*, it implies that the buffer is full and **decoder**() must wait:

```
while ( !quit ) {
   SDL_LockMutex (mutex); //CondWait releases mutex before sleep
   while ( head == tail && !quit )  //shared Buffer empty
     SDL_CondWait ( condVar, mutex );
   ....
}
```

Modulo *NSlots* is taken on *head* and *tail* to point to the actual buffer location. Also, the SDL function **SDL_GetTicks**() is used to give an estimate of the time delay between two frames as shown in the following piece of code where a frame rate of 20 frames per second (fps) is assumed:

```
Uint32 prev_time, current_time;
current_time = SDL_GetTicks();          //ms since library starts
if ( current_time - prev_time < 50 ) //20 fps ~ 50 ms / frame
   SDL_Delay ( 50 - ( current_time - prev_time ) );
prev_time = current_time;
```

The variable *quit* is global. All threads check the state of *quit* periodically; if it is **true**, the threads terminate. (The producer thread sets *quit* to **true** when there is no more data. The consumer thread needs to empty the buffer, consuming all data before terminating.) It is set to **true** when the key 'ESC' or 'q' is pressed or when there are no more data. The complete code of **tplayer.cpp** can be found in the web site of this book. You may compile it with the command:

```
$g++ -o tplayer tplayer.cpp  -L/usr/local/lib -lSDL
```

Simply executing the command **tplayer** palys the raw video "../data/sample_video.raw".

Program **tplayer.cpp** of uses some hard-coded parameters and plays video data that are not compressed. Figure 10-3 shows a sample output frame of the program. If we need to play compressed data, we only have to change the **decoder()** thread, which decodes data and acts as the producer. Instead of using hard-coded parameters, we can read in the parameters from the file containing the encoded data. Also, in order to test or perform experiments on our encoder and decoder, we need to download some video files which are saved in a standard video format. We shall address these problems in the next chapter.

Figure 10-3 A Frame of Sample Raw Video

Chapter 11

Video File Formats and Codec Player

11.1 Introduction

In Chapter 10, we have discussed how to play a video using data saved in the raw format of a file. In reality, video data are saved in a predefined format. There have been numerous video formats around and the data of most of them are saved in compressed form. In this Chapter, we shall give a brief discussion on some popular formats and do a case study on the **.avi** file format. Just as raw pixel data are often saved in **.bmp** format, and raw PCM sound samples in **.wav** format, raw video data are often saved in **.avi** format. We shall learn how to extract the raw video data from a .avi file so that we can play the video as we discussed in Chapter 10 or process them in our own way. There exists utilities in the Internet that allows one to convert from other video formats to uncompressed .avi format. With the help of those utilities, we can download a video file saved in any format from the Internet, convert it to uncompressed .avi and experiment the converted uncompressed data with our own encoder, decoder, and video player.

11.2 Video Storage Formats

11.2.1 Requirements of Video File Format

There exists a large number of video file formats in the market not only because competing companies create their own formats, hoping to push out competitors and to make their formats standards, but also because there are legal needs of not overstepping competitors' so called intellectual property. The following sections examine some common characteristics between the popular file formats. We summarize the requirements for video file format to be successful as follows. A video file format should be able to

1. store video and audio data,
2. provide fast, real-time playback on target viewing platforms,
3. provide efficient scrubbing (fast-forward and rewind while previewing),
4. store metadata (e.g. copyright, authorship, creation dates ...),
5. store additional tracks and multimedia data like thumbnails, subtitle tracks, alternate language audio tracks ...,
6. allow for multiple resolutions,
7. provide file locking mechanisms,
8. allow for video editing,

9. provide integrity checking mechanism, and
10. perform segmentation of audio and video portions into packets for efficient Internet transmission.

11.2.2 Common Internet Video Container File Format

A container file format is hierarchical in structure, and can hold different kinds of media (audio, video, text ..) synchronized in time. The following are some popular container formats, which can save various types of media data:

1. AVI (Audio Video Interleaved) – standard audio / video file format under Windows; not suited for streaming as it does not have any standard way to store packetization data.
2. MOV – Apple's Quick Time format, better than AVI in syncing audio and video; also supports Windows, and Linux.
3. ASF (Advanced Streaming Format) – Microsoft's proprietary format (.WMV, .WMA), designed primarily to hold synchronized audio and video.
4. NSV (NullSoft Video) – by NullSoft (a division of AOL) for streaming.
5. RM (RealMedia) – Real's streaming media files; can be extended to hold all types of multimedia; supports Windows, and Linux platforms and many standards, including MPEG-2, MPEG-4, Real, H263.
6. MP4 (MPEG-4) – almost identical to MOV but MPEG-4 players can handle only MPEG-4 related audio, video and multimedia.
7. SWF, SWV (Shockwave Flash) – for Flash movies, typically containing vector-drawn animations with scripting controls; also supports video codecs, JPEG still images, remote loading of SWF files, XML data and raw text.

11.2.3 Simple Raw or Stream Video Format

Simple raw storage or stream formats store the compressed data without extra headers or metadata. These are essentially live audio-video streams saved to disk. Below are some examples:

1. MPEG-1, MPEG-2 – streams are composed of interleaved audio and video data arranged into groups of pictures.
2. MP3 – encode audio; part of MPEG-1
3. DV (Digital Video) – used by modern digital cameras and video editing software.
4. .263 – video compressed with H.263 codec.
5. .RTP – Real Time Protocol data.

11.2.4 Internet Playlist, Index, and Scripting Format

Index formats have pointers linking to other resources. The following are some of this kind:

1. MOV – has several formats that do not contain actual video or audio data, but merely point to other files.
2. RAM (RealAudio Metafile) – points to the URL of the actual media file (RealMedia .RM or RealAudio .RA).
3. ASX (Active Streaming Index) – index files that work in Windows Media system and point to the content held in an ASF media file.
4. SMIL (Synchronized Multimedia Integration Language) – provides instructions to a media player on how to present a multimedia interface and what content to display.

11.3 Case Study: AVI Files (.avi)

AVI (Audio Video Interleaved) is a file format defined by Microsoft for use in applications that capture, edit and play back audio-video sequences. Just as raw pixel data are often saved in .bmp format, and raw PCM sound samples in .wav format, raw video data are often saved in .avi format. It is a special case of **RIFF** (Resource Interchange File Format) and is the most commonly used format for storing audio/video data in a PC. An AVI file can be embedded in a web page using a link like:

< A HREF="http://www.*somedomain*.com/movie.avi" > A Movie </A>

In order that your Apache Web server is able to handle avi files, you need to add in the configuration file the following statement:

AddType video/avi .avi

AVI is considered as an obsolete video/audio file format as it lacks many contemporary and crucial features to support streaming and image processing. However, it has been extended by OpenDML to include some of those features.

11.3.1 RIFF File Format

The AVI file format is based on the RIFF (resource interchange file format) document format. A RIFF file consists of a RIFF header followed by zero or more lists and chunks; it uses a FOURCC (four-character code) to denote a text header. A FOURCC is a 32-bit unsigned integer created by concatenating four ASCII characters. For example, 'abcd' = 0x64636261. The AVI file format uses FOURCC code to identify stream types, data chunks, index entries, and other information. The RIFF file format has the following form.

1. A RIFF header consists of
   'RIFF' *fileSize fileType (data)*
   where
   - 'RIFF' is the literal FOURCC code 'RIFF',
   - *fileSize* is a 4-byte value indicating the size of the data in the file including the size of the *fileType* plus the size of the data that follows,
   - *fileType* is a FOURCC that identifies the specific file type,
   - *data* consists of chunks and lists in any order.
2. A **chunk** consists of
   chunkID chunkSize chunkData
   where
   - *chunkID* is a FOURCC that identifies the data contained in the chunk,
   - *chunkSize* is a 4-byte value giving the size of data in chunkData not including padded values,
   - *chunkData* is zero or more bytes of data, padded to nearest WORD boundary.
3. A **list** consists of
   'LIST' *listSize listType listData*
   where

- ‘LIST’ is the literal FOURCC code ‘LIST’,
- *listSize* is a 4-byte value, indicating the size of the list,
- *listType* is a FOURCC code specifying the list type,
- *listData* consists of chunks or lists, in any order.

Table 11-1 shows some sample data from an AVI file. The data are displayed in hexadecimal; the corresponding ASCII characters are printed on the right if they are printable otherwise a dot is printed. Some comments are shown at the far right to indicate what the data represent.

Table 11-1 Sample AVI Data

```
 0  1  2  3  4  5  6  7  8  9 10 11 12 13 14 15  0123456789012345]
52 49 46 46 DC 6C 57 09 41 56 49 20 4C 49 53 54 |RIFF.lW.AVI LIST|RIFF fileSize
                                                                 fileType LIST
CC 41 00 00 68 64 72 6C 61 76 69 68 38 00 00 00 |.A..hdrlavih8...|listSize
                                                    listType avih structSize
50 C3 00 00 00 B0 04 00 00 00 00 00 10 00 00 00 |P...............|
                                              microSecondPerFrame maxBytesPerSec
A8 02 00 00 00 00 00 00 01 00 00 00 00 84 03 00 |................|totalFrames
                                        initFrames streams suggestedBufferSize
40 01 00 00 F0 00 00 00 00 00 00 00 00 00 00 00 |@...............|width height
00 00 00 00 00 00 00 00 4C 49 53 54 74 40 00 00 |........LISTt@..|
73 74 72 6C 73 74 72 68 38 00 00 00 76 69 64 73 |strlstrh8...vids|
00 00 00 00 00 00 00 00 00 00 00 00 00 00 00 00 |................|
64 00 00 00 D0 07 00 00 00 00 00 00 A8 02 00 00 |d...............|
00 84 03 00 10 27 00 00 00 00 00 00 00 00 00 00 |.....’..........|
40 01 F0 00 73 74 72 66 28 00 00 00 28 00 00 00 |@...strf(...(...|
40 01 00 00 F0 00 00 00 01 00 18 00 00 00 00 00 |@...............|
00 84 03 00 00 00 00 00 00 00 00 00 00 00 00 00 |................|
00 00 00 00 69 6E 64 78 F8 3F 00 00 04 00 00 00 |....indx.?......|
01 00 00 00 30 30 64 62 00 00 00 00 00 00 00 00 |....00db........|
00 00 00 00 0C 44 00 00 00 00 00 00 40 00 00 00 |.....D.......@..|
.
.
4C 49 53 54 38 F9 56 09 6D 6F 76 69 69 78 30 30 |LIST8.V.moviix00|LISTlistSize
                                                          listType indexBlock
F8 3F 00 00 02 00 00 01 A8 02 00 00 30 30 64 62 |.?..........00db|
                                                  ....00db(uncompress frame)
```

As we can see from the sample avi data of Table 11-1, a two-character code is used to define the type of information in the chunk:

Two-character code	**Description**
db	Uncompressed video frame
dc	Compressed video frame
pc	Palette change
wb	Audio data

For example, if stream 0 contains audio, the data chunks for that stream would have the FOURCC ‘00wb’. If stream 1 contains video, the data chunks for that stream would have the FOURCC ‘01db’ or ‘01dc’.

11.3.2 AVI RIFF Format

As shown in Table 11-1, the FOURCC 'AVI ' in a RIFF header identifies the file to be an AVI file. An AVI file has two mandatory LIST chunks, defining the format of the streams and the stream data, respectively. An AVI file might also include an index chunk, indicating the address of the data chunks of the file; it has the following form (Table 11-2):

Table 11-2 AVI RIFF Format

```
RIFF ('AVI '
        LIST ('hdrl' ... )
        LIST ('movi' ... )
        ['idx1' () ]
     )
```

The 'hdrl' list defines the format of the data and is the first mandatory LIST chunk. The 'movi' list contains the data for the AVI sequence and is the second required LIST chunk. An optional index ('idx1') chunk can follow the 'movi' list. The index contains a list of the data chunks and their location in the file. If we expand 'hdrl' and 'movi' in Table 11-2, we shall get a form as shown below:

```
RIFF ('AVI '
      LIST ('hdrl'//header length
            'avih' ()
            LIST ('strl'//stream length
                  'strh' ()
                  'strf' ()
                  [ 'strd' () ]
                  [ 'strn' () ]
                  ...
                 )
            ...
           )
      LIST ('movi'
            {SubChunk | LIST ('rec '
                                 SubChunk1
                                 SubChunk2
                                 ...
                              )
                ...
            }
            ...
           )
      ['idx1' () ]
     )
```

The 'hdrl' list begins with the main AVI header, which is contained in an 'avih' chunk. The main header contains global information for the entire AVI file, such as the number of streams within the file and the width and height of the AVI sequence. This main header structure is shown below:

```
typedef struct _avimainheader {
    FOURCC fcc;      //'avih'
    DWORD  cb;       //size of structure, not including 1st 8 bytes
    DWORD  dwMicroSecPerFrame;
    DWORD  dwMaxBytesPerSec;
    DWORD  dwPaddingGranularity;
    DWORD  dwFlags;
    DWORD  dwTotalFrames;
    DWORD  dwInitialFrames;
    DWORD  dwStreams;
    DWORD  dwSuggestedBufferSize;
    DWORD  dwWidth;
    DWORD  dwHeight;
    DWORD  dwReserved[4];
} AVIMAINHEADER;
```

One or more 'strl' lists follow the main header. A 'strl' list is required for each data stream. Each 'strl' list contains information about one stream in the file, and must contain a stream header chunk ('strh') and a stream format chunk ('strf'). In addition, a 'strl' list might contain a stream-header data chunk ('strd') and a stream name chunk ('strn'). The stream header chunk ('strh') consists of an AVISTREAMHEADER structure as shown in Table 11-3.

Table 11-3 AVI Main Stream Header

```
typedef struct _avistreamheader {
     FOURCC fcc;
     DWORD  cb;
     FOURCC fccType;//'vids'-video, 'auds'-audio, 'txts'-subtitle
     FOURCC fccHandler;
     DWORD  dwFlags;
     WORD   wPriority;
     WORD   wLanguage;
     DWORD  dwInitialFrames;
     DWORD  dwScale;
     DWORD  dwRate;
     DWORD  dwStart;
     DWORD  dwLength;
     DWORD  dwSuggestedBufferSize;
     DWORD  dwQuality;
     DWORD  dwSampleSize;
     struct {
         short int left;
         short int top;
         short int right;
         short int bottom;
     }  rcFrame;
} AVISTREAMHEADER;
```

One can also express Digital Video (DV) data in the AVI file format. The following example shows the AIFF RIFF form for an AVI file with one DV data stream, expanded with completed header chunks.

Example AVI File With One DV Stream

```
00000000 RIFF (0FAE35D4) 'AVI '
0000000C     LIST (00000106) 'hdrl'
00000018         avih (00000038)
                   dwMicroSecPerFrame     : 33367
                   dwMaxBytesPerSec       : 3728000
                   dwPaddingGranularity   : 0
                   dwFlags             : 0x810 HASINDEX|TRUSTCKTYPE
                   dwTotalFrames          : 2192
                   dwInitialFrames        : 0
                   dwStreams              : 1
                   dwSuggestedBufferSize  : 120000
                   dwWidth                : 720
                   dwHeight               : 480
                   dwReserved             : 0x0
00000058         LIST (0000006C) 'strl'
00000064             strh (00000038)
                         fccType                : 'iavs'
                         fccHandler             : 'dvsd'
                         dwFlags                : 0x0
                         wPriority              : 0
                         wLanguage              : 0x0 undefined
                         dwInitialFrames        : 0
                         dwScale          : 100 (29.970 Frames/Sec)
                         dwRate                 : 2997
                         dwStart                : 0
                         dwLength               : 2192
                         dwSuggestedBufferSize  : 120000
                         dwQuality              : 0
                         dwSampleSize           : 0
                         rcFrame                : 0,0,720,480
000000A4             strf (00000020)
                         dwDVAAuxSrc      : 0x........
                         dwDVAAuxCtl      : 0x........
                         dwDVAAuxSrc1     : 0x........
                         dwDVAAuxCtl1     : 0x........
                         dwDVVAuxSrc      : 0x........
                         dwDVVAuxCtl      : 0x........
                         dwDVReserved[2]  : 0,0
000000CC     LIST (0FADAC00) 'movi'
0FADACD4     idx1 (00008900)
```

11.4 Utility Program for Reading AVI Files

In order to extract the data from an AVI file, we need a program that can understand the AVI format. Rather than reinventing the wheel and developing such a program, which is not directly related to video compression, we shall make use of some existing open-source libraries and code to help us do the job. We shall utilize the code from **MPEG4IP** (*http://mpeg4ip.sourceforge.net/*), which is an open-source package consisting of tools for streaming video and audio. MPEG4IP is small and is standards-oriented and free from proprietary protocols and extensions. Its development is focused on the Linux platform, and has been ported to Windows, Solaris, FreeBSD, BSD/OS and Mac OS X. It can handle MPEG-4, H.261, MPEG-2, H.263, MP3, AAC, and AMR file formats. When you download the package from its site and unpack it, you will find the utility program "avilib.c" and its header file "avilib.h" in the subdirectory "./lib/avi". You also need the header file "mpeg4ip.h" and some other related header files in the subdirectory "./include" to compile "avilib.c". Some minor modifications, such as data type casting need to be made to these files for "avilib.c" to be compiled by "g++". We shall also present another open-source utility, **ffmpeg** in the Appendix, which is more powerful and popular in handling compressed data. Here, we utilize the functions provided by "avilib.c" to read an AVI file. The main AVI structure is defined in "avilib.h" and is named **avi_t**. As shown below, **avi_t** basically covers all the crucial features of an AVI file:

```
typedef struct
{
   long   fdes;               /* File descriptor of AVI file */
   long   mode;               /* 0 for reading, 1 for writing */

   long   width;              /* Width  of a video frame */
   long   height;             /* Height of a video frame */
   double fps;                /* Frames per second */
   char   compressor[8];      //Type of compressor,4 bytes+padding
                              //  for 0 byte
   long   video_strn;         /* Video stream number */
   long   video_frames;       /* Number of video frames */
   char   video_tag[4];       /* Tag of video data */
   long   video_pos;          /* Number of next frame to be read
                                 (if index present) */

   long   a_fmt;              /* Audio format, see #defines below */
   long   a_chans;            /* Audio channels, 0 for no audio */
   long   a_rate;             /* Rate in Hz */
   long   a_bits;             /* bits per audio sample */
   long   audio_strn;         /* Audio stream number */
   long   audio_bytes;        // Total number of bytes of audio data
   long   audio_chunks;       /* Chunks of audio data in the file */
   char   audio_tag[4];       /* Tag of audio data */
   long   audio_posc;         /* Audio position: chunk */
   long   audio_posb;         /* Audio position: byte within chunk*/

   long   pos;                /* position in file */
   long   n_idx;              //# of index entries actually filled
   long   max_idx;            //# of index entries actually allocated
   unsigned char (*idx)[16]; /* index entries (AVI idx1 tag) */
   video_index_entry * video_index;
   audio_index_entry * audio_index;
   long   last_pos;           /* Position of last frame written */
   long   last_len;           /* Length of last frame written */
   int    must_use_index;     /* Flag if frames are duplicated */
   long   movi_start;
} avi_t;
```

To read an AVI file, we can first use the function **AVI_open_input_file**() of "avilib.c" to open the AVI file:

avi_t ***AVI_open_input_file**(const char **filename*, int *getIndex*);

where *filename* points to the filename of the AVI file to be opened and *getIndex* determines if we need the indexing information of the file; a nonzero value indicates we want the information while a value of 0 indicates we don't. If opened successfully, it returns a pointer to an **avi_t** structure containing relevant information of the AVI file for further processing.

We provide a sample program named **avi_to_raw.cpp** that makes use of the avilib functions to extract the video and audio information from an AVI file. Readers can obtain the program along with the mpeg4ip library source code from the website of this book. The program is simple and straightforward and the code is self-explained. However, it has to be compiled with the **avilib.c** program. For example, we can use the following command for compilation to obtain the executable **avi_to_raw**:

```
$g++ -o avi_to_raw avi_to_raw.cpp ../lib/avilib.c -I../lib
```

assuming that the **avilib** files are in the directory "../lib". We can execute it with the following format:

$./avi_to_raw *avi_file* [*raw_video_output_file* *raw_audio_output_file*]

If the input *avi_file* is in uncompressed format, we will obtain the video raw data to be saved in *raw_video_output_file*. The program will also output other relevant data of the video and audio data. The following is a sample output:

```
Video Frame Rate:          20   fps
Number of Frames:         680
File Duration:             34   sec
Video width:              320   pixels
Video height:             240   pixels
Compressor type:
Audio channels:             0
Audio sample rate:          0   Hz
Bits per audio sample:      0
Video starts at:        17420 ( 0x440c )
```

We provide an uncompressed avi file, **sample_video.avi** for you to experiment with the program. The file can be also downloaded from the web site of this book:

http://www.forejune.com/vcompress .

It does not have an audio channel. Therefore, when you execute

```
$ ./avi_to_raw sample_video.avi
```

only the file **sample_video.rawv** consisting of raw video data will be created.

11.5 A Simple Video Codec for Intra Frames

In previous chapters, we have discussed the encoding and decoding of intra-frames of a video as well as playing videos using a solution for the producer-consumer problem. In this section, we combine all the code and put together a simple video codec (coder-decoder) that does intra-frame coding and decoding. At this point, our codec does not consider inter-frame coding that utilizes Motion Estimation (ME) and Motion Compensation (MC). Also, the pre-calculated Huffman code is very brief and is far from optimized. However, as we did before, we use integer arithmetic in the implementation to speed up the computing and utilize the C/C++ Standard Template Library (STL) to simplify the program and make it more robust. As usual, SDL is mainly used for rendering images and creating multi-threads. The codec can compress an uncompressed AVI file and play it back. We assume that the video data of the avi file are saved using the 24-bit RGB colour model. Most of the code presented here have been discussed in previous sections or Chapters.

11.5.1 Compressed File Header

We first define our own header of the compressed file. The header contains the basic information of the compressed data and consists of 27 bytes as listed in Table 11-4.

Table 11-4	
Bytes	**Information**
0 - 9	contains "FORJUNEV" as I.D. of file
10 - 11	frame rate (frames per second)
12 - 15	number of frames
16 - 17	width of an image frame
18 - 19	height of an image frame
20	bits per pixel
21	quantization method
22	extension, 0 for uncompressed data
23	dummy, for byte alignment

The default extension of such a compressed file is **.fjv**. This header can be implemented by defining a class as follows:

```
class Vheader {
public:
  char id[10];           //I.D. of file, should be ``FORJUNEV"
  short fps;             //frame per second
  int   nframes;         //number  of frames
  short width;           //width of video frame
  short height;          //height of video frame
  char  bpp;             //bits per pixel
  char  qmethod;         //quantization method
  char  ext;             //extension
  char  dummy;           //for byte alignment, make header size = 24
  ......
};
```

At present, we set the quantization method variable *qmethod* to 1. The extension variable *ext* is set to 0 if the **.fjv** data are uncompressed and 1 if they are compressed. In summary, at this point the encoding and decoding processes consist of the following steps:

1. **Encoding**:

   1. Read a 24-bit RGB image frame from an uncompressed avi file.
   2. Decompose the RGB frame into 16×16 macroblocks.

3. Transform and down-sample each 16×16 RGB macroblock to six 8×8 YCbCr sample blocks using YCbCr 4:2:0 format.

4. Apply Discrete Cosine Transform (DCT) to each 8×8 sample block to obtain an 8×8 block of integer DCT coefficients.

5. Forward-quantize the DCT block.

6. Reorder each quantized 8×8 DCT block in a zigzag manner.

7. Run-level encode each quantized reordered DCT block to obtain 3D (run, level, last) tuples.

8. Use pre-calculated Huffman codewords along with sign bits to encode the 3D tuples.

9. Save the output bit stream of the Huffman coder in a file.

2. **Decoding**:

1. Construct a Huffman tree from pre-calculated Huffman codewords.

2. Read a bit stream from the encoded file and traverse the Huffman tree to recover 3D run-level tuples to obtain 8×8 DCT blocks.

3. Reverse-reorder and inverse-quantize each DCT block.

4. Apply Inverse DCT (IDCT) to resulted DCT blocks to obtain 8x8 YCbCr sample blocks.

5. Use six 8×8 YCbCr sample blocks to obtain a 16×16 RGB macroblocks.

6. Combine the RGB macroblocks to form an image frame.

We have discussed all of the above steps and their implementations in detail in previous chapters. We just need to make minor modifications to accomplish the task of integrating them.

11.5.2 Modified RGB-YCbCr Transformation

We have discussed in Chapter 3 that if the R, G, and B components of an RGB pixel lie in the range [0, 255], then the transformed components, Y, Cb, and Cr also lie in the range [0, 255] provided that we use Equation (3.18) in our transformation. Aside from rounding errors, the transformation is reversible. Therefore, we can use 8-bit numbers to represent both RGB and YCbCr components. This works fine if the mapping between an RGB pixel and a YCbCr tuple is one-to-one such as the 4:4:4 sampling format. However, when down sampling such as the 4:2:0 format is involved, only one Cb value or one Cr value is calculated for every few pixels. In other words, in the reverse transformation, from YCbCr to RGB, not every Cb or Cr value comes from the same pixel as Y. Consequently, the resulted R, G, and B values are not gauranteed to lie within the range [0, 255]. To minimize the errors introduced by down sampling, we relax our restrictions on the YCbCr values, allowing Cb and Cr to take on negative values. The equations we shall use for RGB-YCbCr transformation is a slight modification of (3.18):

$$\begin{aligned} Y &= 0.299R + 0.587G + 0.114B \\ C_b &= 0.564(B - Y) \\ C_r &= 0.713(R - Y) \\ \\ R &= Y + 1.402C_r \\ G &= Y - 0.714C_r - 0.344C_b \\ B &= Y + 1.772C_b \end{aligned} \tag{11.1}$$

Since Cb and Cr can now take on negative values, we use **short** rather than **unsigned char** to implement the YCbCr components; no change is needed for the data type of the RGB components:

```
class RGB {
public:
    unsigned char R;        //[0, 255]
    unsigned char G;        //[0, 255]
    unsigned char B;        //[0, 255]
};

class YCbCr {
public:
    short Y;                //[0, 255]
    short Cb;               //[-127, 127]
    short Cr;               //[-127, 127]
};

//use 4:2:0 YCbCr
class YCbCr_MACRO {
public:
    short Y[256];           //16x16 ( four 8x8 samples )
    short Cb[64];           //8x8
    short Cr[64];           //8x8
};
```

The following is the code for the integer implementation of (11.1):

```
void rgb2ycbcr( RGB &rgb, YCbCr &ycb )
{
  //coefs summed to 65536 ( 1 << 16 ), so Y is always within [0, 255]
  ycb.Y = (short)((19595 * rgb.R + 38470 * rgb.G + 7471 * rgb.B ) >> 16);
  ycb.Cb = (short)( ( 36962 * ( rgb.B - ycb.Y ) ) >> 16);
  ycb.Cr = (short)(( 46727 * ( rgb.R - ycb.Y ) ) >> 16);
}

void ycbcr2rgb( YCbCr &ycb, RGB &rgb )
{
  int Y = ( int ) ycb.Y << 16;  //same as multiply 65536
  //chop is to truncate a value to lie with [0, 255]
  rgb.R = chop((Y              + (int)91881 * ycb.Cr ) >> 16 );
  rgb.G = chop((Y  - (int)22544 * ycb.Cb - (int)46793 * ycb.Cr ) >> 16);
  rgb.B = chop((Y  + (int) 116129 * ycb.Cb ) >> 16 );
}
```

We save these new declarations and implementations in the files “rgb_ycbcr.h” and “rgb_cbcr.cpp” in the directory **11/**.

11.5.3 Intra Frame Codec Implementation

In implementing our intra frame codec, we reuse most of the code we have developed in previous chapters.

Encoder Class

We group the functions that are used to encode video data into the class *Encoder*:

```
class Encoder {
protected:
  Hcodec hcodec;    //Huffman coder decoder of Chapter 8
public:
  short iwidth;     //image width
  short iheight;    //image height
  //constructors
```

```
    Encoder ();
    Encoder ( short width, short height );
    //save a  DCT block in an array
    void put_one_dct_block(int Y[][8], short dctcoefs[][8][8], int bn);
    //make DCT coeffs for one  macroblock.
    void get_dctcoefs(YCbCr_MACRO &ycbcr_macro, short dctcoefs[][8][8]);
    void encode_one_frame ( char *image,  BitFileIO *bitout );
};
```

The constructor of *Encoder* builds the precalculated Huffman table with its protected data member *hcodec*:

```
Encoder::Encoder ()
{
    hcodec.build_htable();
    iwidth = iheight = 0;
}
```

We use this precalculated table to encode 3D run-level tuples.

The function **put_one_dct_block** is to put an 8×8 block of DCT coefficients into an array. The function **get_dctcoefs** performs DCT operations on the 6 YCbCr sample blocks of a macroblock and makes use of **put_one_dct_block** to save the 6 DCT blocks of a macroblock in a three dimensional array, which is *dctcoefs*[][][].

The function **encode_one_frame** is used to encode one RGB video frame; it divides the RGB frame into macroblocks and calls **macroblock2ycbcr** to converts them to YCbCr sample blocks. It then makes use of **get_dctcoefs** to transform the samples to DCT coefficients which are stored in the 3D array *dctcoefs*. It then carries out the usual quantization, reordering and run-level encoding of the DCT coefficients. Finally, the run-level codewords are encoded by the function **huff_encode** of the class *Hcodec* and the output bit stream is saved in a file.

Decoder Class

We also group the functions for decoding the encoded data into the class *Decoder*:

```
class Decoder {
protected:
    Hcodec hcodec;
    Dtables decode_tables;
    Run3D runs[64];
    Run run;
    Reorder reorder;
    Quantizer quantizer;

public:
    short iwidth;       //image width
    short iheight;      //image height
    Decoder();
    Decoder ( short width, short height );
    bool get_dct_block ( BitFileIO *inputs, int Yi[][8] );
    int get_yccblocks (BitFileIO *inputs, YCbCr_MACRO *ycbcr_macro );
    int decode_one_frame(BitFileIO *inputs, char *image );
};
```

The constructor of *Decoder* builds the precalculated Huffman table using the function **build_htable** of the class *Hcodec*. This precalculated table is then used to construct the Huffman tree for decoding; this is done by the function **build_huff_tree** of *Hcodec*. The tree is saved in the *Dtables* object *decode_tables*:

```
Decoder::Decoder()
{
    hcodec.build_htable();
    hcodec.build_huff_tree ( decode_tables );
    iwidth = 0;
    iheight = 0;
}
```

The Huffman tree stored in *decode_tables* is used to decode the bit stream read from the input file.

The function **get_dct_block** reads the bit stream from the input file, and uses **huff_decode** of class *Hcodec* to decode it to obtain a sample block. It then run-level decodes it to obtain an 8×8 sample block, which will be reverse-reordered and inverse-quantized to a DCT block. The resulted 8×8 DCT sample block is sent back to the calling function via the array *Yi*.

The function **get_yccblocks** makes use of **get_dct_block** to obtain DCT sample blocks. It converts the DCT coefficients to YCbCr samples and put four 8×8 Y sample blocks, one 8×8 Cb sample block and one 8×8 Cr sample block into the arrays of the YCbCr object specified by the calling function.

The function **decode_one_frame** makes use of **get_yccblocks** to obtain macroblocks of YCbCr samples; it uses an external function, **ycbcr2macroblock** to convert the YCbCr macroblocks to RGB macroblocks. The RGB macroblocks are joined together to form a frame.

vcodec.cpp

The file "vcodec.cpp" contains the entry point **main** function of our codec. It also has a few other functions, **player**, **encode_thread**, and **decode_thread**. The **main** asks for an AVI file as input to encode. If a switch "-d", or "-s" is provided, it tries to decode the input file whose data are saved in the **.fjv** format mentioned above. If the **.fjv** file is uncompressed (i.e. value of "ext" of its header is 0), the program simply plays the video, otherwise it decodes the data and plays the video. If the switch is "-s" and the **.fjv** file is compressed, it decodes the data and save the uncompressed data in an output file again in the **.fjv** format with *ext* set to 0. If no argument is provided, it simply presents a simple menu showing its usage similar to the following:

```
Usage: vcodec [-d|-s] infile [outfile]
  Default is encoding, encoded data saved.
  -d : Decoding, decoded data not saved
  -s : Decoding, decoded data saved
Examples:
        vcodec sample.avi        ;output in sample.fjv
        vcodec -d sample.fjv     ;output not saved
        vcodec -s sample.fjv     ;output in sample_d.fjv
```

The **main** function makes use of the functions of **avilib** library to read in the avi file parameters such as frame width and height. It creates four buffers, each of which is large enough to hold one frame of data; the data memory buffer is pointed by the array of pointers *buf*[]. As discussed before, our implementation uses the producer-consumer paradigm to separate the video display from the encoding or decoding process by creating a consumer thread to play the video and a producer thread to supply and process the data. The function **player** is always the consumer thread. It simply lets the screen-display-pointer pointing to one of the data buffer *buf*[i] that *head* pointer is pointing at; it then advances *head*. If *head* catches up with *tail* where data are inserted, **player** sleeps and releases the semaphore *mutex*. It is awaken by the producer **encode_thread**, when it has put a frame in the buffer and executes **SDL_CondSignal**:

```
while ( !quit ) {
  SDL_LockMutex ( mutex );    // CondWait releases mutex before sleep
  while ( head == tail && !quit )         //shared Buffer empty
    SDL_CondWait ( condVar, mutex );
```

```
    if ( head == tail ){                    //no more data
      SDL_CondSignal ( condVar );
      SDL_UnlockMutex ( mutex );
      return 0;
    }
    SDL_UnlockMutex ( mutex );

    //consumes the data
    screen->pixels = buf[head%NSlots];
    if ( current_time - prev_time < frame_time )
      SDL_Delay ( frame_time - ( current_time - prev_time ) );
    prev_time = current_time;

    SDL_UpdateRect ( screen, 0, 0, 0, 0 ); //update whole screen
    SDL_LockMutex ( mutex );   //acquire lock before changing head
    head++;
    SDL_CondSignal ( condVar );//wake up any sleeping producer
    SDL_UnlockMutex ( mutex ); //release lock
  } //while
```

The function **encode_thread**() is a producer thread and is the entry point for the encoding process. It first creates an *Encoder* object, *encoder*, whose consturctor builds the precalculated Huffman table. The function **encode_one_frame** of *encoder* is used to encode an image frame. This thread is a producer and is supposed to put data in one of the memory buffers pointed by *buf*. Actually, it obtains the image data from the input file via the MPEG4IP avi function **AVI_read_frame**(). If the four buffers at *buf* are full, it goes to sleep and will be awaken by the *player* thread. When there is no more data, it sets the variable *quit* to true and executes **SDL_CondBroadcast**() to wake up any sleeping thread.

The function **decode_thread** is also a producer thread and is the entry point for the decoding process. It first creates a *Decoder* object, *decoder*, whose constructor builds the Huffman tree for decoding. The function **decode_one_frame** of *decoder* is used to decode a frame from the input bit stream and to put the decoded data in a memory buffer of *buf*[]. It may also save the decoded data in an output file.

Again, the whole package along with a couple sample AVI files are provided in the book's web site at

http://www.forejune.com/vcompress.

The programs presented here are for intra-frame coding. No temporal correlations have been considered. However, it forms the basis for implementations of more advanced compression techniques. In the next two chapters, we discuss the implementations of inter-frame coding and codecs that exploit temporal redundancies. A lot of the code presented here will be reused in those implementations.

Chapter 12

DPCM Video Codec

12.1 Introduction

Frame differencing is a simple technique that exploits temporal redundancy in a video sequence to achieve good compression. In the method, we code the difference between one frame and the next. In other words, the predicted frame for the current frame is equal to the previous frame, and we code the difference between the two frames. Again, as we have discussed before, if the encoding process is lossy, we obtain the predicted frame by reconstructing it from the decoded difference so that both the encoder and the decoder use the same predicted frame. We refer to this method as differential pulse code modulation (**DPCM**) coding, a term borrowed from signal processing. Figure 12-1a shows a block diagram of DPCM encoding and Figure 12-1b shows the corresponding decoder.

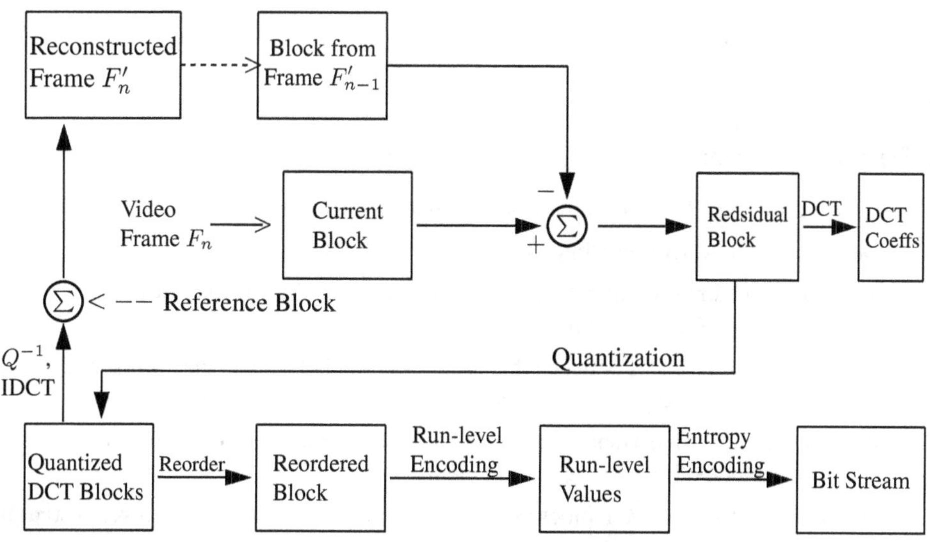

Figure 12-1a. DPCM Video Encoder

If there is little motion between successive frames, DPCM yields a difference image that is mostly uniform and can be coded efficiently. However, if there is rapid motion between frames or when a scene changes sharply, DPCM does not give good results.

12.2 DPCM Encoding and Decoding

As shown in Figure 12-1, the DPCM encoder processes the n-th video frame F_n to produce a compressed bitstream, and the decoder decompresses the encoded bitstream to the n-th reconstructed video frame F'_n, which is usually not identical to the original source video frame F_n. Many of the decoding functions are actually contained within the encoder as the encoder needs to reconstruct F'_n to be used as the predictor for the next source frame. The following steps describe the encoding and decoding processes of such a codec.

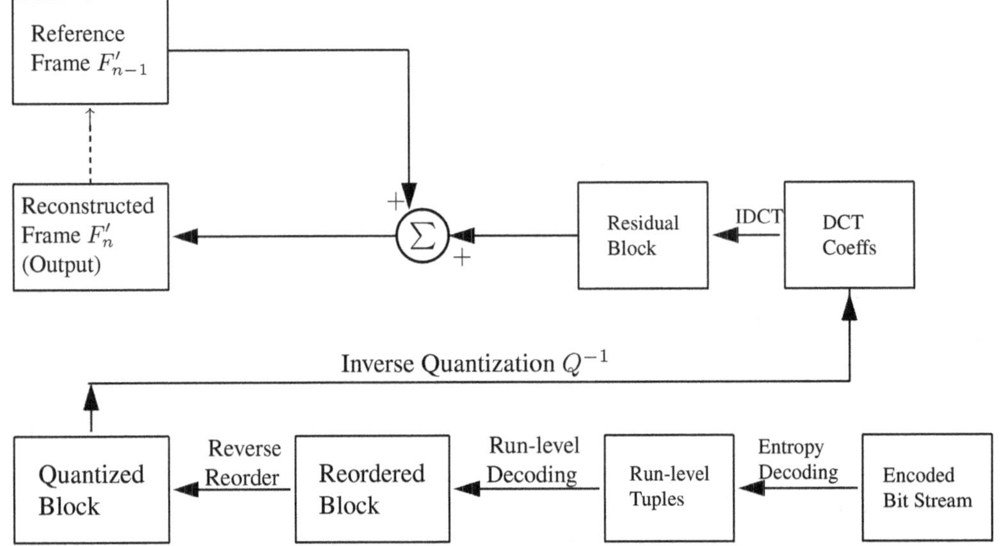

Figure 12-1b. DPCM Video Decoder

Encoder:

1. **Forward Encoding**:

   1. Read a 24-bit RGB image frame from an uncompressed avi file.
   2. Decompose the RGB frame into 16×16 macroblocks.
   3. Transform and down-sample each 16×16 RGB macroblock to six 8×8 YCbCr sample blocks using YCbCr 4:2:0 format.
   4. Calculate the differences between the current sample blocks and the corresponding sample blocks from the previously encoded-and-reconstructed frame.
   5. Apply Discrete Cosine Transform (DCT) to each 8×8 difference sample block to obtain an 8×8 block of integer DCT coefficients.
   6. Forward-quantize the DCT block; reconstruct the block as described in **reconstruction process**.
   7. Reorder each quantized 8×8 DCT block in a zigzag manner.
   8. Run-level encode each quantized reordered DCT block to obtain 3D (run, level, last) tuples.
   9. Use pre-calculated Huffman codewords along with sign bits to encode the 3D tuples.

10. Save the output bitstream of the Huffman coder in a file.

2. **Reconstruction Process**:

   1. Inverse-quantize each quantized DCT block. (Note that quantization is a lossy process and therefore, the recovered block is not identical to the one before quantization.)

   2. Apply Inverse DCT (IDCT) to resulted DCT blocks to obtain 8×8 YCbCr difference sample blocks.

   3. Add the difference sample blocks to the corresponding reference sample blocks that were previously encoded and reconstructed.

   4. Save the reconstructed sample blocks which will be used as the reference blocks when we encode the next frame.

Decoder:

1. Construct a Huffman tree from pre-calculated Huffman codewords.
2. Read a bit stream from the encoded file and traverse the Huffman tree to recover 3D run-level tuples to obtain 8×8 DCT blocks.
3. Reverse-reorder and inverse-quantize each DCT block.
4. Apply Inverse DCT (IDCT) to resulted DCT blocks of Step 3 to obtain 8×8 YCbCr difference sample blocks.
5. Add the difference sample blocks to the corresponding reference sample blocks that were previously encoded and reconstructed.
6. Save the decoded sample blocks which will be used as the reference blocks when we decode the next frame.
7. Use six 8×8 YCbCr sample blocks to obtain a 16×16 RGB macroblock.
8. Combine the RGB macroblocks to form an image frame.

The above descriptions and Figure 12-1 clearly present the requirement of a decoding path in the encoding process. This is necessary to ensure that the encoder and decoder use the same reference sample blocks to calculate residuals.

12.3 Implementation of DPCM Codec

To implement the DPCM codec, we just need to make minor modifications to the codec presented in the previous chapter (Chapter 11). Actually, the main difference between the current codec and the previous one is that the current codec encodes the residuals (differences) between two adjacent frames as opposed to encoding the frame directly in the previous case. Note that we calculate the residuals in the YCbCr space rather than in the RGB space. A simple way to accommodate this feature is to reconstruct the YCbCr macroblock from the quantized difference DCT blocks and save it using a vector; the saved macroblock will be used as the reference block when we process the next frame. Initially, the reference block sample values are set to zero.

C++ Vector

The C++ vector class implements a growable array of objects. In C++, a **vector** is a collection of data items of the same type. We can access every element of the collection separately. Unlike arrays, vectors expand automatically when new data is added to them. The name **vector** here is somewhat unconventional. Some other programming languages call a sequence of values an **array**. Readers should not confuse the term vector here with the physical vector we will discuss in the next chapter (Chapter 13). To utilize the vector class, one has to add the statement "#include <vector>" at the beginning of the program.

Reference Vector

We use C++ vector to construct the class *RefVector* that rebuilds the reference frames. The constructor of *RefVector* creates a vector (*ycc_refv*) that is big enough to hold all the YCbCr macroblocks of one frame; it also sets all sample values in each block to zero. The member function **calculate_diff**() calculates the residuals of a YCbCr macroblock in the current frame as compared to a corresponding one in the previous frame. This member function is used only by the encoder. The member function **reconstruct_macro**() reconstructs the YCbCr macroblock from the quantized DCT coefficients. As discussed above, both the encoding and decoding processes need to reconstruct reference frames. Thus this function is used by both the encoder and the decoder. Note that inverse DCT and inverse quantization take place at this function. Therefore, the *Decoder* class does not need to perform these operations any more. Listing 12-1 shows the interface of this class:

Program Listing 12-1 Reference Vector

```
-----------------------------------------------------------------------
class RefVector {
public:
  //vector of YCbCr Macro blocks of reference (previous) frame
  vector<YCbCr_MACRO> ycc_refv;
  //initialize the YCbCr Macro reference vectors
  void init_ref ( int width, int height );
  void calculate_diff(const YCbCr_MACRO *mp, YCbCr_MACRO &diff, int nm);
  void reconstruct_macro ( short dctcoefs[][8][8], int nm );
};
-----------------------------------------------------------------------
```

The data member *ycc_refv* of *RefVector* is a vector that holds the YCbCr macro blocks of the reference (previous) frame in sequence. When processing a frame, these reference blocks are used to calculate the residuals between the current frame and the reference frame or used to reconstruct a frame from the residuals. Each time a frame is processed, all its YCbCr macro blocks are saved in this vector and will be used for reference when processing the next frame.

The encoding process has a reconstruction path. The function **reconstruct_macro()** reconstructs the YCbCr macroblock from the DCT coefficients of the residuals of a current macroblock; it first inverse-quantizes the coefficients, applies IDCT to them to obtain the residuals, and then adds the residuals to the reference sample values to reconstruct the macroblock. The newly reconstructed macroblock replaces the one in the vector *ycc_refv*; this macroblock will be used as the reference block when we encode the next frame.

Note that we do **not** need to transform the YCbCr samples back to RGB values because in the DPCM codec, we always operate in the YCbCr space when we calculate the residuals.

Encoding:

To encode one frame of a video, we only need to make minor modifications to the function **encode_one_frame** of the *Encoder* class discussed in the previous chapter. A convenient way to implement the new features is to declare a new class, say, *Encoder_dpcm* that extends the class *Encoder*. The original class, *Encoder* is referred to as the parent class, superclass or base class; the extended class, *Encoder_dpcm* is called the child class, subclass or derived class. In C++ terminology, the extending process is called **inheritance**, which is a mechanism for enhancing existing, working classes. If a new class needs to be implemented and a class representing a more general concept is already available, then the new class can **inherit** from the existing class.

Figure 12-2 is a class diagram showing the relationship between these classes. Note that inheritance is a relationship between classes, not objects. The two simple boxes show the two classes and the arrow with a hollow head indicates inheritance.

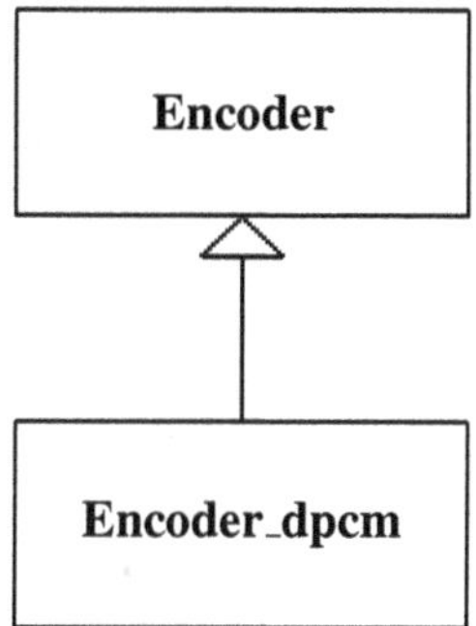

Figure 12-2. Inheritance Diagram

Listing 12-2 shows the declaration of the new class *Encoder_dpcm*:

Program Listing 12-2 *Encoder_dpcm* class

```
class Encoder_dpcm : public Encoder
{
private:
  RefVector refVector;
public:
  //constructor
  Encoder_dpcm ( short width, short height );
  void encode_one_frame ( char *image, BitFileIO *bitout );
};
```

The : symbol denotes inheritance. The keyword **public** is required for a technical reason; if we omitt this keyword, the inheritance becomes private. That is, only member functions of **Encoder_dpcm** get to call member functions of **Encoder**. If the inheritance is private, whenever we invoke an **Encoder** member function on an **Encoder_dpcm** object elsewhere, error occurs:

```
int main()
{
     Encoder_dpcm  encoder;
     ....
     encoder.get_dctcoefs( ycbcr_macro, dctcoefs );  //error
}
```

Private inheritance is rarely used as it violates the spirit of inheritance, which creates objects to be usable just like parent class objects.

The following shows the constructor of **Encoder_dpcm**:

```
Encoder_dpcm::Encoder_dpcm( short w, short h ) : Encoder( w, h )
{
  refVector.init_ref ( iwidth, iheight );
}
```

In general, the constructor of a child class has two tasks:

- Initialize the parent object
- Initialize all data members

The second task is straightforward but the first one is more complicated. We have to construct the parent object and tell it to use the image width and height. Very often, a child class constructor must invoke the parent class constructor before initializing the child class data. The code segment ": Encoder(w, h)" shown in the *Encoder_dpcm* constructor above is a special syntactical construct to denote the parent construction; it means "call the *Encoder* constructor with parameters *w* and *h* before executing the code inside the braces {}". In our case, it builds a precalculated Huffman table and set the image width and height to *w* and *h* respectively. It then initializes the reference vector *refVector* with the values of the image width and height.

The member function **encode_one_frame** of **Encoder_dpcm** has the same parameter list as that of its parent, *Encoder*. We say that the parent class method is overridden by the child class. (For more advanced C++ readers, if you want to use dynamic binding and to ensure that the child class method rather than the parent method is called, you may add the keyword **virtual** in front of the function of the parent class.) Listing 12-3 shows the implementation of this function.

Program Listing 12-3 Method encode_one_frame of Encoder_dpcm

```
------------------------------------------------------------------------
void Encoder_dpcm::encode_one_frame ( char *image,  BitFileIO *bitout )
{
  short row, col, i, j, r;
  YCbCr_MACRO ycbcr_macro;        //macroblock for YCbCr samples
  YCbCr_MACRO ycc_diff;           //difference between current and
                                  //  reference YCbCr macroblocks
  short dctcoefs[6][8][8];        //DCT coefficients for 6 sample blocks
  RGB macro16x16[256];            //16x16 pixel macroblock; 24-bit RGB
  short Y[8][8], Yr[8][8], bn;
  Quantizer quantizer;
  Reorder   reorder;
  Run3D     runs[64];
  Run       run;
  RGB *p;                         //pointer to an RGB pixel
 int nm = 0;                      //for indexing macroblock
  for ( row = 0; row < iheight; row += 16 ) {
    for ( col = 0; col < iwidth; col += 16 ) {
      p = ( RGB *) image  +  ( row * iwidth + col );
      r = 0;
      for ( i = 0; i < 16; ++i ) {
        for ( j = 0; j < 16; ++j ) {
          macro16x16[r++] = (RGB) *p++;
        }
        p += ( iwidth - 16 );  //points to next row within macroblock
      }
      macroblock2ycbcr ( macro16x16,  &ycbcr_macro );    //RGB to YCbCr
      //obtain difference between current and reference
      refVector.calculate_diff ( &ycbcr_macro, ycc_diff, nm );
```

```
        get_dctcoefs( ycc_diff, dctcoefs );   //get 6 dct coefs blocks
                                              //  from 1 YCbCr macroblock
        for ( bn = 0; bn < 6; bn++ ) {
          quantizer.quantize_block ( dctcoefs[bn] );//quantize 1 dct block
          reorder.reorder(dctcoefs[bn], Yr); //reorder the quantized sample block
          run.run_block ( Yr, runs );         //encode reordered DCT coefs with
                                              //  3D run-level code
          hcodec.huff_encode (runs, bitout); //Huffman-encode and save
        } //for bn

        //reconstruct YCbCr macroblock from quantized DCT coefficients;
        //  save block in ycc_refv[nm]
        refVector.reconstruct_macro( dctcoefs, nm );
        nm++;                                 //next macroblock
      } //for col
    } //for row
}
```

The function uses **calculate_diff** of **refVector** to obtain the residuals of the current macroblock from that of the reference frame. It then applies DCT transform to the residuals, and most of other encoding processes are the same as those discussed in Chapter 11. At the end, it uses the function **reconstruct_macro** to reconstruct the macroblock and save it in the vector *ycc_refv* of **refVector**, which will be used as the reference block (or predictor) when we process the corresponding macroblock of the next frame. Since we use this function to encode each frame of a video and it has the same name and parameter list as that of the parent, we only have to change one statement of the encoder thread; we just need to change

```
Encoder encoder(avi->width, avi->height);
```

to

```
Encoder_dpcm encoder(avi->width, avi->height);
```

All other code of the thread remains the same.

Decoding:

The decoder requires more modifications because of the reconstruction procedure. Just like the encoding process, we extend *Decoder* class to *Decoder_dpcm*:

Program Listing 12-4 Decoder_dpcm class

```
class Decoder_dpcm : public Decoder
{
private:
  RefVector refVector;
public:
  //constructor
  Decoder_dpcm ( short width, short height);
  bool get_dct_block ( BitFileIO *inputs, int Yi[][8] );
  void copy_dct_block ( int Y[][8], short D[][8] );
  int get_yccblocks( BitFileIO *inputs, YCbCr_MACRO *ycbcr_macro, int nm );
  int decode_one_frame (  BitFileIO *inputs, char *image );
};
```

Figure 12-3 shows the relation between *Decoder* and *Decoder_dpcm*. We need to override the functions **get_dct_block**, **get_yccblocksde**, and **decode_one_frame** though the modifiications to each of them are very minor. We also define a new function, named **copy_dct_block** to copy a DCT block into an array of DCT blocks (a macroblock). The main change is in the **get_yccblocks**() function. It uses **get_dct_block**() to get a residual DCT sample block by reading from the input bitstream, and carrying out the Huffman decoding, run-level decoding and reverse-reordering. However, **get_dct_block**() does not perform the task of inverse-quantization, which has been moved to the function **reconstruct_macro**(). The function **get_yccblocks**() gathers six quantized sample DCT blocks into the array *dctcoefs* with the help of **copy_dct_block**() and calls **reconstruct_macro**() to reconstruct the corresponding YCbCr macro block, which will be held by the vector *ycc_refv* of **RefVector**. Vector *ycc_refv* contains all reference YCbCr macroblocks:

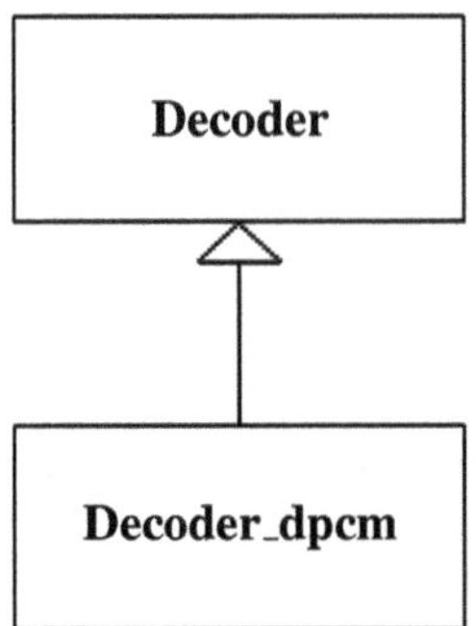

Figure 12-3. Extending Decoder

Program Listing 12-5 Function get_yccblocks of Decoder_dpcm class

```
----------------------------------------------------------------------
\begin{verbatim}
int Decoder_dpcm::get_yccblocks( BitFileIO *inputs,
                                  YCbCr_MACRO *ycbcr_macro,int nm)
{
  short i, j, k, n, block;
  int   Y[8][8];
  short dctcoefs[6][8][8];

  n = 0;
  //read data from file, perform IDCT, put them in 4 8x8 Y sample blocks
  for ( block = 0; block < 4; block++ ) {
  if ( !get_dct_block ( inputs, Y ) )    //read in one DCT block
      return 0;
    copy_dct_block ( Y, dctcoefs[block] );
  } //for block

  if ( !get_dct_block ( inputs, Y ) )    //read in one DCT block
    return 0;
  copy_dct_block ( Y, dctcoefs[4] );
  //now do that for 8x8 Cr block
  if ( !get_dct_block ( inputs, Y ) )    //read in one DCT block
    return 0;
  copy_dct_block ( Y, dctcoefs[5] );
  refVector.reconstruct_macro ( dctcoefs, nm );
  //copy the YCbCr Macro
  for ( i = 0; i < 256; i++ )
    ycbcr_macro->Y[i] = refVector.ycc_refv[nm].Y[i];
```

```
    for ( i = 0; i < 64; i++ ) {
      ycbcr_macro->Cb[i] = refVector.ycc_refv[nm].Cb[i];
      ycbcr_macro->Cr[i] = refVector.ycc_refv[nm].Cr[i];
    }
    n = 6 * 64;
    return n;                              //number of bytes read
}
--------------------------------------------------------------------
```

The function **decode_one_frame**() makes use of **get_yccblocks**() and **ycbcr2macroblock**() to recover the RGB samples. It is almost identical to the overrided function of its parent. The only change is the statement

```
n = get_yccblocks( inputs, &ycbcr_macro, nm++ );
```

where the parameter "nm++" is added and is used to specify that the "nm-th" macroblock saved in the reference vector needs to be retrieved to do the reconstruction.

Just like the case of the encoding process, we only need to change one statement in the decoding thread. We simply change

```
Decoder decoder (hp->width, hp->height);
```

to

```
Decoder_dpcm decoder (hp->width, hp->height);
```

All other code of the thread remains the same.

Consequently, we only need to make two changes to the main entrance file "vcodec.cpp" of Chapter 11, one to change "Decoder" to "Decoder_dpcm" and the other to change "Encoder" to "Encoder_dpcm". Again, condition variables and semaphores are used to synchronize events of a producer and a consumer.

We rename the modified file as "vcodec_dpcm.cpp" and call the executable of this codec "vcodec_dpcm". For example, the following command,

```
./vcodec_dpcm ../data/sample_video.avi
```

generates the compressed file "sample_video.fjv". We may check the file sizes with the "ls" command:

```
$ ls -l ../data/sample_video.*
-rw-r--r-- 1 user user  5762656 ../data/sample_video.avi
-rw-r--r-- 1 user user   446687 ../data/sample_video.fjv
```

The file has been compressed by a factor of $5762656/446687 = 12.9$. Figure 12-4 compares a frame of the original video and the corresponding decoded frame from the compressed file "sample_video.fjv". To decode and play the video of "sample_video.fjv", we can run vcodec_dpcm with the "-d" switch:

```
./vcodec_dpcm -d ../data/sample_video.fjv
```

In the next chapter, we will discuss the implementation of a codec that includes more formal motion estimation and compensation.

Figure 12-4. Comparison of original frame (left) and decompressed frame (right)

Chapter 13

Implementation of Video Codec with ME and MC

13.1 Introduction

The DPCM video codec introduced in the previous chapter can be considered as a simple inter-frame codec, which extends the intra-frame codec presented in Chapter 11. It usually gives better compression ratio compared to intra-frame coding. To make further improvement, we have to include both motion estimation (ME) and motion compensation (MC) in the coding process. This can be done by extending and making minor modifications to the DPCM codec. In the DPCM codec implementation, we do **not** have to reconstruct a reference frame in the RGB space. We only have to reconstruct it in the YCbCr space as we only have to find the residuals between macroblocks of two frames at fixed positions. Because of the inclusion of Motion Estimation, here we need to search for the 'best-matched' macroblocks for each frame and their positions may vary from frame to frame. Therefore, we need to reconstruct a reference frame in the RGB space to accommodate the searching; for each macroblock considered, it is transformed to the YCbCr space before calculating the residuals for comparison. You can see that motion estimation is computing intensive. As an illustration of the technique, we use a simple Three Step Search (TSS) as our searching algorithm. Motion estimation and compensation involve the search of locations and the transmission of motion vectors. We consider a location as a point and a motion vector as a vector. Before moving on, we discuss briefly the distinction between a point and a vector.

13.2 Points and Vectors

In our implementation, we shall use two classes to define points and vectors. You may ask: "Why do we need two classes? Isn't a point the same as a vector as both of them are specified by a 2-tuple (x, y)? Isn't one class good enough to describe both of them?"

First of all, a point is **not** the same as a vector. A **point** denotes a position or a location; it does not have any direction. On the other hand, a **vector** specifies a direction rather than a location; it has a magnitude and directional components. It makes sense to add two vectors but it does **not** make any sense to add two points. In some situations, a vector may be considered as a special point located at infinity. A common way to distinguish between a point and a vector denoted by (x, y) is to introduce an additional component, usually expressed as 'w', with '$w = 1$' denoting a point and '$w = 0$' denoting a vector. Therefore, in two-dimensional space, (x, y, 1) represents a point and (x, y, 0) represents a vector. If we consider three-dimensional situations, (x, y, z, 1) represents a point and (x, y, z, 0) represents a vector. With this representation, the operations on points and vectors are consistent with our intuition or understanding of points and vectors. For example, a point $(x_1, y_1, 1)$ plus a vector $(x_2, y_2, 0)$ is a point $(x_1 + x_2, y_1 + y_2, 1)$, and a point $(x_1, y_1, 1)$ minus a point $(x_2, y_2, 1)$ is a vector $(x_1 - x_2, y_1 - y_2, 0)$. A point $(x_1, y_1, 1)$ plus another point $(x_2, y_2, 1)$ gives $(x_1 + x_2, y_1 + y_2, 2)$, which is an invalid representation and therefore, adding two points is an illegal operation. Table 13-1 summarizes the operations.

Though it is illegal to add two points, we may form linear combinations of points:

$$P = c_0 P_0 + c_1 P_1 + ... + c_{n-1} P_{n_1} \tag{13.1}$$

where $P_i = (x_i, y_i, 1)$ is a point and c_i's are constant coefficients. The combination is legitimate if the summing coefficients are summed up to 1, and the combination gives a valid new point. i.e.,

$$c_0 + c_1 + ... + c_{n-1} = 1 \tag{13.2}$$

This is the principle behind point interpolation and extrapolation. Linear combination of points satisfying (13.2) is in general referred to as affine combination of points. (The word "affine" has the Latin root "affinis" meaning "connected with"; "finis" means border or end, and "af" means sharing a common boundary.) To construct a valid interpolation or extrapolation of points, the combination must be affine.

Table 13-1 Point and Vector Operations

Operation			Result
Vector	+	Vector	Vector
Vector	-	Vector	Vector
Vector	+	Point	Point
Vector	-	Point	Illegal
Point	+	Point	Illegal
Point	-	Point	Vector
Point	+	Vector	Point
Point	-	Vector	Point

From the above discussion, we see that actually we can use one class to define both points and vectors by introducing and incorporating a third component 'w' in the implementation. However, it is a lot clearer, especially for illustrating concepts discussed, to separate points from vectors, by declaring two classes, one defining points, and the other defining vectors. The users will not mix up the two types of variables and the program becomes easier to read and understand.

For the purpose of implementing the video codec, we define the *Point2* class to represent two-dimensional points and the *Vec2* class to represent two-dimensional vectors. (Alternatively, one can define a parent class *XY* that contains common attributes of points and vectors, and let both *Point2* and *Vec2* extend *XY*.) For more advanced C++ readers, you may overload operators '+' and '-' in defining theses two classes so that the the operators can operate on *Point2* and *Vec2* objects. However, to avoid any confusion for those who have not used C++ before, we simply define the operations using function names **plus** and **minus**. The following is the implementation of the *Vec2* class:

Program Listing 13-1 Implementation of *Vec2* class

```
---------------------------------------------------------------
\begin{verbatim}
Vec2::Vec2 ()
```

```
{
  x = y = 0;
}

Vec2::Vec2 ( int x0, int y0 )
{
  x = x0;     y = y0;
}

Vec2::Vec2 ( const Vec2 &v )
{
  x = v.x;    y = v.y;
}

void Vec2::set ( int x0, int y0 )
{
  x = x0;     y = y0;
}

void Vec2::set ( const Vec2 &v )
{
  x = v.x;    y = v.y;
}

//negation of this vector
void Vec2::neg ()
{
  x = -x;
  y = -y;
}

//vector - vector --> vector
Vec2 Vec2::minus ( const Vec2 &v )
{
  Vec2 v1;

  v1.x = x - v.x;
  v1.y = y - v.y;

  return v1;
}

//vector + vector --> vector
Vec2 Vec2::plus ( const Vec2 &v )
{
  Vec2 v1;

  v1.x = x + v.x;
  v1.y = y + v.y;

  return v1;
}

//vector + point --> point
Point2 Vec2::plus ( const Point2 &p )
```

```
{
  Point2 p1;

  p1.x = x + p.x;
  p1.y = y + p.y;

  return p1;
}
```

The implementation of *Point2* is very similar to that of *Vec2*. Of course, the implementations have to follow the rules shown in Table 13-1.

13.3 Three Step Search (TSS)

As mentioned above, we use a simple three-step search (TSS) (see Chapter 9) as our searching algorithm in the motion estimation process. A search is divided into three stages. The adjacent searching centers are 4 pixels apart in the first stage, and are 2 and 1 apart in the second and third stages respectively. We label the searching positions from 0 to 8 as shown in Figure 13-1, which shows the searching coordinates of stage 1.

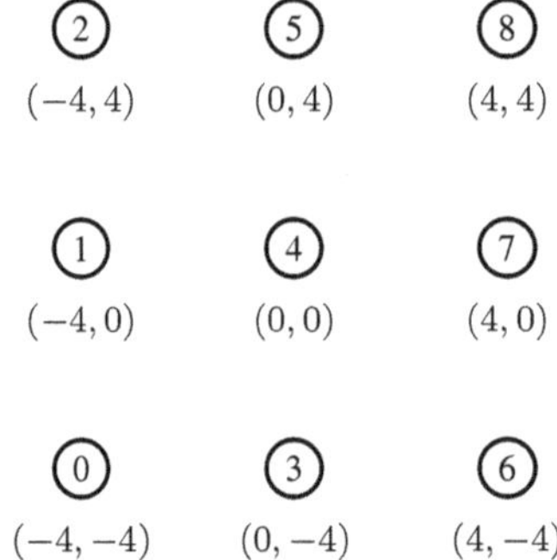

Figure 13-1. Stage 1 Searching Centers of TSS

The vector of a location is measured relative to the origin (0, 0) (node 4 in Figure 13-1). Therefore, the position and the vector of a searching center have the same values. For example, both the position and the vector of node 1 are represented by (-4, 0) or if we include the 'w' component in our representation, the position of node 1 is (-4, 0, 1) and the vector of node 1 relative to the origin is (-4, 0, 0). We define a class called *Tss* to perform Three Step Search, where we use the method **setLevel**() to set the searching centers at the three different levels. It sets the coordinates of the searching positions with the origin (node 4 of Figure 13-1) as an input parameter. Another input parameter is for specifying one of the three levels that we want to set. This is shown in Listing 13-2 below.

Program Listing 13-2 Three Stage Search Implementation

```
//Three Stage Search
//upper-left corner of macroblock is location of macroblock
Tss::Tss ( int w, int h )
{
```

```
  width = w;  height = h;
}

void Tss::set_dim ( int w, int h )
{
  width = w;  height = h;
}

//Set the searching locations of stage n; p is location of origin.
void Tss::setLevel ( const Point2 &p, int n )
{
  //searching centers for stage 0
  int rx[] = { -4, 0, 4, -4, 4, -4, 0, 4 };
  int ry[] = { -4, -4, -4, 0, 0, 4, 4, 4 };
  int m;                            //scaling factor of (rx, ry)
                                    //  for stage 0, 1, and 2
  if ( n == 0 ) m = 1;              //stage 0
  else if ( n == 1 ) m = 2;         //stage 1
  else m = 4;                       //stage 2
  if ( p.x < 0 || p.y < 0 ){        //not valid position
    for ( int i = 0; i < 8; ++i )
    level[n][i].set(-1, -1);
    return;
  }
  //set the searching locations
  for ( int i = 0; i < 8; ++i ) {
    int locx = p.x - rx[i] / m;
    int locy = p.y - ry[i] / m;
    //skip the out-of-bound locations
    if (locx < 0||locx >= (width-16)||locy < 0||locy >= (height-16))
      level[n][i].set( -1, -1 );
    else
      level[n][i].set ( locx, locy );
  }
}
```

We use Sum of Absolute Difference (SAD) as our searching criterion. Its implementation is straightforward. We name it **sad**() in the *Tss* class:

```
//Sum of absolute differences between macroblocks
int Tss::sad( const YCbCr_MACRO *p1, const YCbCr_MACRO *p2 )
{
  int s = 0;
  for ( int i = 0; i < 256; ++i )
    s += abs ( p1->Y[i] - p2->Y[i] );
  for ( int i = 0; i < 64; ++i ) {
    s += abs ( p1->Cb[i] - p2->Cb[i] );
    s += abs ( p1->Cr[i] - p2->Cr[i] );
  }

  return s;
}
```

Note that we operate in YCbCr space rather than in RGB space. We define a method named **getRGB-macro**() to obtain an RGB macroblock at a specified location of an RGB image. The function basically copies the RGB data of a 16 × 16 region at the specified location of the RGB image to an RGB array:

Program Listing 13-3 Function **getRGBmacro**() of *Tss* class

```
---------------------------------------------------------------------------
void Tss::getRGBmacro ( const char *image, const Point2 &p,
                                           RGB macro16x16[256] )
{
  RGB *rgbp;                    //points to an RGB pixel
  //points to specified RGB macroblock
  rgbp = ( RGB *) image + ( p.y * width + p.x );
  int r = 0;
  for ( int i = 0; i < 16; ++i ) {
    for ( int j = 0; j < 16; ++j )
      macro16x16[r++] = (RGB) *rgbp++;
    rgbp += ( width - 16 );  //points to next row (pointer arithmetic)
  }
}
---------------------------------------------------------------------------
```

Now we can implement the TSS search. The method **search**() of *Tss* presented in Listing 13-4 shows the implementation. An RGB image frame and the search origins are inputs to the method. It starts from the origin and uses the strategy discussed above to search the minimal point at each level. The difference between a minimal point and the search origin gives the desired motion vector. (Note that the difference between two points is a vector as shown in Table 13-1.) The resulted motion vectors (MVs) at the three levels are returned in the integer array mvs[]:

Program Listing 13-4 Function **search**() of *Tss* class

```
---------------------------------------------------------------------------
void Tss::search ( const char *ref_frame, const Point2 &origin,
                          const YCbCr_MACRO &yccm,  Vec2 mvs[] )
{
  Point2 p, cp;
  int d, dmin;
  RGB *rgbp, macro16x16[256];
  YCbCr_MACRO yccm_ref;          //YCbCr Macro from reference frame
  for ( int i = 0; i < 3; ++i )
    mvs[i].set ( 0, 0 );         //Set alll motion vectors to (0, 0)
  cp = origin;                   //Set current point to origin
  for (int k = 0; k < 3; ++k) { //Find minimal points at three levels
    p = cp;
    setLevel ( cp, k ); //Calculate all searching locations of stage k
    //Get an RGB macroblock from Reference frame
    getRGBmacro (ref_frame, cp, macro16x16);
    macroblock2ycbcr ( macro16x16,  &yccm_ref );//convert to YCbCr
    dmin = sad (  &yccm, &yccm_ref );    //calculate SAD between current
                                         //  and reference macroblocks
    for ( int i = 0; i < 8; ++i ) {      //test all valid search points
      if ( level[k][i].x < 0 || level[k][i].y < 0 )
        continue;                        //invalid search point
     getRGBmacro ( ref_frame, level[k][i], macro16x16 );
      macroblock2ycbcr ( macro16x16,  &yccm_ref ); //convert to YCbCr
      d = sad ( &yccm, &yccm_ref );
```

```
        if ( d < dmin ) {
          p = level[k][i];
          dmin = d;
        }
      }
      //p is the 'minimal' point
      if ( p.x == cp.x && p.y == cp.y ) //if origin is minimal, we're done
        break;
      mvs[k] = p.minus( cp );        //motion vector is difference between
                                     //  minimal point and origin
      cp = p;                        //p becomes the new search center
    } //for k
}
--------------------------------------------------------------------------
```

Note that unlike the DPCM codec where we only need to reconstruct a reference frame in YCbCr, in **search**() of *Tss*, we have to reverse the transformations all the way to RGB to reconstruct a reference frame. It searches a fixed number of positions, specified by **setLevel** (cp, k) and obtains the RGB macroblock of the reference frame using
getRGBmacro(); for each selected RGB macroblock, it transforms it to YCbCr using the external function **macroblock2ycbcr**() before calculating the SAD between the current and reference macroblocks.

13.4 Reconstructing Frames

We reconstruct an RGB frame from a vector of YCbCr macroblocks. Each time when we transform and encode a YCbCr macroblock of a frame, we reverse the transformations to reconstruct it and save the reconstructed YCbCr macroblock in a vector (see also the reconstruction algorithm described in Section 13.6 below). After we have gathered all the YCbCr macroblocks of one frame, we use the function **ycbcr2macroblock**() to convert each YCbCr macroblock saved in the vector to an RGB macroblock; we then combine all the RGB macroblocks to form an RGB reconstructed frame. We extend the class *RefVector* discussed in Chapter 12 to *RefVectorMV* to implement these features; the interface is shown in Listing 13-5 below. Figure 13-2 shows the inheritance diagram for these two classes.

Program Listing 13-5 RefVectorMV extends RefVector for ME and MC

```
--------------------------------------------------------------------------
class RefVectorMV : public RefVector
{
public:
  Tss tss;
  int width;
  int height;
  RefVectorMV();                              //constructor
  RefVectorMV ( int width, int height );      //constructor
  void set_dim ( int width, int height );
  void get_ref_point(const Point2 &cp,const Vec2 mvs[],Point2 &ref_point);
  //for encoding
  void current_ref_diff ( const YCbCr_MACRO *mp, const char *ref_frame,
                          const Point2 &ref_point, YCbCr_MACRO &diff, int nm);
  void reconstruct_frame ( char *ref_frame, int number_of_macros );
  //for decoding
```

```
  void current_ref_sum (YCbCr_MACRO *mp, char *ref_frame,
              const Point2 &ref_point, const YCbCr_MACRO &diff, int nm);
};
```

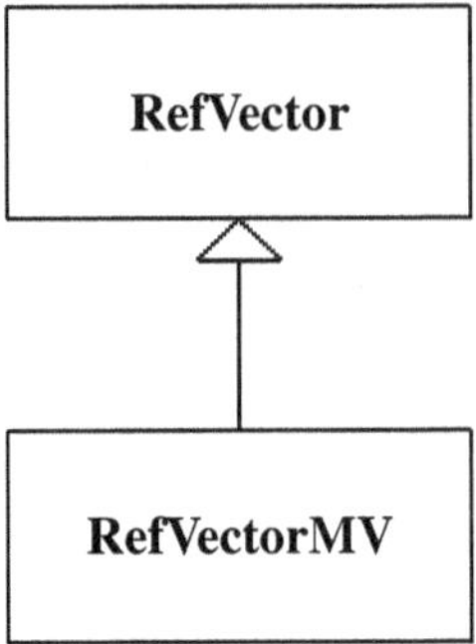

Figure 13-2. Extending *RefVector* to *RefVectorMV*

The function **get_ref_point**() is to obtain the location at which the reference block is located. It is given by the sum of the current location and the motion vectors of the three levels:

```
void RefVectorMV::get_ref_point( const Point2 &cp,
                      const Vec2 mvs[], Point2 &ref_point )
{
  ref_point.set ( cp );
  for ( int i = 0; i < 3; i++ )
    ref_point = ref_point.plus( mvs[i] );
}
```

The function **current_ref_diff**() calculates the residuals between the current macroblock and the reference macroblock. It is used in the encoding process. At the end, the reference macroblock is updated with the current one:

```
void RefVectorMV::current_ref_diff ( const YCbCr_MACRO *mp,
          const char *ref_frame,  const Point2 &ref_point,
          YCbCr_MACRO &diff, int nm  )
{
  RGB rgb_macro[256];
  YCbCr_MACRO refm;

  tss.getRGBmacro ( ref_frame, ref_point, rgb_macro );
  macroblock2ycbcr ( rgb_macro,  &refm ); //from RGB to YCbCr
  for ( int i = 0; i < 256; ++i )
    diff.Y[i] = (short) mp->Y[i] - (short) refm.Y[i];
  for ( int i = 0; i < 64; ++i ) {
    diff.Cb[i] = (short) mp->Cb[i] - (short) refm.Cb[i];
    diff.Cr[i] = (short) mp->Cr[i] - (short) refm.Cr[i];
  }
  //save the reference macroblock for reconstruction
  for ( int i = 0; i < 256; ++i )
    ycc_refv[nm].Y[i] = refm.Y[i];
  for ( int i = 0; i < 64; ++i ) {
    ycc_refv[nm].Cb[i] = refm.Cb[i];
    ycc_refv[nm].Cr[i] = refm.Cr[i];
  }
}
```

The function **current_ref_sum**() is the opposite of **current_ref_diff**(). It adds the residuals of the current macroblock to the reference macroblock to recover the original values. Its implementation is similar to that of **current_ref_diff**().

The function **reconstruct_frame**() is to reconstruct an RGB frame from the vector of reconstructed YCbCr macroblocks. It scans all the YCbCr macroblocks saved in the vector *ycc_refv* and uses the external function **ycbcr2macroblock** to convert each of them to an RGB macroblock. It puts the RGB macroblocks one by one onto an image frame, which will be used as the reference frame for searching when processing the next frame:

```
-------------------------------------------------------------------------
void RefVectorMV::reconstruct_frame(char *ref_frame,int number_macros)
{
  RGB *p, macro16x16[256];
  int row, col, i, j, k, r;

  row = col = 0;
  for ( k = 0; k < number_macros; ++k ){
    ycbcr2macroblock( &ycc_refv[k], macro16x16 );   //converts to RGB
    int offset = row * width + col;
    p = ( RGB *) ref_frame  +  offset; //points to start of macroblock
    r = 0;
    for ( i = 0; i < 16; ++i ) {
      for ( j = 0; j < 16; ++j ) {
        *p++  = macro16x16[r++];
      }
      p += ( width - 16 );                //next row within macroblock
    }
    col += 16;
    if ( col >= width ){
      row += 16;                          //next row of frame
      col = 0;
    }
  } //for k;
}
-------------------------------------------------------------------------
```

13.5 Encoding Motion Vectors

Like encoding 3D run-level tuples, we use pre-calculated 'Huffman codes' to encode motion vectors. We also use this as an example to elaborate more on our implementation of Huffman Trees. Since objects are more likely to have left-right motion than up-down movements, we assign higher probabilities to nodes 1 and 7 of the TSS searching positions shown in Figure 13-1. Eventually, we come up with the pre-calculated Huffman Tree for TSS motion vectors of stage 0 shown in Figure 13-3. This tree is based on very brief estimates. Readers should be able to improve it by gathering real statistics. The same tree structure is also used for stage 1 and stage 2.

The codewords corresponding to the Huffman Tree of Figure 13-3 are shown in Table 13-2. In general, we express Huffman codeword bits from left to right corresponding to the traversal of the tree from the root to a leaf. However, in our program, we send out the rightmost bits first. Therefore, in Table 13-2, we flip the bits of each codeword to make things consistent. The flipped codewords are the ones we actually use to encode motion vectors.

As Table 13-2 and Figure 13-1 show, the total number of symbols is $n_0 = 9$. Based on the discussions of Chapter 8, there are $n_0 - 1$ internal nodes. If the table holds all internal node pointers and symbols, the size of the table N'_T required to implement the Huffman tree is $N'_T = 2 \times (n_0 - 1) + n_0 = 3 \times n_0 - 2 = 3 \times 9 - 2 = 25$. As discussed in Chapter 8, actually we do not need to save the symbols. Under this situation, the table size required is :

$$N_T = N'_T - n_0 = 25 - 9 = 16 \tag{13.1}$$

The locations of the table can be indexed as $N_T - 1, ..., 1, 0$ (or $15, 14, ..., 1, 0$ here).

The root starts at location $N_T - 1$. However, to distinguish if a location contains an internal node or a symbol, we need to add n_0 back to a saved pointer so that if its value is smaller than n_0, we know that it is a symbol, otherwise it is a pointer, and when we actually access a table location, we need to subtract n_0 from the pointer value. Thus, the initial value of the root is $root = (N_T - 1) + n_0 = 3 \times n_0 - 3 = 24$. We develop the class **MvCodec** which is similar to **Hcodec** discussed in Chapter 8 to handle the encoding of motion vectors using the Huffman code. Besides encoding different kinds of 'symbols' (motion vectors vs. runs), the main difference between **MvCodec** and **Hcodec** is that **MvCodec** needs three sets to handle the three levels of motion vectors, one for each level. Listing 13-6 shows the function prototypes of this class along with the **MVtables** class for storing the motion vectors and the pre-calculated Huffman Tree of the motion vectors:

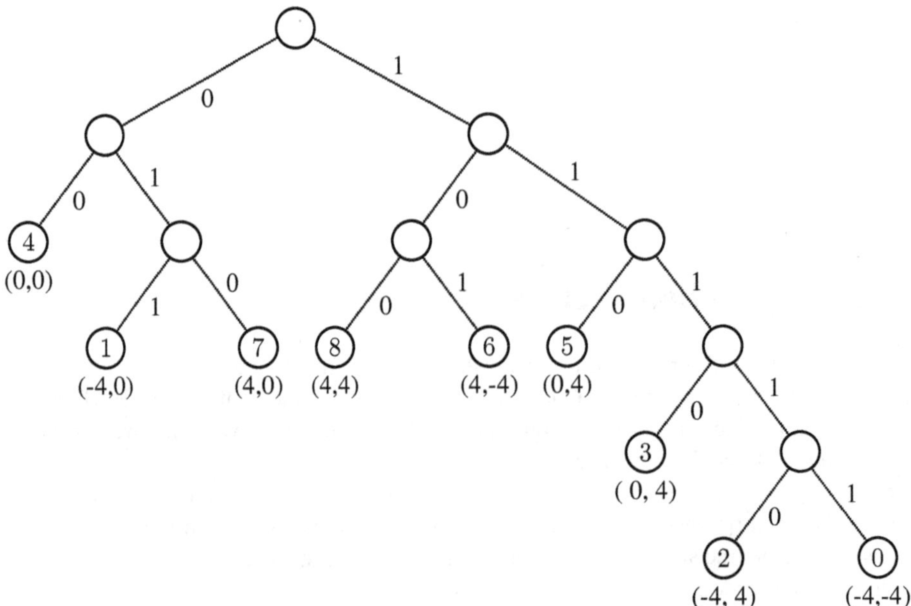

Figure 13-3. A Huffman Tree of Three Step Search (TSS) MVs

Table 13-2 Pre-calculated Huffman Codewords of TSS Motion Vectors

Index	MV	Codeword (Binary)	Flipped Codeword	Codeword in Hex	Codeword Length
0	(-4, -4)	11111	11111	1f	5
1	(-4, 0)	010	010	02	3
2	(-4, 4)	11110	01111	0f	5
3	(0, -4)	1110	0111	07	4
4	(0, 0)	00	00	00	2
5	(0, 4)	110	011	03	3
6	(4, -4)	101	101	05	3
7	(4, 0)	011	110	06	3
8	(4, 4)	100	001	01	3

Program Listing 13-6 Structure of Class *MvCodec*

```
---------------------------------------------------------------------------
class MVtables {
public:
  short mv_tree[1024];          //table containing Huffman Tree for MVs
  Vec2  mv_table[512];          //table containing MVs
};

class MvCodec {
public:
  set<MvHuff> mvtables[3];
  MVtables mv_decode_tables[3];
  MvCodec();
  //use a set (mvtable) to collect all pre-calculated motion vector (MV)
  //codewords. There are totally 9 motion vectors.
  void build_mvtables ();
  void mv_encode ( Vec2 mvs[], BitFileIO *outputs );
  void build_huff_tree ( int nlevel );
  short mv_decode( BitFileIO *bf,  Vec2 mvs[] );
};
---------------------------------------------------------------------------
```

In Listing 13-6, the constructor calls **build_mvHtables**() to build an array of three sets of *MvHuff*. The class *MvHuff* is similar to the *RunHuff* class discussed in Chapter 8, except that the *Run3D* data member *r* of *RunHuff* is replaced by the *Vec2* data member *mv* (for encoding motion vectors). (See below for its implemenation.) The *MvHuff* objects are used in both the encoding and decoding processes. The constructor also calls **build_huff_tree**() to build the Huffman trees of motion vectors for decoding; these trees are only used in the decoding process but not in the encoding process because in the encoding process we do not have to traverse a tree and we only need to encode a 'symbol' with its codeword. Actually, it is better not to build the trees in the constructor but build them in the *Decoder*.

The function **build_huff_tree**() takes a set of *MvHuff* that contains the pre-calculated Huffman codewords of *Vec2* at a specified level to construct a Huffman tree for that search level. The outputs are saved in the specified locations of the data member array *mv_decode_tables*[] with data type *MVtables*. The class *MVtables* uses a short array *mv_tree*[] to hold the Huffman tree and a *Vec2* array *mv_table*[] to hold the motion vectors as shwon in Listing 13-6.

We define the class *MvHuff* to hold a row of information of Table 13-2 that contains the pre-calculated Huffman codes and motion vectors:

```
class MvHuff {
public:
  Vec2 mv;
  unsigned int codeword;
  char  hlen;             //length of code
  short index;            //table index where codeword saved
  MvHuff() {}             //constructors
  MvHuff ( Vec2 a, unsigned c, char len, short idx )
  {
    mv = a, codeword = c, hlen = len; index = idx;
  }
  //'<' operator is to order motion vectors so that they can be
  //  saved in a binary tree ( set )
  friend bool operator < ( MvHuff left, MvHuff right ) {
    if ( left.mv.x < right.mv.x )
      return true;
    if ( left.mv.x > right.mv.x )
      return false;
    //x values equal
    if ( left.mv.y < right.mv.y )
      return true;
    if ( left.mv.y > right.mv.y )
      return false;
    //both x and y values equal
    return false;             //so left is not smaller than right
  }
};
```

We use a set of MvHuff objects to save the relevant information of all the entries of Table 13-2, which has a total of 9 entries. We also use the other two sets to save the corresponding information of the other two search levels (Level 1 and Level 2) of TSS. These sets are utilized by **build_huff_tree**() and are constructed by the function **build_mvtables**(), where we use the variable *scale* to find the motion vectors of Level 1 and Level 2 from those of Level 0. For example, at Level 0, $scale = 1$ and $(x_0, y_0) = (-4, -4)$; at Level 1, $scale = 2$, and $(x_0, y_0) = (-4/2, -4/2) = (-2, -2)$; at Level 2, $scale = 4$, and $(x_0, y_0) = (-4/4, -4/4) = (-1, -1)$. The code of this function is shown below:

Program Listing 13-7 Building MV Tables

```
------------------------------------------------------------------------
void MvCodec::build_mvtables ()
{
  short i, j, k, N = 9;          //N = # of possible motion vectors
  char hlen[] = {5, 3, 5, 4, 2, 3, 3, 3, 3};//lengths of MV codewords
  //Huffman codewords: no codeword is a prefix of another
  unsigned short hcode[] = { 0x1f, 0x02, 0x0f, 0x07, 0x00,
                                             0x03, 0x05, 0x06, 0x01 };

  //Level 0  motion vectors (x, y)
  int x[] = { -4, -4, -4,  0, 0, 0,  4,  4,  4 };
  int y[] = { -4,  0,  4, -4, 0, 4, -4,  0,  4 };

  Vec2 mv;                //an MV vector
  MvHuff mvf[3][128];     //table containing MvHuff objects
```

```
  int scale = 1;          //for calculating MVs of all levels
  for ( j = 0; j < 3; ++j ) {
    k = 0;
    for ( i = 0; i < N; ++i ) {
      mv.set( x[i]/scale, y[i]/scale );
      mvf[j][k] = MvHuff ( mv, hcode[i], hlen[i], i );
      k++;
    }
    scale *= 2;
  }
  //insert all N MvHuff objects into a set
  for ( k = 0; k < 3; ++k ) {
    for ( i = 0; i < N; ++i )
      mvtables[k].insert ( mvf[k][i] );
  }
}
-------------------------------------------------------------------------
```

We then use the *mvtables*[] built by the function to encode the three motion vectors found by TSS:

```
-------------------------------------------------------------------------
void MvCodec::mv_encode ( Vec2 mvs[], BitFileIO *outputs )
{
  int nlevels = 3;

  set<MvHuff>::iterator itr;   //iterator to traverse mvtable

  for ( int  i = 0; i < nlevels; ++i ) {
    //construct an MvHuff object; only mvs[k] is relevant here
    MvHuff mvf ( mvs[i], 0, 0, 0 );
    if ((itr = mvtables[i].find (mvf)) != mvtables[i].end()) //found
      outputs->outputBits ( itr->codeword, itr->hlen );
    if ( itr->mv.x == 0 && itr->mv.y == 0 )
      break;                   //best match at position 0, done
  }
}
-------------------------------------------------------------------------
```

13.6 Encoding One Frame

After we have developed the utility functions discussed above, we are ready to implement a function that encodes a frame. As shown in Figure 9-5a, encoding of a frame consists of a forward path and a reconstruction path. The goal of the reconstruction process is to obtain a reference frame for motion compensations of the macroblocks of the next frame. Many of the reconstruction functions are also used in the decoding process. We present the algorithms of the two stages used in our implementations where we have used TSS in searching:

Encoding:

1. **Forward Encoding**:

    1. Read a 24-bit RGB image frame from an uncompressed avi file.

2. Decompose the RGB frame into 16×16 macroblocks.
3. Transform and down-sample each 16×16 RGB macroblock to six 8×8 YCbCr sample blocks using YCbCr 4:2:0 format.
4. Use TSS to search the reference frame for a 'best-matched' YCbCr macroblock, which we call it reference macroblock.
5. Encode the motion vector (MV) of the reference macroblock found by TSS using pre-calculated Huffman codes and transmit the codewords.
6. Calculate the residuals between the current macroblock and the reference macroblock.
7. Apply Discrete Cosine Transform (DCT) to the residuals.
8. Forward-quantize the DCT block; reconstruct the block as described in **reconstruction path**.
9. Reorder each quantized 8×8 DCT block in a zigzag manner.
10. Run-level encode each quantized reordered DCT block to obtain 3D (run, level, last) tuples.
11. Use pre-calculated Huffman codewords along with sign bits to encode the 3D tuples.
12. Transmit the codewords.

2. **Reconstruction Path**:

1. Inverse-quantize each quantized DCT block. (Note that quantization is a lossy process and therefore, the recovered block is not identical to the one before quantization.)
2. Apply Inverse DCT (IDCT) to resulted DCT blocks to obtain 8×8 YCbCr residual sample blocks.
3. Add the residual sample blocks to the corresponding reference sample blocks that were previously encoded and reconstructed to obtain the reference macroblock.
4. Save the reconstructed reference macroblock in a vector which will be used to construct one frame.
5. Convert each of the YCbCr macroblock saved in the vector to an RGB macroblock, which is then saved in a buffer. The buffer is the reconstructed frame. (See Section 13.4 for the implementation of reconstructing one frame.)

We extend the class *Encoder* of Chapter 11 to *Encoder_mv* to implement the function **encode_one_frame**() that encodes one frame of video data. The relations between the three encoders we have discussed or mentioned, *Encoder*, *Encoder_dpcm*, and *Encoder_mv* are shown in Figure 13-4. The function prototypes of *Encoder_mv* is shown in Listing 13-8 below:

Program Listing 13-8 Encoder_mv class

```
------------------------------------------------------------------------
class Encoder_mv : public Encoder
{
private:
  RefVectorMV refVectorMV;
  Hcodec hcodec;
  MvCodec mvCodec;
  Tss tss;
  char *ref_frame;
public:
```

```
  //constructors
  Encoder_mv ( short width, short height );
  void encode_one_frame ( char *image, BitFileIO *bitout );
  //destructor
  ~Encoder_mv();
};
--------------------------------------------------------------------------
```

The constructor of *Encoder_mv* initializes various objects, allocates memory for holding the RGB data of one frame, and construct the Huffman table:

```
Encoder_mv::Encoder_mv( short w, short h ) : Encoder( w, h )
{
    refVectorMV.set_dim ( iwidth, iheight );
    refVectorMV.init_ref ( iwidth, iheight );
    hcodec.build_htable();
    tss.set_dim ( iwidth, iheight );
    int frameSize = iwidth * iheight * 3;
    ref_frame = new char[frameSize];
    for ( int i = 0; i < frameSize; i++ ) {
      ref_frame[i] =  0;
    }
}
```

The symbol ~ in front of the member function of a C++ class denotes a destructor. So in Listing 13-8, ~**Encoder_mv**() is a destructor function. A destructor of a C++ class is a functon that is always called when an object is about to go out of scope. In our case, the constructor of **Encoder_mv** allocates memory to hold one image frame and the memory buffer is pointed by the pointer variable *ref_frame*. Our destructor frees this memory before the program terminates otherwise memory leak will occur in the system that runs our codec:

```
Encoder_mv::~Encoder_mv()
{
    if ( ref_frame != NULL )
    free ( ref_frame );
}
```

Note that the name of the destructor is the name of the class, prefixed by the symbol ~. Listing 13-9 shows the code of **encode_one_frame**() of the class *Encoder_mv*.

Program Listing 13-9 Encoding One Frame

```
--------------------------------------------------------------------------
void Encoder_mv::encode_one_frame (char *image, BitFileIO *outputs)
{
  short row, col, i, j, r;
  YCbCr_MACRO ycbcr_macro; //macroblock for YCbCr samples
  YCbCr_MACRO ycc_diff;    //difference between current & ref. blocks
  short dctcoefs[6][8][8]; //DCT coefficients for 6 sample blocks
  RGB macro16x16[256];     //16x16 RGB 24-bit pixel macroblock
  short Y[8][8], Yr[8][8], bn;
  Quantizer quantizer;
  Reorder   reorder;
  Run3D     runs[64];
  Run       run;
  RGB *p;                  //pointer to an RGB pixel
  Point2 cp;               //current position of macroblock
```

```
  Point2 ref_point;          //point at which ref. block is subtracted
  int nm = 0;                //for indexing macroblock
  Vec2 mvs[3];               //motion vectors

  for ( row = 0; row < iheight; row += 16 ) {       //scan all rows
    for ( col = 0; col < iwidth; col += 16 ) {      //scan all columns
      p = ( RGB *)image + ( row * iwidth + col ); //begin of macroblock
      cp.set ( col, row ); //set x, y values of current position
      r = 0;                 //note pointer arithmetic
      for ( i = 0; i < 16; ++i ) {
      for ( i = 0; i < 16; ++i ) {
        for ( j = 0; j < 16; ++j ) {
          macro16x16[r++] = (RGB) *p++;
        }
        p += (iwidth - 16);//next row within macroblock
      }
      macroblock2ycbcr(macro16x16, &ycbcr_macro); //from RGB to YCbCr

      //motion estimation and motion compensation
      tss.search ( ref_frame, cp, ycbcr_macro, mvs );
      mvCodec.mv_encode ( mvs, outputs );

      //obtain the point at which the reference block is subtracted
      refVectorMV.get_ref_point (  cp, mvs, ref_point );

      //obtain difference between current and reference;
      //  save reference YCC macro in  ycc_refv[nm] of refVectorMV
      refVectorMV.current_ref_diff ( &ycbcr_macro, ref_frame,
                                          ref_point, ycc_diff, nm );
      //get 6 dct coefs blocks from 1 YCbCr macroblock
      get_dctcoefs( ycc_diff, dctcoefs );
      for ( bn = 0; bn < 6; ++bn ) {
        quantizer.quantize_block(dctcoefs[bn]); //quantize 1 dct block
        reorder.reorder ( dctcoefs[bn], Yr );
        run.run_block ( Yr, runs );          //encode reordered DCT coefs
        hcodec.huff_encode ( runs, outputs );    //encode and save
      } //for bn

      //reconstruct YCbCr macroblock from quantized DCT coefficients;
      //  save block in ycc_refv[nm]  of refVectorMV
      refVectorMV.reconstruct_macro( dctcoefs,  nm );
      nm++;                                 //next macroblock
    } //for col
  } //for row
  //reconstruct a frame from all YCbCr macroblocks saved in vector
  //  ycc_refv. (Converts to RGB first.)
  refVectorMV.reconstruct_frame ( ref_frame,  nm );
}
-------------------------------------------------------------------
```

The function **encode_one_frame**() walks through a frame to decompose it to 16 × 16 RGB macroblocks. It uses **macroblock2ycbcr**() to convert each RGB macroblock to a YCbCr macroblock in 4:2:0 format, and employs **search**() of the *Tss* class to find the three vectors (or positions) of the macroblocks in the reference frame that best-matches the current macroblock using TSS. (Keep in mind that TSS is a three-level search and this is why we have three vectors.) It then encodes the vectors and sends the codewords to the output file by **mv_encode**() of *MvCodec*. Given the three vectors, it obtains the point at which the reference block will be subtracted using **get_ref_point**() of *RefVectorMV* and uses this information to calculate the residuals between the current macroblock and the reference macroblock. After finding the residuals, it transforms them to DCT coefficients using **get_dctcoefs**() of *Encoder*, which are then quantized, reordered, and run-level encoded respectively by the functions **quantize_block**(), **reorder**(), and **run_block**() of various classes that we have discussed in previous chapters. Utilizing pre-calculated Huffman codewords, it employs **huff_encode**() to encode the 3D run-level tuples and to send the codewords to the output file. Each time it encodes a macroblock, **encode_one_frame**() uses **reconstruct_macro**() to reconstruct a YCbCr macroblock from the quantized DCT coefficients and save the macroblock in the vector *ycc_refv* of the class *refVectorMV*. Finally, after it has finished encoding one frame, it reconstructs the next reference frame from the vector *ycc_refv* using **reconstruct_frame**(), which first converts the YCbCr macroblocks in the vector to RGB macroblocks.

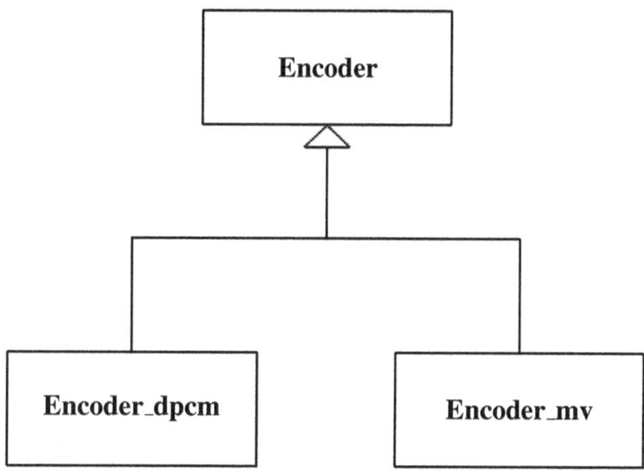

Figure 13-4. Relations between encoders

13.7 Decoding a Frame

The process of decoding a frame is shown in Figure 9-5b. It consists of the following steps, some of which overlap with the reconstruction path of the encoding stage:

Decoding:

1. Construct a Huffman tree from pre-calculated Huffman codewords for decoding 3D run-level tuples.

2. Construct a Huffman tree from pre-calculated Huffman codewords for decoding motions vectors (MVs).

3. Read the bits of the bit stream from the encoded file and traverse the MV Huffman tree to recover the TSS MVs of a macroblock.

4. Read the bits from the encoded file and traverse the 3D run-level Huffman tree to recover 3D run-level tuples to obtain 8×8 DCT blocks.

5. Reverse-reorder and inverse-quantize each DCT block.

6. Apply Inverse DCT (IDCT) to resulted DCT blocks of Step 5 to obtain 8×8 YCbCr residual sample blocks.

7. Add the residual sample blocks to the corresponding reference sample blocks that were previously encoded and reconstructed. frame.

8. Save the reconstructed reference macroblock in a vector which will be used to construct one frame.

9. Convert each of the YCbCr macroblock saved in the vector to an RGB macroblock, which is then saved in a buffer. The buffer is the reconstructed frame.

We extend the class *Decoder* of Chapter 11 to **Decoder_mv** to implement the function **decode_one_frame**() that decodes one frame of video data. The relations between the three decoders we have discussed or mentioned, *Decoder*, *Decoder_dpcm*, and *Decoder_mv* are shown in Figure 13-5. The function prototypes of *Decoder_mv* are shown in Listing 13-10 below:

Program Listing 13-10 Decoder_mv Class Structure

```
------------------------------------------------------------------------
class Decoder_mv : public Decoder
{
private:
  RefVectorMV refVectorMV;
  Hcodec hcodec;
  MvCodec mvCodec;
  Tss tss;
  char *ref_frame;
public:
  //constructors
  Decoder_mv ( short width, short height );
  //destructor
  ~Decoder_mv();
  bool get_dct_block ( BitFileIO *inputs, int Yi[][8] );
  int  get_yccblocks(BitFileIO *inputs, YCbCr_MACRO *ycbcr_macro,
                                                 Point2 cp, int nm);
  int  decode_one_frame ( BitFileIO *bitout, char *image );
};
------------------------------------------------------------------------
```

In our implementation, the function **get_yccblocks**() of the Decoder class does most of the work in the decoding process. It fetches DCT data using the function **get_dct_block**() which does the Huffman decoding to obtain 3D run-level tuples, then performs run-level decoding, reverse ordering and inverse quantization. After obtaining a DCT block from **get_dct_block**(), **get_yccblocks**() does IDCT to obtain YCbCr sample blocks and put them in a YCbCr macroblock structure. These are actually the residual values. The function add the residual values to the corresponding YCbCr macroblock in the reference vector:

Program Listing 13-11 Function **get_yccblocks**() of *Decoder_mv* class

```
------------------------------------------------------------------------
int Decoder_mv::get_yccblocks( BitFileIO *inputs,
                  YCbCr_MACRO *ycbcr_macro, Point2 cp, int nm )
{
  short i, j, k, n, block;
```

```
short *py;
int   Y[8][8], X[8][8];
short dctcoefs[6][8][8];
YCbCr_MACRO ycc_diff;  //difference between current & ref. blocks
Point2 ref_point;      //point at which ref block is subtracted

Vec2 mvs[3];           //motion vectors
if ( mvCodec.mv_decode ( inputs,  mvs )  <  0 ){
  printf("\nError in mv_decode\n");
  return -1;
}
n = 0;
//read data from file, perform IDCT, put them in 4 8x8 Y blocks
for ( block = 0; block < 4; block++ ) {
  if ( !get_dct_block ( inputs, Y ) )    //read in 1 DCT block
    return 0;
  idct ( (int *) Y,(int *) X );  //perform IDCT, output in X
  k = 0;
  //let py point to beginning of block
  if ( block < 2 )
    py = ( short * ) &ycc_diff.Y + 8*block;
  else
    py = (short *)&ycc_diff.Y + 128 + 8*(block-2);
  for ( i = 0; i < 8; i++ ) {    //one sample-block
    if ( i > 0 ) py += 16;       //advance py by 16 (one row)
    for ( j = 0; j < 8; j++ ) {
      *(py+j) = (short) X[i][j]; //put sample value in macroblock
      n++;
    } //for j
  } //for i
} //for block

//now do that for 8x8 Cr block
if ( !get_dct_block (inputs, Y)) //read in one DCT block
  return 0;
idct ((int *) Y, (int *) X );    //perform IDCT, output in X
k = 0;
for ( i = 0; i < 8; ++i ) {
  for ( j = 0; j < 8; ++j ) {
    ycc_diff.Cb[k] = X[i][j];    //put Cr value in macroblock
    k++;
    n++;
  }
}
//now do that for 8x8 Cr block
if (!get_dct_block (inputs, Y))  //read in one DCT block
  return 0;
idct ((int *) Y, (int *) X );    //perform IDCT, output in X
k = 0;
for ( i = 0; i < 8; ++i ) {
  for ( j = 0; j < 8; ++j ) {
    ycc_diff.Cr[k] = X[i][j];    //put Cr values in macroblock
    k++;
    n++;
  }
```

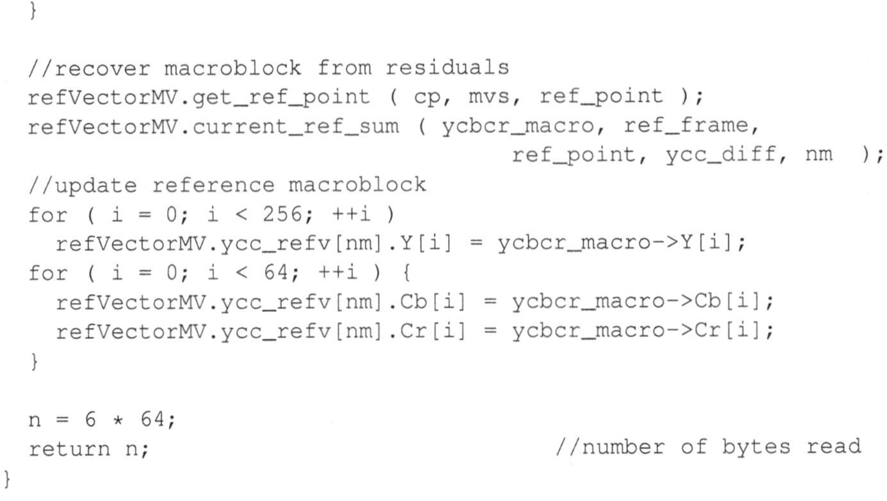

```
  }

  //recover macroblock from residuals
  refVectorMV.get_ref_point ( cp, mvs, ref_point );
  refVectorMV.current_ref_sum ( ycbcr_macro, ref_frame,
                               ref_point, ycc_diff, nm  );
  //update reference macroblock
  for ( i = 0; i < 256; ++i )
    refVectorMV.ycc_refv[nm].Y[i] = ycbcr_macro->Y[i];
  for ( i = 0; i < 64; ++i ) {
    refVectorMV.ycc_refv[nm].Cb[i] = ycbcr_macro->Cb[i];
    refVectorMV.ycc_refv[nm].Cr[i] = ycbcr_macro->Cr[i];
  }

  n = 6 * 64;
  return n;                          //number of bytes read
}
```

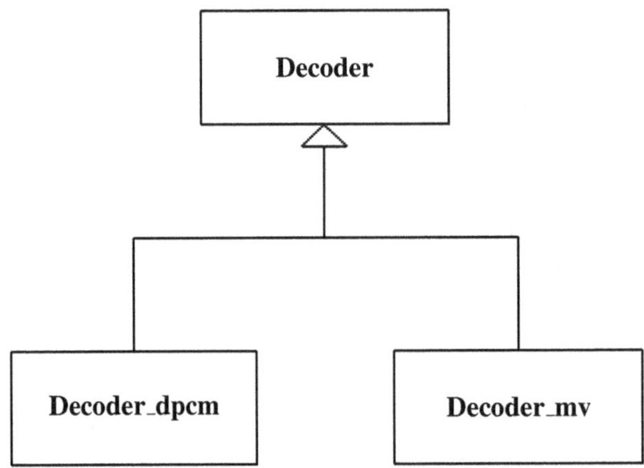

Figure 13-5. Relations between decoders

Finally, the function **decode_one_frame**() rounds up our implementation of decoding one frame. The function uses **get_yccblocks**() to fetch one YCbCr macroblock from the encoded bit-stream. It then employs **ycbcr2macroblock**() to convert the YCbCr macroblock to RGB. At the end, it uses **reconstruct_frame**() to reconstruct the next reference frame from the vector *ycc_refv* of the class **RefVectorMV**.

Program Listing 13-12 Function **decode_one_frame**() of *Decoder_mv*

```
int Decoder_mv::decode_one_frame( BitFileIO *inputs, char *image )
{
  short r, row, col, i, j, k, block;
  int n, numBytes = 0;
  RGB *p, macro16x16[256];
  YCbCr_MACRO ycbcr_macro;
  int nm = 0;               //for indexing macroblock
  Point2 cp;                //current position of macroblock

  for ( row = 0; row < iheight; row += 16 ) {
```

```
    for ( col = 0; col < iwidth; col += 16 ) {
      cp.set ( col, row );
      n = get_yccblocks( inputs, &ycbcr_macro, cp, nm++ );
      if ( n <= 0 ) return n;
      ycbcr2macroblock( &ycbcr_macro, macro16x16 );//converts to RGB
      //points to beginning of macroblock
      p = ( RGB *) image  +  ( row * iwidth + col );
      r = 0;
      for ( i = 0; i < 16; ++i ) {
        for ( j = 0; j < 16; ++j ) {
          *p++ =  macro16x16[r++];
        }
        p += ( iwidth - 16 ); //points to next row within macroblock
      }
      numBytes += 768;          // 768 = 16x16x3
    } //for col
  } //for row
  refVectorMV.reconstruct_frame ( ref_frame, nm );
  return numBytes;
}
-----------------------------------------------------------------------
```

Just like the case of developing the DPCM codec in Chapter 12, we only need to make two changes to the main entrance file "vcodec.cpp" of Chapter 11; one modification is to change *Decoder* to *Decoder_mv* and the other modification is to change *Encoder* to *Encoder_mv*. We rename the modified file to "vcodec_mv.cpp" and call the executable of this codec "vcodec_mv". For example, the following command,

```
./vcodec_mv ../data/sample_video.avi
```

generates the compressed file "sample_video.fjv". Again, we may check the file sizes with the "ls" command:

```
$ ls -l ../data/sample_video.*
-rw-r--r-- 1 user user  5762656 ../data/sample_video.avi
-rw-r--r-- 1 user user   446174 ../data/sample_video.fjv
```

We can see from the sample outputs that the originial video file size is 5762656 bytes and the compressed file size is 446174 bytes. This implies that the compression ratio R is

$$R = \frac{5762656}{446174} = 12.9$$

which is better than that of the DPCM codec.

Figure 13-6 below shows a frame of the original sample video and Figure 13-7 shows the corresponding decoded frame from the compressed file. A quantization factor of 12 has been used in the compression.

Figure 13-6 Original Sample Image Frame

Figure 13-7 Decoded Image Frame of Figure 13-6

Chapter 14

Hybrid Coding

14.1 Introduction

In the past two decades, a new development in video compression is to utilize synthesized images to represent some natural scenes that do not change much for a substantial period of time. For example, in a TV news announcement like the one shown in Figure 14-1, the major scene change is the lip movement of the announcer. The background of the scene is fixed and in many cases may not be very important. This is also true for the situation of a video conference.

Figure 14-1 News Announcer

To compress this kind of frames, one can use a graphics model to synthesize the announcer; the encoder just has to send the parameters of the lip movements of the announcer. Upon receiving the parameters, the decoder reconstructs the scene using the parameters and the graphics model. Of course, the parameters can be compressed before sending. One can easily see that this can give a very high compression ratio of the video as the encoder does not need to send the details of the images. It only has to send some parameters that will be used by the graphics model of the decoder to reconstruct the scene. As computer graphics software and hardware technologies advance, the use of graphics techniques will play a more important role in video compression. The recent success of real 3D movies such as "Avatar" and "Alice and Wonderland" will further accelerate this trend.

In the 1990s, MPEG began to integrate synthetic audio and video data into audio and visual samples acquired from the natural world. The MPEG Synthetic-Natural Hybrid Coding was based on technologies developed by the Virtual Reality Modeling Language (VRML) Consortium (now Web3D). In the later versions of MPEG-4 International Standard, efficient coding of shape and animation of human faces and bodies is specified. The specifications include standardizing Facial Animation (FA) and Face and Body Animation (FBA). MPEG-4 Visual specifies support for animated face and body models within the Simple Face Animation and simple FBA. A face model described by Facial Definition Parameters (FDPs) and animated using Facial Animation Parameters (FAPs) is specified. The body is described by body animation parameters (BAP). The basic idea of these technologies is to use graphics models to create synthesized human bodies or faces, which are modified or deformed by parameters extracted from the real scene. Figure 14-2 shows an example of such a model. (The image is taken from *http://coven.lancs.ac.uk/mpeg4/* .).

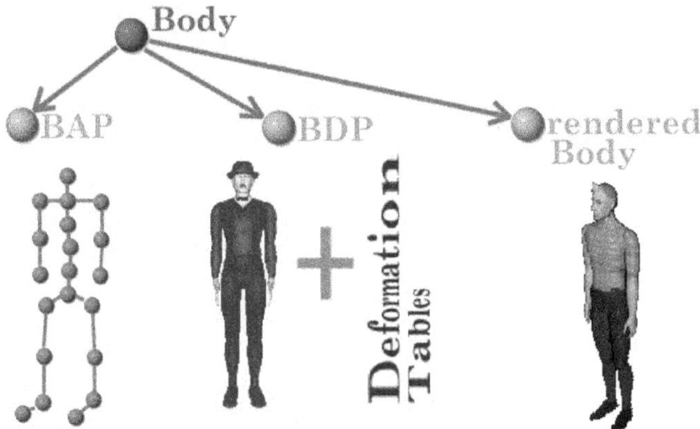

Figure 14-2 MPEG-4 Body Animation

The next question is: *how do we generate synthesized human bodies or in general graphics objects?* It turns out that most 3D objects can be described using polygon meshes. Polygon meshes (or simply meshes) are collections of polygons that fit together to form the skin of the object. They have become a typical way of representing a broad class of solid graphical shapes. The simplest polygon is the triangle, which is one of the most useful geometric figures. The triangle is commonly used in the construction of buildings and bridges as it is the strongest geometric figure. Moreover, the vertices of a triangle always lie on the same plane. Therefore, it is the most popular polygon used to construct 3D graphical objects. The left image of Figure 14-3 shows the triangles that are used to construct a human face and the upper body. The right two images of Figure 14-3 show the use of triangles to represent a rabbit; by deforming a triangle, one can change the shape of the object.

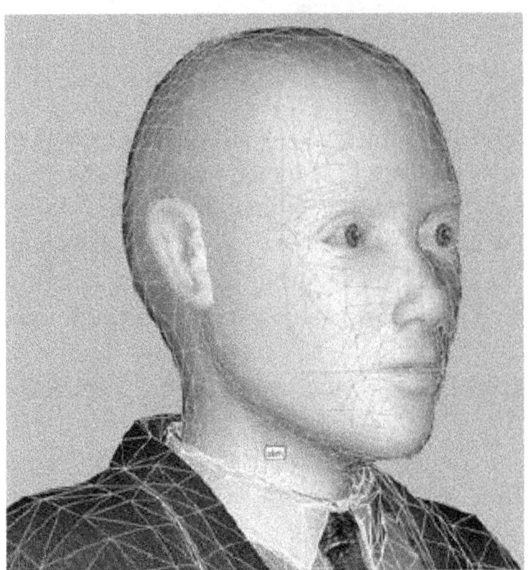

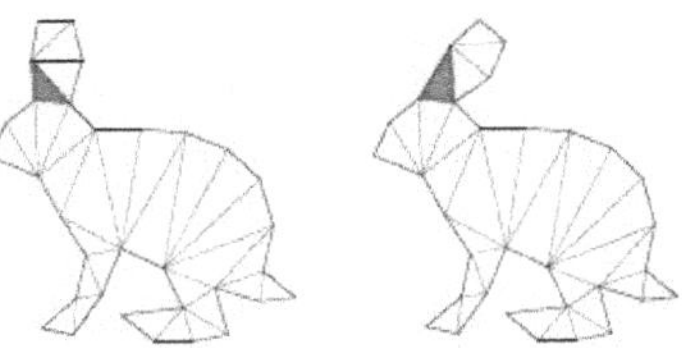

Figure 14-3 Human Face Formed by Polygon Mesh and Changing a Rabbit's Shape by Deforming a Polygon

There exist a lot of geometric modeling software packages that construct a model from some object, which can be a surface or a solid; it tries to capture the true shape of the object in a polygonal mesh. By using a sufficient number of polygons, a mesh can approximate the underlying surface to any desired degree of accuracy. For example, 3D Max is one of such 3D modeling software packages that run on Windows. Blender (*http://www.blender.org/*) is a popular free open-source 3D creation suite that lets users create sophisticated 3D graphical objects and do animation, and is available in all major operating systems, including Linux, Windows, and Mac OS/X. Typically, an artist creates an object using one of those packages and save it as a mesh in a file. A programmer writes programs in a computer language such as C/C++ or java to parse the polygons and manipulate the object. Artists may even post their graphical objects on some 3D graphics sites such as 3D Cafe (*http://www.3dcafe.com/*) for sale or for sharing. Specifically, **MakeHuman** (*http://www.makehuman.org/*) is an open-source tool for making 3D characters. Using MakeHuman, a photorealistic character can be modeled in less than 2 minutes and the character can be saved as a polygon mesh. MakeHuman is released under an Open Source Licence (GPL3.0) , and is available for Windows, Mac OS X and Linux. Xface is an MPEG4-based open-source toolkit for 3D facial animation. .

Figure 14-4 shows two more synthetic images for video compression taken from the web site *http://coven.lancs.ac.uk/mpeg4* that does Synthetic-Natural Hybrid Coding (SNHC) conformed to the MPEG-4 standard.

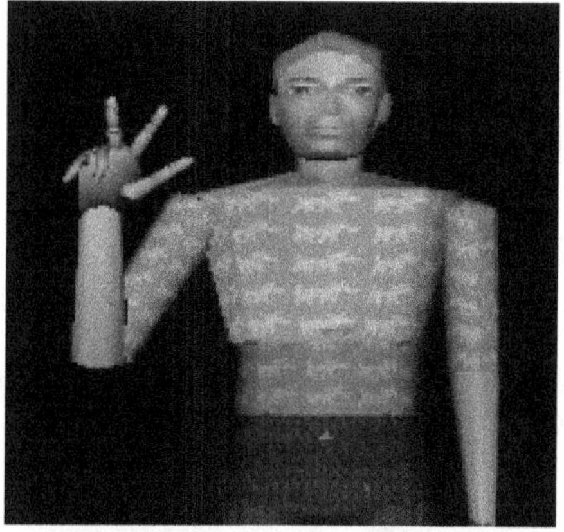

Figure 14-4a Animating Sign Language

Figure 14-4b Animating Business Meeting

14.2 MPEG-4 Facial Animation

To accomplish the representation of synthetic visual objects, MPEG-4 had to choose a scene description language to describe the scene structure. MPEG-4 selected Virtual Reality Modeling Language (VRML) standard as the basis with some additional new nodes to form the scene description language. Rather than constructing an object using purely triangles, the standard composes human face or body and other generic objects using a variety of geometric primitives such as cones, rectangles, triangles, and spheres. This makes the task of creating an object easier, and the object may look more realistic with the same number of polygons. To make the processing of the geometric primitives more efficient, the standard uses an indexed face set to define vertices and surface patches. It also uses nodes such as Transform to define rotation, scale, or translation and uses IndexedFaceSet nodes to describe the 3-D shape of an object. There are three problems that one has to address in animating human faces: a head needs to be specified; facial expressions have to be animated in real-time; animation and speech need to be synchronized.

MPEG-4 Facial Animation (FA) specifies the procedures to create a talking agent by standardizing various necessary parameters. The procedures of creating a talking agent consist of two phases.

Phase one specifies the feature points on a static 3D model that defines the regions of deformation on the face. Phase two involves generation and interpolation of parameters that are used to modify the feature points to produce the actual animation. The two phases are cleanly separated from each other so that application developers can focus on their field of interest.

Face Definition Parameters (FDPs) and Face Animation Parameters (FAPs) are used to define head models and primitive facial expressions respectively. FDPs define the texture shape and texture of and FAPs are used to animate the face. FAPs are based on the study of minimal perceptible actions (MPA) and are closely related to muscle actions, including movements of lips, jaw, cheek and eyebrows. They make up a complete set of basic facial actions that represent the most natural facial expressions. Exaggerated parameter values may be used for Cartoon-like characters. Figure 14-5 shows some common facial expressions.

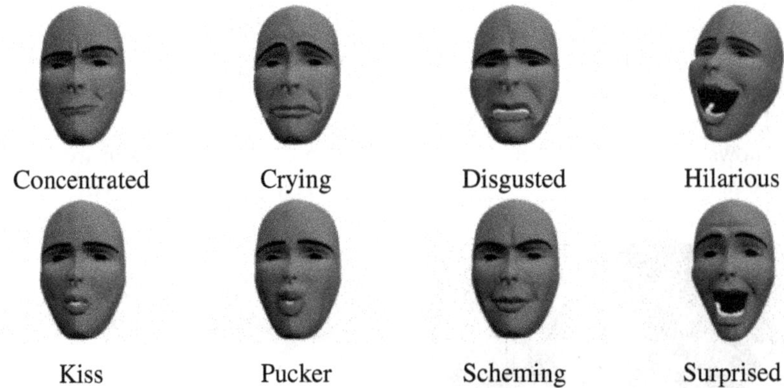

Figure 14-5 Common Facial Expressions

The FAP values are usually defined and normalized in face animation parameter units (FAPUs) so that interpolations of the FAPs on any facial model are made in a consistent way. FAPUs measure spatial distances of facial expressions from its neutral state and are defined in terms of the fractions of distances between the marked key features. MPEG-4 defines a generic face model in its neutral state along with some feature points as shown in Figure 14-6. The neutral state of a face model may be defined by the following features:

1. gaze is along the Z-axis,
2. all face muscles are relaxed,
3. eyelids are tangent to the iris,
4. the pupil is one third of the diameter of the iris,
5. lips are in contact,
6. the mouth is closed and the upper teeth touch the lower ones,
7. the tongue is flat, horizontal with the tip of tongue touching the boundary between upper and lower teeth,
8. FAPUs (Face Animation Parameter Units) are defined as fractions of distances between key facial features in the neutral state as shown in the Table 14-1.

Iris diameter	IRISD = IRISD0 / 1024
Eye Separation	ES = ES0 / 1024
Eye-nose Separation	ENS = ENS0 / 1024
Mouth-nose Separation	MNS = MNS0 / 1024
Mouth width	MW = MW0 / 1024
Angle unit (AU)	10^{-5} rad

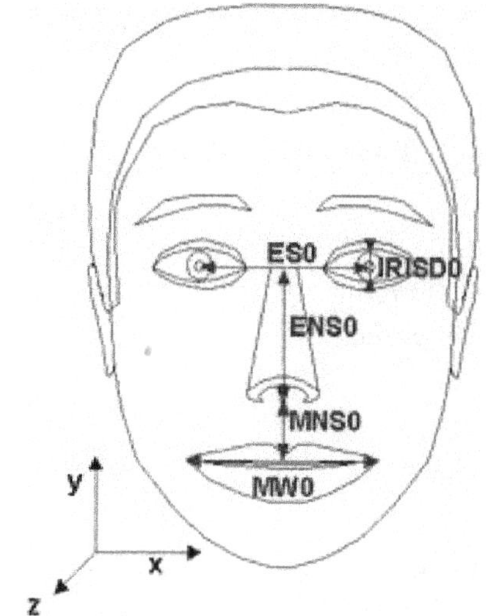

Figure 14-6 A Face Model in Neutral State

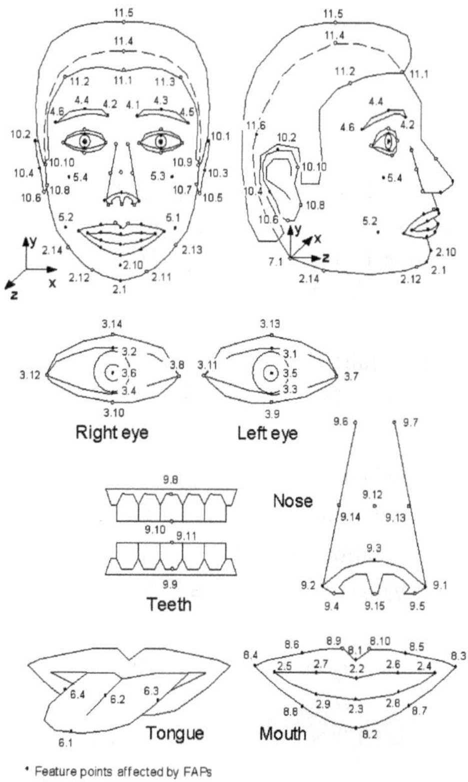

Figure 14-7 MPEG-4 Feature Points

For creating a standard conforming face, MPEG-4 specifies 84 feature points (FPs) on the neutral face. Feature points are arranged in groups such as cheeks, eyes and mouth. Applications need to define the locations of these feature points in order to conform to the standard. The feature points provide spatial references for defining FAPs as well as calibration between models when switched from one player to another. Figure 14-7 shows the set of FPs which are used to provide spatial reference for defining FAPs. The 68 FAPs are classified into 10 groups as shown in the following table:

Table 14-1 FAP Groups

Group	Number of FAPs
1. visemes and expressions	2
2: jaw, chin, inner lowerlip, cornerlips, midlip	16
3. eyeballs, pupils, eyelids	12
4. eyebrow	8
5. cheeks	4
6. tongue	5
7. head rotation	3
8. outer lip positions	10
9. nose	4
10. ears	4
Total	68

14.3 Computing Face Mesh Vertices

We use FAP values to animate a facial model, creating desired facial expressions. MPEG-4 further divides the FAPs into two subgroups. The first subgroup consists of FAPs that control simple motion of human face such as rotation, translation and scaling. The second subgroup FAPs are used for animating more complex motions that do not have any regular order such as frowning, blinking, and mouth-opening.

The first subgroup FAP values are fairly easy to process. For example, FAP23 is used to animate horizontal orientation of left eyeball. Suppose we have the following parameters,

$$\begin{aligned} \text{AU (Angle Unit)} &= 10^{-5} \text{ rad} \\ \text{Rotation Axis} &= (0, \text{-}1, 0) \\ \text{Rotation factor } \theta &= 1 \\ \text{Value of FAP23} &= 10000 \end{aligned}$$

then the left eyeball needs to be rotated by an angle α given by,

$$\alpha = 10^{-5} \times 10000 \times 1 = 0.1\ radian$$

The mesh vertice coordinates are more difficult to obtain from the second subgroup of FAPs. We have to perform a piecewise linear interpolation to obtain the new vertex coordinates of the mesh in the affected region. Figure 14-8 shows two phases of a left eye blink along with the neutral phase. The eyelid motion is controlled by FAP19. In the blinking animation, the eyelid movement is along an acred trajectory but we can use 2D coordinates to specify the trajectory as shown in the figure.

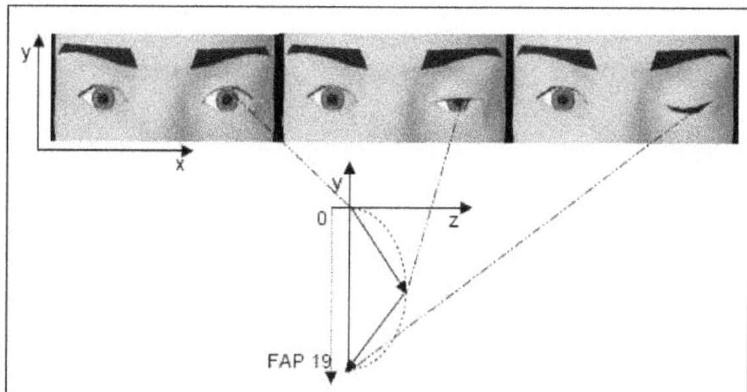

Figure 14-8 Two Phases of Movement of Upper Left Eyelid

In general, we can compute the displacements of mesh vertices using piecewise linear interpolation. We approximate the motion trajectory of each mesh vertex as a piecewise linear one as shown in the figure below:

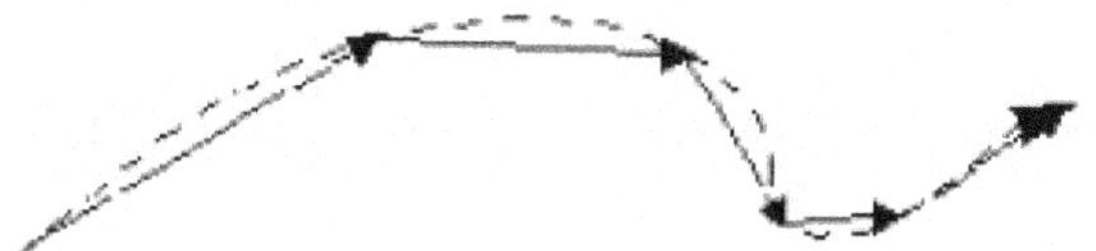

Suppose P_m is the position of vertex m when the face is in neutral state (FAP = 0) and $D_{m,k}$ is the 3D displacement that defines the piecewise linear function in the kth interval as shown in Figure 14-9. If P'_m is the new position of the same vertex after animation with the gvien FAP value, we can compute P'_m according to the following algorithm which is slightly different from that of MPEG-4, which requires 0 to be on an interval boundary all the time.

1. Assume that the range of FAP is divided into max intervals:

$$[I_0, I_1], [I_1, I_2], [I_2, I_3], ..., [I_{max-1}, I_{max}]$$

where

$$I_0 = -\infty, \; I_{max} = +\infty$$

2. Assume that the received FAP is in the jth interval, $[I_j, I_{j+1}]$, and 0 is in the kth interval, $[I_k, I_{k+1}]$, with $0 \leq j, k < max$. (See Figure 14-9.)

3. If $j > k$, we compute the new position P'_m of the mth vertex by:

$$\begin{aligned} P'_m = \; & P_m + FAPU \times [(I_{k+1} - 0) \times D_{m,k} + (I_{k+2} - I_{k+1}) \times D_{m,k+1} \\ & +... + (I_j - I_{j-1}) \times D_{m.j-1} + (FAP - I_j) \times D_{m,j}] \end{aligned} \quad (14.1)$$

4. If $j < k$, we compute P'_m by:

$$\begin{aligned} P'_m = \; & P_m + FAPU \times [(I_{j+1} - FAP) \times D_{m,j} + (I_{j+2} - I_{j+1}) \times D_{m,j+1} \\ & +... + (I_k - I_{k-1}) \times D_{m.k-1} + (0 - I_k) \times D_{m,k}] \end{aligned} \quad (14.2)$$

5. If $j = k$, we compute P'_m by:

$$P'_m = P_m + FAPU \times FAP \times D_{m,k} \quad (14.3)$$

6. If the range of FAP contains only one interval, the motion is strictly linear, and we compute P'_m by:

$$P'_m = P_m + FAPU \times FAP \times D_{m,0} \tag{14.4}$$

For example, suppose the FAP range is divided into three intervals:

$$[-\infty, 0], [0, 500], [500, +\infty].$$

The coordinates (x, y, z) of the displacements of vertex m controlled by the FAPs in these intervals are:

$$\begin{pmatrix} 1 \\ 0 \\ 2 \end{pmatrix}, \quad \begin{pmatrix} 0.8 \\ 0 \\ 0 \end{pmatrix}, \quad \begin{pmatrix} 1.5 \\ 0 \\ 4 \end{pmatrix}$$

respectively. The coordinates of vertex m in neutral expression is P_m. Suppose the received FAP value is 600 and the corresponding FAPU is Mouth Width, MW = 0.1. Since this FAP value is in the third interval [500, $+\infty$] and 0 is in the second interval [0, 500], we have the situation $j > k$. Thus we apply (14.1) to calculate the new position P'_m of vertex m:

$$P'_m = P_m + 0.1 \times [(500 - 0) \times \begin{pmatrix} 0.8 \\ 0 \\ 0 \end{pmatrix} + (600 - 500) \times \begin{pmatrix} 1.5 \\ 0 \\ 4 \end{pmatrix}] = P_m + \begin{pmatrix} 55 \\ 0 \\ 40 \end{pmatrix}$$

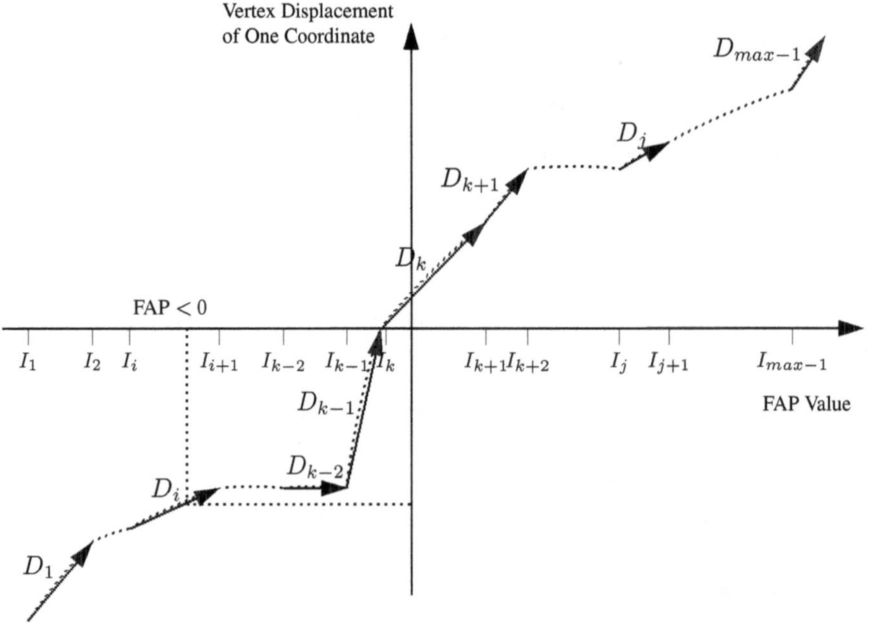

Figure 14-9. Piecewise Linear Interpolation of FAP Values

To speed up the animation process, we may save the relation between FAP intervals and 3D displacements in the so called *FaceDefTables*. When we get the value of an FAP, we need to look up the *FaceDefTables* to get information about the control region of the FAP and the three dimensional displacements of vertices within the control region to convert the FAP into facial animation as shown in the figure below:

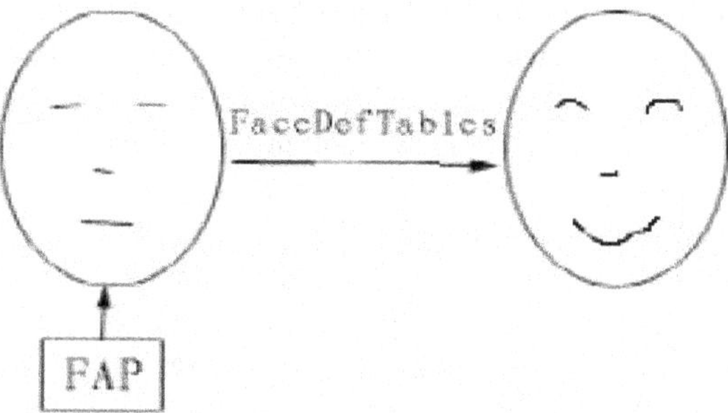

14.4 Keyframing

To animate realistic facial expressions, one can first calculate the animation parameters for key frames from photographs. A key frame in animation and film making is an image that defines the starting and ending points of any smooth transition. **Keyframing** is the process of creating animated motion by specifying objects at key frames and then interpolating the motion in intermediate frames. For traditional animation of movies, the key frames, also known as keys, are drawn by a senior artist. Other artists, *inbetweeners* and *inkers*, draw the intermediate frames and fill in the complete detailed drawings. The key frames are drawn for critical poses or when there is a sharp change in motion. At the beginning, the key frames could be very brief without fine details. The inbetweener would draw the intermediate poses to ensure that the motion appear fluid and natural.

Keyframing is particularly important in the animation of a full-length movie, which plays 24 frames per second. A 90-minute movie consists of 129,600 frames, which are way too many for a single artist to handle. On the other hand, if many artists draw different portions of the movie, the style or even appearance could be inconsistent. The movie has much better look if the production company employs a few senior animators to draw the key frames and a larger number of inbetweeners and linkers to draw the frames in between. A single senior animator can draw all the key frames of a particular character in a movie, producing more consistency of style.

In a similar spirit, computer animation uses interpolation to do keyframing. We specify the crucial parameters like positions, orientations, and shapes of objects in the scene at key frames. Then, we obtain the parameters as smooth functions of time using interpolating curves. This often can be done fully automatically but manual editing may be needed at some stages.

14.5 Extracting FAPs From Video

We have discussed how to use FAPs to animate facial expressions. This actually is a relatively easy part. When the animation parameters are given, one can basically use any appropriate model to perform animation. The more difficult problem is how to extract the FAPs from a given video. The extraction of facial parameters from video is not a completely solved problem. The process involves face detection, identification, recognition and tracking which are still active research topics in the academic and the industry. Automatic and accurate location of facial features is always difficult. The variety of human faces, expressions, facial hair, glasses, poses, and lighting contribute to the complexity of the problem.

A quick and simple way to find a human face in an image is to search for some common characteristics of human faces, such as color and shape. Some people use Delaunay triangulation and Voronoi diagrams to locate facial features of humans. However, this method is usually not very robust.

More sophisticated methods in general involve some statistical techniques and deformable models. A human is a deformable object and the tracking and recognition of it is usually tackled by making simplified assumptions concerning the motion or imposing constraints on it. Very often, the first step towards human tracking is to segment human figures from the background. A popular and relatively simple method to extract and track a deformable object in an image is the Active Contour Model (also called "snake"), which finds the contour of an object by balancing the effects of several energy terms. Variations of the Active Contour Model also exist. The gradient vector flow (GVF) snake is an improved model that includes the gradient vector flow, a new non-irrotational external force field. Another approach for tracking a deformable object is to employ deformable templates to automatically detect the objects. In general, retrieval by shape requires object detection and segmentation. Some researchers had used model-based region-grouping techniques to detect and retrieve deformable objects and found that using this method along with perceptually-motivated splitting strategy yields good image segmentation results of deformable shapes. In this section, we present a practical and popular technique for extracting FAPs from a video, the active appearance model (AAM).

14.5.1 Active Appearance Model (AAM)

An active appearance model (AAM) considers a face as a pattern in an image and makes use of a statistical model to match its appearance and shape with a pattern in the image. The approach is widely used for matching and tracking faces and for medical image interpolation.

AAM is an extension of the active shape model (ASM), which is a statistical model of the shape of objects that iteratively deform to fit to an example of the object in a new image. The shapes are constrained by the PDM (point distribution model) Statistical Shape Model to vary only in ways seen in a training set of labelled examples.

The shape of an object can be represented by a mesh of polygons or represented by a set of points (controlled by the shape model). Typically, it works by alternating the following steps:

1. Look in the image around each point for a better position for that point.
2. Update the model parameters to best match these new found positions.

To locate a better position for each point one may need to look for strong edges, or a match to a statistical model of what is expected at the point.

Usually, the points that represent a shape are referred to as *landmarks*. In general, a *landmark* is a distinguishable point present in most of the images under consideration and people use landmarks to locate features of an image. In our case, we locate facial features by locating landmarks. Figure 14-10 shows an image with correctly positioned landmarks.

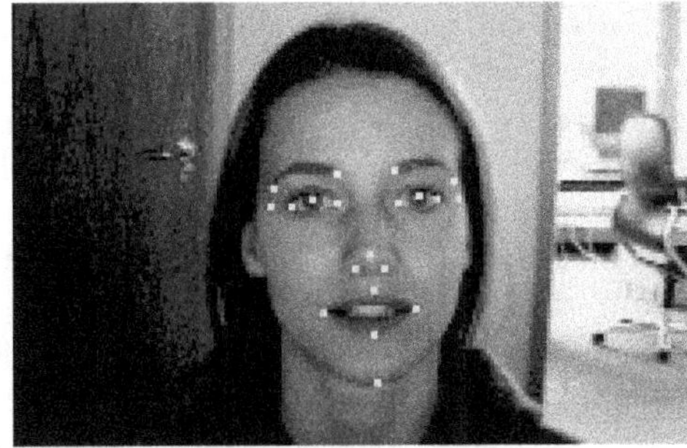

Figure 14-10 A face with correctly positioned landmarks

A set of landmarks forms a shape. Therefore, a shape s consists of a set of points. We can express s as an n-tuple:

$$s = \begin{pmatrix} p_1 \\ p_2 \\ . \\ . \\ . \\ p_n \end{pmatrix} \tag{14.5}$$

where

$$p_i = \begin{pmatrix} x_i \\ y_i \\ z_i \end{pmatrix} \tag{14.6}$$

is a point with three coordinates if we consider 3D space. The z_i component of (14.6) will be dropped if we consider 2D space. In general, the points of a shape are vertices of a mesh composed of triangles.

One can align one shape to another with an affine transformation (translation, scaling, or rotation) that minimizes the average Euclidean distance between shape points. The mean shape is the mean of the aligned training shapes, which are manually landmarked faces. (Note that the average of points is a linear affine combination of points and thus the average is also a valid point.) In general, a shape s is typically controlled by adding a linear combination of shape/deformation modes to the average shape $\overline{s}$:

$$s = \overline{s} + \Phi b \tag{14.7}$$

where b is a set of vectors consisting of deformation parameters and Φ is a matrix whose columns contain the deformation modes. A deformation is a displacement of a point and can be regarded as a vector. The operation Φb gives us another set of vectors. Therefore, in (14.7) we add a set of points to a set of vectors and the operation is legitimate; the result is another set of points as the sum of a point and a vector yields another point.

We can generate various shapes with Equation (14.7) by varying the deformation parameters in b. By keeping the elements of b within limits (determined during model building) we ensure that the generated face shapes are lifelike. Conversely, given a suggested shape s, we can calculate the parameter b that allows Equation (14.7) to best approximate s with a model shape s'. One can use an iterative algorithm to find b and T that minimize a 'distance' D described by

$$D = ||s, T(\overline{s} + \Phi b)|| \tag{14.8}$$

where T is an affine transformation that maps the model space into the image space.

ASM is relatively fast but it is too simplistic, not robust when new images are introduced. It may not converge to a good solution. Another disadvantage of ASM is that it only uses shape constraints and does not take advantage of all the available information such as the texture of the target object.

It turns out that an equation similar to (14.7) can be also used to describe the texture of objects based on statistical models. A texture t of an object is also a set of points at various locations of the objects:

$$t = \overline{t} + \sigma w \tag{14.9}$$

where $\overline{t}$ is the average texture, σ describes texture modes and w is a set of texture parameters.

Active appearance models (AAMs), also known as "smart snakes" as they conform to some explicit shape constraints like what an active contour model (snake) does, combine shape and texture into a single statistical model. We can express an AAM as

$$\begin{aligned} s &= \overline{s} + \phi \mathbf{v} = \overline{s} + \sum_{j=1}^{n} \phi_{ij} v_j \\ t &= \overline{t} + \sigma \mathbf{v} = \overline{t} + \sum_{j=1}^{n} \sigma_{ij} v_j \end{aligned} \tag{14.10}$$

That is, we use the same displacement vectors to control both shape and texture. In (14.10), each v_i is a vector and the coefficients ϕ_i and σ_i are shape and texture parameters respectively. Note that

$$v_i = \begin{pmatrix} v_{ix} \\ v_{iy} \\ v_{iz} \end{pmatrix}$$

AAMs are normally computed from training data. The standard approach is to apply Principal Component Analysis (PCA) to the training meshes. The mean shape $\overline{s}$ is usually referred to as the base shape. Figure 14-11 shows an example of AAM, where $\overline{s}$ is the average shape and v_i's are shape vectors.

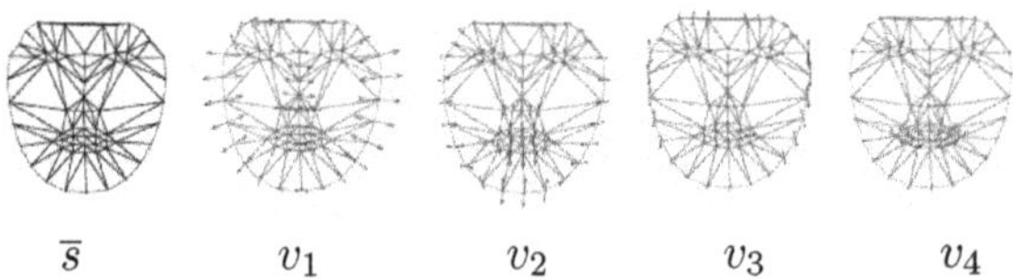

$\overline{s}$ v_1 v_2 v_3 v_4

Figure 14-11 An Example of AAM. $\overline{s}$ is the average shape. v_i's are shape vectors.

14.5.2 An AAM Search Algorithm

Face modeling has been the most frequent application of AAMs. Typically an AAM is first fit to an image of a face. That is, we search for model parameters that maximize the "match" between the model instance and the input image. The model parameters are then used in whatever the application is. Fitting an AAM to an image is a non-linear optimization problem. The usual approach is to iteratively solve for incremental additive updates to the parameters (the shape and appearance coefficients.) We breifly describe an AAM search algorithm here that is based on such an iterative update.

For an input image I and a model parameter vector $\mathbf{v}$, we can map the image onto the model and reshape the model to the standard shape to create a normalized image J:

$$J = J(I, s(\mathbf{v})) \tag{14.11}$$

For simplicity, we assume that the input image I is fixed. Therefore, the normalized image J is a function of $\mathbf{v}$ only. The residual image R is given by

$$R(\mathbf{v}) = J(\mathbf{v}) - s(\mathbf{v}) \tag{14.12}$$

We want to find $\mathbf{v}$ so that the error measure

$$E(\mathbf{v}) = ||R(\mathbf{v})||^2 \tag{14.13}$$

is minimized. Suppose we roughly know that the optimal $\mathbf{v}$ is near $\mathbf{v_o}$. Then the optimization process can be approximated by finding $\delta\mathbf{v}$ so that $E(\mathbf{v_o}+\delta\mathbf{v})$ is optimized. We can make a Taylor expansion of $R(\mathbf{v_o} + \delta\mathbf{v})$ and simplify the expression by retaining only the first two terms:

$$R(\mathbf{v_o} + \delta\mathbf{v}) \approx R(\mathbf{v_o}) + D\delta\mathbf{v} \tag{14.14}$$

where

$$D = \frac{\partial R(\mathbf{v})}{\partial \mathbf{v}}$$

is evaluated at $\mathbf{v} = \mathbf{v_0}$. Thus, our optimization is reduced to minimizing

$$E(\mathbf{v_0} + \delta\mathbf{v}) \approx ||R(\mathbf{v_0}) + D\delta\mathbf{v}||^2 \tag{14.15}$$

The least square solution to Equation (14.15) is

$$\delta\mathbf{v} = -(D^T D)^{-1} D^T R(\mathbf{v_0}) \tag{14.16}$$

We can use Equation (14.16) to update $\mathbf{v}$ in the search space; we use the $\delta\mathbf{v}$ to compute a new vector $\mathbf{v}$ and a new error measure:

$$\begin{aligned} \mathbf{v}' &= \mathbf{v_0} + \delta\mathbf{v} \\ E' &= E(\mathbf{v}') \end{aligned} \tag{14.17}$$

If $E' < E$, we update $\mathbf{v}$ accordingly ($\mathbf{v}' \rightarrow \mathbf{v_0}$) and repeat the steps until convergence occurs. If $E' > E$, we do not perform the update but try smaller update steps. If the smaller steps still do not improve the error measure, we assume that convergence has reached.

We can estimate the gradient matrix D from a set of training data. For example, the ith row of D can be estimated as:

$$D_i = \sum_k [R(\mathbf{v} + \delta\mathbf{v}_{ik}) - R(\mathbf{v})] \tag{4.18}$$

where $\delta\mathbf{v}_{ik}$ is a vector that perturbs $\mathbf{v}$ in the ith component to the amount of $k \times c$ for some suitable constant c. We can then compute the update matrix U as the negative pseudoinverse of D:

$$U = -D^* = -(D^T D)^{-1} D^T \tag{14.19}$$

We can apply a similar procedure to the texture of Equation (14.10).

Some tools for studying AAM can be downloaded from the web site of Professor Tim Cootes (*http://personalpages.manchester.ac.uk/staff/timothy.f.cootes/default.htm*).

14.6 3DS File Format

We mentioned in the Introduction of this chapter that a 3D graphical object is composed of polygons and we can deform, rotate, scale or translate the object by changing the polygons. In general the tasks of creating nice-looking 3D objects are done by artists using some software such as the open-source 3D suite Blender. After creating the objects, the artists would pass them to software developers who could write programs to parse the objects that can be used for the 3D animation modeling discussed above. Or sometimes, a programmer may simply purchase or download the objects from the Internet, which may be sold as finished 'products' by the creators. In order that the programmers can use files created by artists effectively, they need to communicate in a standard agreed upon way. There are quite a lot of 'standard' 3D graphical object formats. Though MPEG-4 chose VRML as their scene description language, we shall discuss one of the more pupular ones, the 3ds file format so that readers can start doing experiments on this topic and may better integrate their work with the 3D graphics community.

File format of 3ds Max (formerly 3D Studio Max), is a full-featured 3D graphics animation package developed by Autodesk Media and Entertainment. The native file format used by 3D Studio for storing the 3D vector animations are binary files with the extension .3ds. A 3ds-file contain all information from the 3D editor and the keyframer (meshes, materials, cameras, tracks, etc.). The internal structure of a 3ds-file is hirerchical. The hirearchy is made up of data chunks, which can contain subchunks which in turn can contain new subchunks. Each data chunk starts with a 6-byte header which consists of a 2-byte id field and 4-byte length field. The length field includes the size of the header (6 byte). After the header follows an optional payload field that can contain new subchunks or data related to the 3D vector animation.

In addition to its modeling and animation tools, the latest version of 3ds Max also features advanced shaders (such as ambient occlusion and subsurface scattering), dynamic simulation, particle systems, radiosity, normal map creation and rendering, and global illumination. The open-source 3D grahics package Blender also supports this format. Figure 14-12 shows a 3ds image, which is made up of numerous number of triangles:

Figure 14-12 3ds max living room rendered with V-Ray

As mentioned above, 3ds data are organized into chunks with each chunk containing a 2-byte chunkname and a 4-byte length, and each chunk may have subchunks. The following list shows some of the chunks and subchunks:

1. MAIN3DS

   0x4D4D : The main chunk in the .3ds file, containing all other chunks

2. EDIT3DS

   0x3D3D : Most interested, containing EDIT_OBJECT chunks, which define the objects in the .3ds scene (lights, geometry, etc...)

3. EDIT_OBJECT

   0x4000 : Containing data and OBJ_TRIMESH; immediately followed by an object name, which is a NULL terminated string

4. OBJ_TRIMESH

   0x4100 : Containing the geometric information about the object: the vertices, triangles, and texture coordinate chunks

5. TRI_VERTEXL

   0x4110 : Containing a list of vertices, a 2-byte unsigned integer vertex count followed by vertex count float triplets that define the x, y, z coordinates

6. TRI_FACEL1

0x4120 : Defining the triangles of the model, similar to the vertex list, starting out with a 2-byte unsigned integer that gives a count of how many triangles there are, followed by sets of four 2-byte unsigned integers, the first three indixing to one of the vertices in the vertex list, the last containing a few bit-flags; a triangle consists of three vertices in counter-clockwise order

7. TRI_TEXCOORD

0x4140 : Giving a series texture coordinates, starting out with a 2-byte unsigned integer like the last couple lists which defines how many entries are in this list

The following is an example of some sample data of a 3ds file:

```
00000:  4D 4D 29 D2 00 00        |MAIN3DS chunk length
        02 00 0A 00 00 00        |BOTTOM subchunk length
        03 00 00 00              |LEFT
00016:  3D 3D 39 D1 00 00 3E 3D  |EDIT3DS sibling chunk length
        0A 00 00 00 03 00 00 00

00032: 00 01 0A 00 00 00 00 00 80 3F 00 40 1F D1 00 00 |.........?.@....|
00048: 54 6F 72 75 73 20 4B 6E 6F 74 00 00 41 0E D1 00 |Torus Knot..A...|
00064: 00 10 41 C4 49 00 00 25 06 3D 09 61 42 40 3E 05 |..A.I..%.=.aB@>.|
00080: C0 E7 75 01 42 6A 93 6D 42 F2 1F 0E C1 38 E3 1C |..u.Bj.mB....8..|
00096: 42 C5 E3 67 42 40 BC 5D C1 D5 D4 3F 42 59 80 51 |B..gB@.]...?BY.Q|
00112: 42 97 CF 7A C1 C6 ED 60 42 DF 68 30 42 87 8F 5D |B..z...`B.h0B..]|
00128: C1 BA 4F 77 42 46 7B 0D 42 7C D2 0D C1 5C FB 7C |..OwBF{.B|...\.||
00144: 42 E2 26 E4 41 81 D8 03 C0 B3 6B 70 42 88 12 CB |B.&.A.....kpB...|
00160: 41 81 B4 97 40 64 FE 54 42 D0 71 D6 41 8F 76 1B |A...@d.TB.q.A.v.|
00176: 41 C7 0C 32 42 53 9C 01 42 E9 89 38 41 D6 F3 10 |A..2BS..B..8A...|
00192: 42 CC B3 22 42 DD 49 1B 41 C1 23 F5 41 66 A1 45 |B.."B.I.A.#.Af.E|
00208: 42 AC 19 97 40 7C CC E9 41 3B 09 61 42 13 3E 05 |B...@|..A;.aB.>.|
00224: C0 E5 75 01 42 AD 0E 6E 42 04 51 AA 3F 38 97 0D |..u.B..nB.Q.?8..|
00240: 42 BA 90 7B 42 F4 63 84 C0 C9 08 2D 42 A6 99 76 |B..{B.c....-B..v|
      [ 0  1  2  3  4  5  6  7  8  9 10 11 12 13 14 15  0123456789012345]
```

In the example,

(a) Chunk name = "MAIN3DS" (0x4D4D)
(b) Length of main chunk = 0x0000D229 = 53801 bytes (equals length of file)
(c) Subchunk name = "BOTTOM" (0x0002)
(d) Length of subchunk = 0x00000A = 10 (bytes)
(e) Sibling subchunk = "LEFT" (0x0003)
(f) Sibling subchunk = "3DSEDIT" (0x3D3D)
(g) Length of "3DSEDIT" = 0x3D3E0000 = 15678 (bytes)

It is not too difficult to write a program to parse a 3ds file. However, again we are not interested in studying file formats in details. We shall use existing free libraries to parse 3ds files; we discuss this in the next section.

14.7 Parsing 3DS Files

Free 3ds file parsers are available in the Internet. The library that we use to process 3ds files is **Lib3ds**, a simple free toolkit for processing 3D model files saved in 3ds format. It is written in C and its main goal is to simplify creation of 3ds import and export filters. The official **Lib3ds** homepage can be found at (*http://www.lib3ds.org*).

Program listing 14-1 is a simple sample program that makes use of the file "3dsdump.cpp" provided by Lib3ds to parse 3ds files and display the scenes using OpenGL, which is a popular open-source graphics API. The program input 3ds file name is hard-coded and is set to "../data/objects.3ds". It makes use of the functions provided by "3dsdump.cpp" to print out the information of the 3ds objects in the file and renders them on the screen. You can rotate the objects around the x, y, and z axis by pressing keys 'x' or 'X', 'y' or 'Y', 'z' or 'Z' respectively. Also, you can translate them by pressing keys 'a', 'b', and 'c' or 'A', 'B', and 'C' along the x, y, and z directions. The program is somewhat incomplete as it has not considered the texture of the objects and has not handled the lighting in a proper way. Nevertheless, it illustrates the basic usage of Lib3ds and serves as a starting point for rendering 3ds files.

Program Listing 14-1 Loading and Parsing 3ds File Using "lib3ds"

```
#include <stdio.h>
#include <GL/gl.h>
#include <GL/glu.h>
#include <GL/glut.h>
#include <stdlib.h>
#include <malloc.h>
#include <string.h>
#include <assert.h>
#include <stdlib.h>
#include <stdio.h>
#include <lib3ds.h>
#include <string.h>
#include <math.h>

#define WINWIDTH 400
#define WINHEIGHT 300

//hard-coded input filename
char *file_3ds = "../data/objects.3ds";

struct Vertex {
  float x;
  float y;
  float z;
};

static int window;

//rotation angles,
int anglex, angley, anglez;
//translations
float tx, ty, tz;
//angle increments
float tinc[3] = {0, 0, 0};

//from dump3ds.cpp
Lib3dsFile *f;
void set_io_func ( Lib3dsIo *io );

Lib3dsFile *get3dsFile ( char *filename )
{
```

```
  FILE *fp;
  Lib3dsFile *f = 0;
  Lib3dsIo io;
  int result;

  fp = fopen ( filename, "rb" );
  if (!fp) {
        fprintf(stderr, "***ERROR***\nFile not found: %s\n", filename );
        exit(1);
  }
  f = lib3ds_file_new();

  memset(&io, 0, sizeof(io));
  io.self = fp;
  set_io_func ( &io );
  result =  lib3ds_file_read(f, &io);

  fclose(fp);

  if (!result) {
   fprintf(stderr, "***ERROR***\nLoading file failed: %s\n", filename);
   exit(1);
  }

  return f;
}

//get vertices of the mesh
struct Vertex *getVertices( Lib3dsMesh *mesh  )
{
  int i, j;
  float p[3];
  struct Vertex *vs;
  float min[3] = { 1000, 1000, 1000 };
  float max[3] = { -1000, -1000, -1000 };

  assert ( mesh );
  vs = (struct Vertex *)malloc(mesh->nvertices*sizeof(struct Vertex));

  assert ( vs );

  //make appropriate scale of mesh
  for (i = 0; i < mesh->nvertices; ++i) {
    lib3ds_vector_copy(p, mesh->vertices[i]);
    for ( j = 0; j < 3; ++j ) {
      if ( min[j] > p[j] ) min[j] = p[j];
      if ( max[j] < p[j] ) max[j] = p[j];
    }
    vs[i].x = p[0];
    vs[i].y = p[1];
    vs[i].z = p[2];
  }
  for ( j = 0; j < 3; ++j )
    tinc[j] = ( max[j] - min[j] ) / 10.0;
```

```
  return vs;
}

//Find the minimum and maximum x, y, z coordinates
void find_min_max (  Lib3dsFile *f, float min[], float max[] )
{
  Lib3dsMesh *mesh;
  float p[3];
  min[0] = min[1] = min[2] = 100000.0;
  max[0] = max[1] = max[2] = -100000.0;

  for ( int k = 0; k < f->nmeshes; ++k ) {
    mesh = f->meshes[k];

    for (int i = 0; i < mesh->nvertices; ++i) {
      lib3ds_vector_copy(p, mesh->vertices[i]);
      for ( int j = 0; j < 3; ++j ) {
        if ( min[j] > p[j] ) min[j] = p[j];
        if ( max[j] < p[j] ) max[j] = p[j];
      }
    }
  }
}

static const char* node_names_table[] = {
    "Ambient",
    "Mesh",
    "Camera",
    "Camera Target",
    "Omnilight",
    "Spotlight",
    "Spotlight Target"
};

void display_meshes ()
{
  struct Vertex *vs;
  struct Vertex v;
  Lib3dsMesh *mesh;

  glPolygonMode( GL_BACK, GL_LINE );
  glPolygonMode( GL_FRONT, GL_LINE );
  Lib3dsMaterial *mat=0;
   for ( int k = 0; k < f->nmaterials; ++k ) {
    mat = f->materials[k];
    printf("material name: %s\n", mat->name);
    printf("  ambient:          (%f, %f, %f)\n",
        mat->ambient[0], mat->ambient[1], mat->ambient[2]);
    printf("  diffuse:          (%f, %f, %f)\n",
        mat->diffuse[0], mat->diffuse[1], mat->diffuse[2]);
    printf("  specular:         (%f, %f, %f)\n",
        mat->specular[0], mat->specular[1], mat->specular[2]);
  }

  glEnable( GL_CULL_FACE );
```

```
glCullFace ( GL_BACK );
glPolygonMode( GL_FRONT, GL_FILL );
//see mesh names for testing
for ( int k = 0; k < f->nmeshes; ++k ) {
  printf(": %s : ", f->meshes[k]->name );
}
printf("\n");
Lib3dsNode *node;
int l = 0;
for ( node = f->nodes; node != 0; node = node->next ) {
   printf("%d: %s (%s),user_id=%d,node_id=%d\n", l++, node->name,
     node_names_table[node->type],node->user_id, node->node_id );
}
for ( int k = 0; k < f->nmeshes; ++k ) {
  mesh = f->meshes[k];
  vs = getVertices( f->meshes[k] );
  float  (*normals)[3] = (float (*)[3])  malloc ( 3 * 3 *
                              sizeof ( float ) * mesh->nfaces );
  lib3ds_mesh_calculate_face_normals ( mesh,  normals );
  if ( k < f->nmaterials ) {
    mat = f->materials[k];
    if (mat) {
      float s;
      glMaterialfv(GL_FRONT, GL_AMBIENT, mat->ambient );
      glMaterialfv(GL_FRONT, GL_DIFFUSE, mat->diffuse);
      glMaterialfv(GL_FRONT, GL_SPECULAR, mat->specular);
      s = pow(2, 10.0*mat->shininess);
      if (s>128.0) {
        s=128.0;
      }
      glMaterialf(GL_FRONT, GL_SHININESS, s);
    }
  }
  for ( int i = 0; i < mesh->nfaces; ++i ) {
    int k = mesh->faces[i].material;
    mat = f->materials[k];
    if (mat) {
      float s;
      glMaterialfv(GL_FRONT, GL_AMBIENT, mat->ambient );
      glMaterialfv(GL_FRONT, GL_DIFFUSE, mat->diffuse);
      glMaterialfv(GL_FRONT, GL_SPECULAR, mat->specular);
      s = pow(2, 10.0*mat->shininess);
      if (s>128.0) {
        s=128.0;
      }
      glMaterialf(GL_FRONT, GL_SHININESS, s);
    }
    glBegin ( GL_TRIANGLES );
    for ( int j = 0; j < 3; ++ j ) {
      glNormal3fv(normals[3*i+j]);
      int index;
     index = mesh->faces[i].index[j];
      v = vs[index];
      glVertex3f ( v.x, v.y, v.z );
    }
```

```
      glEnd();
    }
    free ( normals );
  }
  free ( vs );
}

void lighting ( Lib3dsFile *f  )
{
  int li = GL_LIGHT0;
  Lib3dsLight *light;

  if ( f->nlights > 0 ) {
    glEnable(GL_LIGHTING);
    for ( int i = 0; i < f->nlights; ++i ) {
      float color[3];
      light = f->lights[i];
      glLightfv( li, GL_DIFFUSE, light->color );
      glLightfv( li, GL_SPECULAR, light->color );
      glLightModelfv(GL_LIGHT_MODEL_AMBIENT, light->color);
      glLightfv(li, GL_POSITION, light->position);
      if ( light->spot_light) {
        glLightfv(li, GL_SPOT_DIRECTION, light->position);
      }
      glEnable(li);
      ++li;
    }
    printf("\n");
  } else {
    printf("no lights provided\n");
    GLfloat light[] = { 1.0, 1.0, 1.0 };
    GLfloat light1[] = { 1.0, 1.0, 1.0 };
    GLfloat light_position[] = { 1.0, 1.0, 1.0, 0.0 };
    GLfloat light_position1[] = { -1, -1, -1, 0.0 };
    GLfloat lmodel_ambient[] = { 0.1, 0.1, 0.1, 1.0 };
    glLightfv(GL_LIGHT0, GL_POSITION, light_position);
    glLightfv(GL_LIGHT0, GL_DIFFUSE, light );
    glLightfv(GL_LIGHT0, GL_SPECULAR, light );
    glLightModelfv(GL_LIGHT_MODEL_AMBIENT, lmodel_ambient);

    glLightfv(GL_LIGHT1, GL_POSITION, light_position1);
    glLightfv(GL_LIGHT1, GL_DIFFUSE, light1 );
    glLightfv(GL_LIGHT1, GL_SPECULAR, light1 );

    glEnable(GL_LIGHTING);
    glEnable(GL_LIGHT0);
    glEnable(GL_LIGHT1);
  }
}

void init()
{
  Lib3dsNode *c,*t;
  glClear(GL_COLOR_BUFFER_BIT | GL_DEPTH_BUFFER_BIT |
                                        GL_STENCIL_BUFFER_BIT);
```

```
glClearColor( 0.8, 0.8, 0.8, 0.5 );

Lib3dsCamera *camera;
glColor3f ( 0.5, 0.5, 0 );
glShadeModel ( GL_SMOOTH );

glEnable(GL_DEPTH_TEST);

f = get3dsFile ( (char *) file_3ds );

lighting( f );

printf("nmeshes=%d\n", f->nmeshes );
printf("nmaterials=%d\n", f->nmaterials );
printf("ncameras=%d\n", f->ncameras);
if ( f->ncameras > 0 ) {
  camera = f->cameras[0];
  printf("  name:       %s\n", camera->name);
  printf("  position:   (%f, %f, %f)\n",
    camera->position[0],camera->position[1],camera->position[2]);
  printf("  target      (%f, %f, %f)\n",
    camera->target[0],camera->target[1],camera->target[2]);
  printf("  roll:       %f\n", camera->roll);
  printf("  fov:        %f\n", camera->fov);
  printf("  see_cone:   %s\n", camera->see_cone ? "yes" : "no");
  printf("  near_range: %f\n", camera->near_range);
  printf("  far_range:  %f\n", camera->far_range);
  printf("\n");
  glMatrixMode ( GL_PROJECTION );
  glLoadIdentity();
  gluPerspective ( 45, 1.0, 100, camera->far_range );
  glMatrixMode ( GL_MODELVIEW );
  glLoadIdentity();
  gluLookAt ( camera->position[0], camera->position[1],
      camera->position[2], camera->target[0], camera->target[1],
      camera->target[2], 0, 1, 0 );
 } else {
   printf("no camera detected, set our own coordinates!\n");
   float min[3], max[3], minx, maxx, miny, maxy, minz, maxz;
   find_min_max ( f, min, max );
   glMatrixMode(GL_PROJECTION);
   glLoadIdentity();
   float delta = 3;
   minx = min[0] - ( max[0] - min[0] ) / delta;
   maxx = max[0] + ( max[0] - min[0] ) / delta;
   miny = min[1] - ( max[1] - min[1] ) / delta;
   maxy = max[1] + ( max[1] - min[1] ) / delta;
   minz = min[2] - ( max[2] - min[2] ) / delta;
   maxz = max[2] + ( max[2] - min[2] ) / delta;
   if ( minz > 0 )
     minz = -minz;
   if ( maxz - minz < 0.1 )
     glOrtho ( minx, maxx, miny, maxy, -10, 10 );
   else
     glOrtho ( minx, maxx, miny, maxy, minz, maxz );
```

```
    printf("..minz=%f,maxz=%f..\n", minz, maxz );
    glMatrixMode(GL_MODELVIEW);
  }
  printf("mesh name:%s,nmeshes=%d\n",f->meshes[0]->name,f->nmeshes);
  printf("nfaces:%d, nvertices:%d\n", f->meshes[0]->nfaces,
                                     f->meshes[0]->nvertices);
}

void display()
{
  glClear(GL_COLOR_BUFFER_BIT | GL_DEPTH_BUFFER_BIT |
                                     GL_STENCIL_BUFFER_BIT);
  glClearColor( 0.8, 0.8, 0.8, 0.5 );
  glPushMatrix();
  glTranslatef ( tx, ty, tz );

  glRotatef( anglex, 1.0, 0.0, 0.0);
  glRotatef( angley, 0.0, 1.0, 0.0);
  glRotatef( anglez, 0.0, 0.0, 1.0);
  display_meshes ();
  glPopMatrix();
  glFlush();
  glutSwapBuffers();
}

//rotate or translate objects
void key_press(unsigned char key, int x, int y)
{
  switch(key) {
    case 'x':
      anglex = ( anglex + 5 ) % 360;
      glutPostRedisplay();
      break;
    case 'X':
      anglex = ( anglex - 5 ) % 360;
      glutPostRedisplay();
      break;
    case 'y':
      angley = ( angley + 5 ) % 360;
      glutPostRedisplay();
      break;
    case 'Y':
      angley = ( angley - 5 ) % 360;
      glutPostRedisplay();
      break;
    case 'z':
      anglez = ( anglez + 5 ) % 360;
      glutPostRedisplay();
      break;
    case 'Z':
      anglez = ( anglez - 5 ) % 360;
      glutPostRedisplay();
      break;
    case 'a':
      tx += tinc[0];
```

```
        glutPostRedisplay();
        break;
      case 'A':
        tx -= tinc[0];
        glutPostRedisplay();
        break;
      case 'b':
        ty += tinc[1];
        glutPostRedisplay();
        break;
      case 'B':
        ty -= tinc[1];
        glutPostRedisplay();
        break;
      case 'c':
        tz += tinc[2];
        glutPostRedisplay();
        break;
      case 'C':
        tz -= tinc[2];
        glutPostRedisplay();
        break;
      default:
//scene_toggle_lighting();
break;
      case 27: /* escape */
glutDestroyWindow(window);
exit(0);
break;
  }
}

void reshape(int w, int h)
{
   glViewport(0, 0, (GLsizei) w, (GLsizei) h);
   glMatrixMode(GL_PROJECTION);
   glLoadIdentity();
   gluPerspective(60.0, (GLfloat) w/(GLfloat) h, 1.0, 30.0);
   glMatrixMode(GL_MODELVIEW);
   glLoadIdentity();
   glTranslatef(0.0, 0.0, -5 );
}

int main(int argc, char *argv[])
{
  if ( argc > 1 ) {
    file_3ds = ( char * ) malloc ( 100 );
    assert ( file_3ds );
    strcpy ( file_3ds, argv[1] );
  }
  glutInit(&argc, argv);
  glutInitDisplayMode(GLUT_RGBA | GLUT_DOUBLE | GLUT_DEPTH );
  glutInitWindowSize(WINWIDTH, WINHEIGHT);

  window = glutCreateWindow(argv[0]);
```

```
#ifdef FULLSCREEN
glutFullScreen();
#endif

  glutKeyboardFunc(key_press);

  /* GL settings */
  glClearColor(1.0f, 1.0f, 1.0f, 1.0f);
  glClearDepth(1.0f);
  glColor4f(1.0f, 1.0f, 1.0f, 1.0f);
  glMatrixMode(GL_PROJECTION);
  glLoadIdentity();
  glOrtho ( 0, 200.0, 0, 200.0, 200, -200 );
  glMatrixMode(GL_MODELVIEW);
  init();
  glutDisplayFunc( display );

  glutMainLoop();
  return 0;
}
---------------------------------------------------------------
```

Though the default input file name for the program is hard-coded, you may override it by supplying a 3ds file name as an input parameter to the program. For example you can run the program using the command,

./parse_3ds ../data/objects.3ds

which loads and parses the 3ds file "objects.3ds" residing in the directory "../data/". It prints out the chunk information and data in text format.

The program needs to link the library "lib3ds.a", which can be compiled from the srouce code obtained from *http://www.lib3ds.org*.

14.7 Conclusions

We have introduced video compression theories and and the corresponding implementations in C/C++ code. The description is far from complete. We have only introduced some basic concepts that help you to establish a solid foundation for further studies in the field. Audio compression and more advanced compression techniques have not been discussed. Though the programs presented are self-contained and executable, they should not be considered as end-applications. They are implemented in a way to help readers understand the theories and concepts. Actually, we have hard-coded some of the parameters and ignored error-checking in a number of places for simplicity and clarity of illustration. The pre-calculated Huffman codes for 3D run-level tuples are very brief and incomplete. Nevertheless, the programs help readers understand basic video compression concepts and interested readers can use the programs as the basis for further development.

The field of video compression is still evolving. However, besides the hybrid coding, the basic techniques are fairly mature. There exists open-source software that compress and decompress videos along with sound using various standards. If your interest is mainly on utilizing existing video compression libraries, you may use open-source video codecs for your applications. One can make use of the libraries to easily integrate videos in a graphics or video game application. The use of these open-source video compression libraries will tremendously shorten your software development cycle. On the other hand, an understanding of the basic principles of video compression helps you more effectively use the libraries or even modify and improve them. Because of the huge advancement and demand of Internet and multi-media applications, the utilization of video compression technologies is ubiquitous. The technologies will be even more important in the coming decades. Their applications are only limited by your imagination.

Bibliography

1. N. Abramson, *Information Theory and Coding*, McGraw-Hill, 1963.

2. R.C. Agarwal, *An In-Place and In-Order WFTA*, ICASSP 83, pp. 190-193, Boston, 1983.

3. J.D. Bruguera and R.R. Osorio, *A United Architecture for H.264 Multiple Block-Size DCT with Fast and Low Cost Quantization*, Proceedings of the 9th EUROMICRO Conference on Digital System Design (DSD06), IEEE Computer Society, pp. 407-414, 2006.

4. D. Genzel and E. Charniak, *Entropy Rate Constancy in Text*, Proceedings of the 40th Annual Meeting of the Association for Computational Linguistics (ACL), Philadelphia, pp. 199-206, July 2002.

5. T. Budd, *Data Structures in C++: Using The Standard Template Library*, Addison Wesley, 1997.

6. S. R. Buss, *3-D Computer Graphics: A Mathematical Introduction with OpenGL*, Cambridge, 2003.

7. G.J. Chaitin, *Algorithmic Information Theory*, Cambridge University Press, 1987.

8. K. Chen, R. Kambhamettu, and D. Goldgof, *Extraction of MPEG-4 FAP Parameters from 3D Face Data Sequences*, CiteSeer, 1998.

9. W. Chen, C. Harrison, and S. Fralick, *A fast computational algorithm for the discrete cosine transform*, IEEE Trans. Com., Vol. COM-25 (9), pp. 1004-1011, Sept. 1977.

10. T. M. Cover and J.A. Cover, *Elements of Information Theory*, Second Edition, John Wiley, 2006.

11. P.F. Drucker, *The Essential Drucker*, Harper Business, 2001.

12. M. Ezhilarasan, and P. Thambidural, *A Hybrid Transform Coding for Video Codec*, 9th International Conference on Information Technology (ICIT06), IEEE Computer Society, 2006.

13. D. Genzel and E. Charniak, *Entropy Rate Constancy in Text*, Proceedings of the 40th Annual Meeting of the Association for Computational Linguistics (ACL), Philadelphia, pp. 199-206, July 2002.

14. A. Gersho and R.M. Gray, *Vector Quantization and Signal Compression*, Kluwer Academic Publishers, 1992.

15. R.G. Gonzalez and R.E. Woods, *Digital Image Processing*, Addison-Wesley, 1992.

16. E. L. Hall, *Computer Image Processing and Recognition*, Academic Press, 1979.

17. B. G. Haskell, A. Puri, and A. N. Netravali, *Digital Video: An introduction to MPEG-2*, Springer, 1996.

18. F.S. Hill, Jr. and S. M. Kelley, Jr., *Computer Graphics Using OpenGL*, Third Edition, Pearson Prentice Hall, 2007.

19. A.K. Jain, *Fundamentals of Digital Image Processing*, Prentice Hall, 1989.

20. R.W. Johnson and C.S. Burrus, *On the Structure of Efficient DFT Algorithms*, ICASSP 83, pp. 163-165, Boston, 1983.

21. T. Koga, K. Iinuma, et al., *Motion-Compensated Inter Frame Coding for Videoconferencing*, IEEE Nat. Telecomm. Conf. 4: pp. 15, 1981.

22. J. Liang and T.D. Tran, *Fast Multiplierless Approximation of the DCT with the Lifting Schemes*, IEEE Transaction on Signal Processing, 49(12), pp. 3032-3044, December 2001.

23. Loki Software with J. R. Hall, *Programming Linux Games: Building Multimedia Applications with SDL, OpenAL, and Other APIs*, Linux Journal Press, 2001.

24. T. Luo et al., *An Improved Three-Step Search Algorithm with Zero Detection and Vector Filter for Motion Estimation*, International Conference on Computer Science and Software Engineering,Vol 2., pp. 967-978, 2008.

25. J.R. Masse and D. Cante, *General - N Winograd D.F.T. Programs with Inverse Option*, ICASSP 83, pp. 1164-1167, Boston, 1983.

26. A. V. Oppenheim and R. W. Schafer, *Digital Signal Processing*, Prentice Hall, 1975.

27. I.S. Pandzic and R. Forchheimer (editors), *MPEG-4 Facial Animation: The Standard, Implementation and Applications*, John Wiley & sons, 2002.

28. M. Peder, *Lecture 6: Winograd's Small DFT: Implementation of DFT Using convolution*,

29. W. B. Pennebaker and J. L. Mitchell, *JPEG: Still Image Data Compression Standard*, Van Nostrand Reinhold, 1993.

30. Recommendations ITU-R BT.601-5, *Studio encoding parameters of digital television for standard 4:3 and wide-screen 16:9 aspect ratios*, ITU-T, 1995.

31. Iain E.G. Richardson, *H.264 and MPEG-4 Video Compression: Video Coding for Next-generation Multimedia*, John Wiley & Sons, 2003.

32. N. Sarris and M. G. Strintzis, *3D Modeling and Animation: Synthesis and Analysis Techniques for the Human Body*, IRM Press, 2005.

33. C. E. Shannon, *A Mathematical Theory of Communication*, The Bell System Technical Journal, 27:379-423, 623-656, July, October, 1948.

34. A. Silberschatz, P.B. Galvin, and G. Gagne, *Operating System Concepts*, Sxith Edition, John Wiley & Sons, 2004.

35. H. Tao and H. H. Chen et. al., *Compression of MPEG-4 Facial Animation Parameters for Transmission of Talking Heads*, IEEE Transactions on Circuits and Systems for Video Technology, 9(2), pp. 264-276, 1999.

36. J.F. Traub, G.W. Waslikowski, and H. Wozniakowski, *Information-Based Complexity*, Academic Press, 1988.

37. G. Wade, *Signal Coding And Processing*, Second Edition, Cambridge University Press, 1994.

38. S. Winograd, *On Computing the Discrete Fourier Transform*, Math. Comput., 32, pp. 175-199, January 1978.

39. T.L. Yu, *A Framework for Very High Performance Compression of Table Tennis Video Clips*, Proceedings of IASTED on Signal and Image Processing, pp. 167-172, Kailua-Kona, Hawaii, August 2008.

40. J. Ziv and A. Lempel, *A Universal Algorithm for Sequential Data Compression*, IEEE Transactions on Information Theory, 23(3), pp. 337343, May 1977.

41. J. Ziv and A. Lempel, *Compression of Individual Sequences Via Variable-Rate Coding*, IEEE Transactions on Information Theory, 24(5), pp. 530-536, September 1978.

42. M. Stokes, et al. *A Standard Default Color Space for the Internet - sRGB*, 1996, http://www.w3.org/Graphi

43. http://www.3dcafe.com/

44. http://www.blender.org/

45. http://coven.lancs.ac.uk/mpeg4

46. http://www.makehuman.org/

47. http://personalpages.manchester.ac.uk/staff/timothy.f.cootes/

48. http://xface.fbk.eu

Index

Books by Fore June:

1. *Windows Fan, Linux Fan*
2. *An Introduction to Video Compression in C/C++*
3. *An Introduction to Digital Video Data Compression in Java*
4. *An Introduction to 3D Computer Graphics, Stereoscopic Image, and Animation in OpenGL and C/C++*
5. *Android Programming and Open Source Tools*

See

http://www.forejune.com/

www.ingramcontent.com/pod-product-compliance
Lightning Source LLC
Chambersburg PA
CBHW080359060326
40689CB00019B/4071
9781451522273